# RETURN TO RUIN

# RETURN TO RUIN

*Iraqi Narratives of Exile and Nostalgia*

ZAINAB SALEH

Stanford University Press
Stanford, California

STANFORD UNIVERSITY PRESS

Stanford, California

© 2021 Zainab Saleh. All rights reserved.

No part of this book may be reproduced or transmitted in any form or by any means, electronic or mechanical, including photocopying and recording, or in any information storage or retrieval system without the prior written permission of Stanford University Press.

Printed in the United States of American on acid-free, archival-quality paper

Library of Congress Control Number: 2020939906

ISBN 978-1-503-60702-6 (cloth)
ISBN 978-1-503-61411-6 (paper)
ISBN 978-1-503-61412-3 (electronic)

Cover design: Angela Moody

Cover art: Dia Azzawi, *Travelling West* (1979), oil on canvas, 60 cm x 80 cm.

Typeset by BookComp, Inc. in 10.25/156 Adobe Caslon Pro

*To my parents, Hayat Sharara and Muhammad Saleh Smeisim,
and my sister, Maha*

# CONTENTS

*Acknowledgments* ix

INTRODUCTION: Empire and Subjectivity  1

*Childhood Stories*  37
1 Emancipation and Revolution  41

*In the Shadow of Fear*  73
2 Revisionist Politics  79

*Memories of Persecution*  109
3 Religious Paths, Secular Pasts  113

*In the Midst of War*  137
4 Itineraries of Homecomings  143

*In the Aftermath of Destruction*  171
5 Dispossession and Authenticity  177

*With No Ray of Hope*  203
CONCLUSION: Enduring Legacies  207

*Notes*  219
*List of References*  233
*Index*  253

# ACKNOWLEDGMENTS

This book would not have seen the light of day if it were not for my Iraqi interlocutors and friends in London. Their generosity, hospitality, and openness over the last fourteen years have made this book possible. I arrived at a time in London (in 2006) when the Iraqi community was suspicious of new faces for fear that they were Saddam Hussein's loyalists. However, they graciously accepted me and shared with me personal stories about their lives in Iraq and in exile, and they were patient with me when I returned again and again to do follow-up interviews. Over the years, they showed me warmth and care, cooked my favorite Iraqi dishes for me, and confided in me much that did not make it into the book. During seven years of visa complications, when I could not leave the United States, they kept in touch with me and sent me updates about their lives. When I was able to travel to London again, they were excited to see me. Growing up in Iraq under Saddam Hussein's regime, I never had friends I could trust, since people were afraid that what they said would be reported back to the authorities. My fieldwork with the Iraqi community in London enabled me to experience true friendships with Iraqis for the first time. Regretfully, due to the need to protect their privacy, I cannot thank them by name.

Nadje al-Ali, Madawi al-Rasheed, and Sami Zubaida frequently met with me to discuss my fieldwork and invited me to their daylong workshops on the Middle East. They offered a much-needed intellectual exchange in London.

I would like to thank the Wenner-Gren Foundation for Anthropological Research for generously funding my research in 2006–2007, with special thanks to Mary Beth Moss, who was patient and considerate as I navigated the logistics of fieldwork when my original plan to go to Iran to do research with Iraqis changed. I am also indebted to the Provost's Office at Haverford College for funding my trips to London over the past three years to do follow-up interviews with my Iraqi interlocutors. The Tri-Co Brainstorming Grants provided funds that enabled a group of colleagues at Haverford, Bryn Mawr, and Swarthmore to meet and discuss our work and themes related to my research on nostalgia and U.S. empire that proved to be invaluable.

My mentors and colleagues at Columbia University showed great enthusiasm for the initial phase of this research. Michael Taussig invited me to take life stories seriously as a writing technique in order to convey the richness of my interlocutors' lives. Many thanks to Sinan Antoon, Nadia Abu El-Haj, Brinkley M. Messick, and Partha Chatterjee, who provided mentorship throughout the years. Neni Panourgia, Lila Abu-Lughod, Mahmood Mamdani, David Scott, Vincent Crapanzano, and Rashid Khalidi offered feedback on my work as well. Many friends commented on this work at various stages, including Thushara Hewage, Fadi A. Bardawil, Danielle Di Novelli Lang, Yogesh Chandrani, Ayça Çubuçu, Alejandra Leal, Trisha Gupta, Lisa Uparesa, Angeliki Rovatsou, Adriana Garriga-López, Patience Kabamba, Nadia Guessous, Nadia Loan, Robert Samet, Nadia Latif, Ryan Chaney, Anush Kapadia, Antina von Schnitzler, Munira Khayyat, Gajendran Ayyathurai, Arafaat A. Valiani, Shahla Talebi, Narges Erami, Maya Mikdashi, Guldem Baykal, Rodney W. J. Collins, Seema Golestaneh, Sophia Stamatopoulou-Robbins, Anand Vivek Taneja, Sue Nahm, Khiara M. Bridges, Siva Arumugam, Ravindran Sriramachandran, Rajan Kurai Krishnan, Nima Paidipaty, Todd Ochoa, Daniella Gandolfo, John Warner, and Maria del Rosario Ferro.

Thanks to my fellowship at the Center for Middle Eastern Studies at the University of California, Berkeley, I met many people who widened my intellectual community, including Stefania Pandolfo, Samera Esmeir, Charles Hirschkind, and Beshara Doumani. I am also thankful for the friendship of Callie Maidhof, Himali Dixit, Patricia Kubala, and Elizabeth Kelley. The administrators at the Center, particularly, Mejgan Massoumi and Priscilla Minaise were always helpful.

## ACKNOWLEDGMENTS

The John B. Hurford '60 Center for the Arts and Humanities at Haverford College provided me with a space that would become an intellectual home. Thoughts and ideas from the insightful and stimulating conversations I had there with Jesse Weaver Shipley, Craig Borowiak, Andrew Friedman, Maris Gillette, Laurie Kain Hart, Gustavus Stadler, and William Williams have found their way into this book years later. I also would like to thank the Department of Anthropology at Haverford College for their unwavering support. Jesse Weaver Shipley, Joshua Moses, Zolani Ngwane, Juli Grigsby, Jacob Culbertson, Patricia Kelly, Maris Gillette, Christopher Roebuck, Ethiraj Dattatreyan, Nikhil Anand, and Laurie Kain Hart are true colleagues and friends. I am also indebted to Brie Gettleson, who always helped me to find the references I needed. Administrators at Haverford College tirelessly responded to my requests. Until her retirement, Kathy McGee offered support and keenly followed my progress. Kelly Kane has been an indispensable asset since she joined the department, with her unflagging enthusiasm pushing me to finish the project. The friendship offered by Aurelia Gomez Unamuno, Nilgün Uygun, Vicky Funari, John Muse, David Watt, and Laura S. Levitt, over the years has enabled me to be myself, thrive, and occasionally take my mind off work.

My friends and colleagues in other institutions have provided me with valuable comments on the book, especially Orit Bashkin, Neha Vora, Sherene Seikaly, and Laleh Khalili, each of whom offered perceptive feedback, friendship, and support. I also would like to thank Toby Craig Jones and Brandon Wolfe-Hunnicutt for their comments and recommendations on Iraqi history. Colleagues at Haverford, Swarthmore, and Bryn Mawr have welcomed me into a supportive intellectual community, strengthening the ideas and themes that appear in the book. Thanks to my colleagues who participated in the Tri-Co Brainstorming Grant on nostalgia, including Maya Nadkarni, Tamsin Lorraine, Sibelan Forrester, Sangina Patnaik, and Farid Azfar; in the Tri-Co Brainstorming Grant on U.S. Empire, including Andrew Friedman, Ahmad Shokr, Madhavi Kale, Anna West, and Megan Brown; and in the Global Ethnographies workshop with Sofia Fenner, Osman, Balkan, Farha Ghannam, Christopher Fraga, and David Harrison, who read chapter 4 and provided thoughtful feedback. I am deeply indebted to Jessica Greenberg, Larisa Kurtovic, Ella Shohat, Rosie Bsheer, Attiya Ahmad, John Willis, Bruce Grant, Nisreen Salti, Jason Price, Aditi Saraf, Nur Amali brahim, Saiba Varma, Omar

Sirri, Dena A Al-Adeeb, Yousef Baker, Khaled Al Hilli, Zahra Ali, Thomas Abowd, Sima Shakhsari, Sara Pursely, Mona Damluji, Bridget Guarasci, Arbella Bet-Shlimon, Ussama Makdisi, Abdel Razzaq Takriti, Mezna Qato, Linda Sayed, Seda Altug, Leena Dallasheh, Dina Rizq Khoury, Ziad Abu-Rish, Ilan Pappe, Haytham Bahoora, and Hala Al-Hoshan for the productive discussions we had about my work during conferences, talks, and seminars.

I would like to thank Kate Wahl, who saw the potential in my book proposal in 2015. Kate provided invaluable support during each stage of writing the manuscript, read many versions of it, and offered critical feedback over years as it developed. I am indebted to Sean Mallin, who has been a meticulous and thorough editor. I also would like to thank the anonymous reviewers for their valuable feedback. Deborah A. Thomas and Sima Shakhsari left their mark on this book when they graciously read the whole manuscript and provided valuable feedback after I had incorporated suggestions made by the external reviewers. Their thoughts on subjectivity and diaspora enabled me to delve into issues that I had only scratched the surface of in the initial draft. I am indebted to Sinan Antoon, who brainstormed titles with me and demonstrated infinite patience, and to Jon Horne Carter, who gave me the title out of his poetic imagination.

I can never thank Jon Horne Carter and his family enough. Jon was the friend I mention in the introduction who was curious about life in Iraq. Since I arrived in the United States in 2002, he has been a supportive and generous friend who was always there for me during moments of doubts. Throughout the years, he was keen to discuss my work with me, push me to approach it from a different angle, and read different drafts. His boundless intellectual ability is combined with uncommon kindness and genuine concern about my well-being. His parents, Peggy and Harold Carter, invited me into their family and home in North Carolina for university breaks, holidays, and anytime I needed shelter and solace during the lonely stretches of working on the book. After Jon married Christina Verano Sornito-Carter, the circle of care and love and intellectual exchange widened. Christina became a fierce friend. We shared many hours talking about the impact of U.S. empire on the Philippines and Iraq. She also made sure I became part of her family in Chicago. Without the love and support the Carters and Sornitos have given me since my arrival in the United States, I would not have been able to survive the predicaments of starting a new project or the difficulties of writing a book.

Ulla Kjellstrand entered my life as I started fieldwork in 2006. She is a gentle soul who has always listened to my stories about fieldwork and research and has shown me unconditional love and support. My relationship with her immediately went beyond that of a landlady and tenant to a strong friendship. Throughout my fieldwork years, I knew that I would return to her house in Queens Park and I would find her waiting for me with a cup of tea, keen to hear how my day had gone. She also made sure that I did not get wrapped up in my research all the time and accompanied me to museums, the theater, and gardens in London. As I was racing to rewrite the introduction and conclusion while in London in the summer of 2019, she did not even allow me to wash a dish so that I could use every moment I had in the morning to write before I went out to interview people or see family. Fieldwork would have been much more difficult and taxing without her.

Victoria Wurman has been a pillar in my life since 2005. She has been instrumental in enabling me to deal with the trauma and anxiety I have experienced. Patiently listening to my stories about life in Iraq and about this project, she has carefully provided me with tools to heal, thrive, and find confidence in myself. I was lucky to have her as a therapist, and I'm fortunate to now call her a friend.

My aunts and their husbands in London, Maream Sharara-Shaw and Jim Shaw, and Balkis Sharara Chadirji and the late Rifat Chadirji, have always been there for me, and I thank them profusely and sincerely. Finally, Andrew Stewart has been a supportive and caring partner, always eager to share the joy and triumph when I finished a chapter and to provide comfort and reassurance in moments of doubt. He taught me to take Saturdays off and to go on vacations. With him, I learned to enjoy the simple things in life, and be more active, which in turn gave me the tools to be more focused and energized when I returned to my desk. Andrew made the journey of writing this book during the last four years a rewarding endeavor. I cannot thank him enough.

# RETURN TO RUIN

❨ INTRODUCTION ❩

# EMPIRE AND SUBJECTIVITY

In the summer of 2002, I left Lebanon to start my doctoral degree at Columbia University in New York City. The atmosphere was charged with war talk. Everyone was discussing the Bush administration's preparations to invade Iraq. The antiwar camp was strong on Columbia's campus. Students and professors demonstrated against the war, organizing sit-ins and lectures to warn of its consequences and expose the hypocrisy of the U.S. government. The pro-war camp, especially outside academia, was more powerful. It agitated about weapons of mass destruction, Saddam Hussein's oppression of Iraqis, and the alleged links between Hussein and al-Qaeda. The camps shouted at each other, and among themselves, about freedom and democracy versus colonialism, sovereignty versus imperialism, and human rights versus oil. Iraqis, who have borne the brunt of Western governments' support of Hussein (and their falling out with his regime), and who were going to bear the brunt of another war, were marginal and faceless in these struggles and debates.

I was surprised to find that no one around me in New York was curious about Iraq or life under Saddam Hussein. I was born and raised in Iraq and had only left the country in the fall of 1997. The prospect of another war haunted me. With the exception of one graduate student, who became a close friend, no one asked me about Iraqis' lives during the Iran-Iraq War (1980–1988) and the 1991 Gulf War or about the catastrophic impact of the sanctions imposed on Iraq by the United Nations in 1990 after Iraqi troops invaded Kuwait.

People around me were reducing a place I knew intimately—the place where I came of age and where I had buried my parents and sister—to talking points. For me, Iraq was a place associated with real people and personal memories. But almost overnight it became the subject of abstract political arguments and theoretical interventions.

Seven months after I arrived in the United States, on March 19, 2003, I left the university library earlier than usual so that I could listen to President George W. Bush deliver a speech following the expiration of the forty-eight-hour ultimatum he had given Saddam Hussein and his sons to leave Iraq. Shortly after I got home, I heard Bush's voice on the radio: "My fellow citizens, at this hour, American and coalition forces are in the early stages of military operations to disarm Iraq, to free its people and to defend the world from grave danger."[1] I thought of the decades of war, dictatorship, and hardship that the Iraqi people had already endured for the sake of U.S. imperial interests in Iraq since the fall of the monarchy in 1958. Iraqis simply did not matter in these decisions, whether in the past or now as the invasion loomed. The dehumanization of Iraqis cut deeply through my heart as I listened to the speech, and I cried uncontrollably.

Over the following months, I faced daily news about the dismantlement of the Iraqi state and its social fabric. The U.S. military watched as Iraqis looted and destroyed state institutions. U.S. Secretary of Defense Donald Rumsfeld hailed the destruction and looting as "creative chaos" out of which a free and democratic Iraq would be born. The Coalition Provisional Authority, which governed Iraq on behalf of the United States, dissolved the Iraqi army and waged a de-Ba'athification campaign to minimize the role of the state and to implement neoliberal policies, which entailed drastically limiting the role of the state in providing social services and jobs, privatizing state industries and institutions, and deregulating markets. Moreover, the United States established a government in Iraq that allocated positions according to a sectarian quota system. This state structure ended up dividing Iraqis, foreclosing the possibilities of forging a unified national identity. Iraqis now had to participate in politics and access services on the basis of their ethnic and sectarian affiliation. Meanwhile, the U.S. military failed to protect the Iraqi borders, and foreign fighters—including members of al-Qaeda—began to infiltrate the country, which exacerbated sectarian violence. I watched

U.S. policies throw Iraq into perpetual violence. News of suicide bombings and other attacks carried out by foreign fighters and Iraqi militias, as well as of violence perpetuated by the U.S. military, became the norm. In this new status quo, Iraqi casualties were reduced to statistics, which warranted little attention from Western audiences.

The erasure of Iraqi individuals from discussions and news about the U.S. occupation prompted me to focus my research on them. As a privileged Iraqi who now lives abroad, I owe it to Iraqis to offer a more nuanced version of their stories, their hopes, their disappointments, and their losses. Since it was almost impossible to do research in Iraq given the deteriorating situation there, I chose London, home to the largest Iraqi diasporic community in Europe at the time. The arrival of thousands of Iraqis in London in the late 1970s and early 1990s to escape Saddam Hussein's reign speaks to the imperial encounter between Iraq and the United States, as well as to the connection between displacement and imperial formations. Moreover, the Iraqi community in London played a major role in shaping post-Hussein Iraq through their agitation for regime change with different U.S. administrations throughout the 1990s and early 2000s. Members of this community, who were part of the exilic Iraqi opposition to Saddam Hussein's regime, also endorsed a sectarian discourse that was eventually implemented in the country.

I arrived in London in the summer of 2006 to begin fieldwork. This turned out to be a pivotal moment for the city's Iraqi community. Iraqis had come to the United Kingdom in large numbers in the late 1970s after Saddam Hussein rose to power, and the vast majority believed that they would return to Iraq once Hussein was gone. To them, the removal of Hussein would herald a return to a utopian past: the Iraq they remembered before Hussein's violent reign. And they hoped that the U.S. invasion would bring social reforms and political stability. However, by the summer of 2006, widespread sectarian violence, which reached its peak between 2006 and 2008, dimmed these hopes that the country might return to the imagined glories of the pre-Hussein era. The scale of destruction the U.S. military inflicted on Iraq left most of the exiles I came to know in a state of shock. Images of violence circulated daily on television, as did stories of killed, kidnapped, and displaced relatives and friends. Their hope and anticipation gave way to disbelief and disappointment.

During my initial phase of fieldwork, from 2006 to 2008, I listened to Iraqis reminisce about anticolonial struggles in the 1940s and 1950s, vibrant political and social spaces defined by demands for equality and women's liberation, radical social reforms, and dreams for a prosperous future for everyone. I also heard stories about death and horror during the CIA-backed first Ba'th coup, in 1963, and radical political transformations with the rise of the one-party regime in Iraq following the second Ba'th coup, in 1968. These narratives of nostalgia and anguish were accompanied by stories about flight and expulsion from Iraq, deaths of family members and close friends, life in exile, yearnings to see Iraq again, and efforts to build homes in diaspora and define Iraqi subjectivities. There were also stories of excitement at visiting Iraq for the first time in decades and bewilderment at seeing how the U.S. occupation, sectarian violence, and decades of war and neglect had left the country, especially Baghdad, unrecognizable.

As I listened to Iraqis, I realized that their narratives of displacement, as well as their general life trajectories, were deeply enmeshed in imperial interventions in Iraq that have taken place since the early twentieth century and continue to the present. Iraqis in London, like those in Iraq, are "imperial subjects," whose lives are inseparable from the histories of Britain and the United States in the region, particularly the latter's efforts to safeguard U.S. oil companies' access to Iraqi oil, to deter Iraq from embracing communism during the Cold War, and to support regimes that would guarantee what the United States perceived as regional stability. These imperial trajectories also became dynamic terrains in which political, gendered, religious, and class differences were inscribed, invoked, and reconfigured in diaspora. This book focuses on how Iraqi political subjectivity—that is, the processes of defining and constructing notions of selfhood and inner lives—in diaspora has been shaped by British colonial rule, U.S. imperial intervention, resource extraction, histories of exile, local and international struggles, and other structures of power. It also explores how Iraqis have responded to these events in culturally specific ways. Moreover, it examines the impact of the U.S. occupation on the diasporic experiences of the Iraqi community in London, as well as the transnational connections it opened and the possibilities it foreclosed.

The story of Iraqi exile and dispossession is closely enmeshed in a genealogy of imperialism. Through its support of authoritarian regimes since the

1960s and fueling of ongoing wars for the past four decades in Iraq, the United States has inscribed itself on the lives of Iraqis. This imperial violence led to the exile of thousands of Iraqis and to the formation of diasporic communities abroad.[2] The effects of the U.S. interventions in Iraq were not contained within the borders of Iraq, but touched Iraqis in diaspora as well. It prolonged their exile, prevented them from enjoying a safe Iraq when they visited after 2003, and caused them anxiety over the fates of relatives and friends and over the possible disintegration of the country. In other words, Iraqis have inhabited an imperial past and present. Scholars have described empire as a "way of life" as far as the United States' foreign policy is concerned, inscribed in its very institutions and practices.[3] But this is also true for Iraqis, who have lived and experienced empire for decades.

The spiraling violence in Iraq brought about by the U.S. occupation and the sectarian conflict raised questions among Iraqis in London about their notion of the self, imagination of the past, and relationship to Iraq. These questions fueled heated discussion among Iraqis about citizenship and the past and intensified their efforts to provide accounts that critiqued the status quo. Iraqis I met in London were avid storytellers who were keen on providing testimonies about their experiences and lives. For them, life stories became a means to bear witness and to write themselves back into a history and a country that was erased constantly by imperial violence. Their narratives provide an alternative account of Iraq and unearth the patterns of systemic violence they endured for decades. Occupying a space of imperial debris became productive of discourses of the self and of nostalgic reminiscences about the past. These practices of re/membering reconnected Iraqis to their national community, produced nostalgic and revisionist accounts of the past to make sense of the present, and highlighted the historical conditions that led to their exile and dispossession.[4] To Iraqis in London, re/membering has become a way to suture together a personal narrative with historical conditions to make sense of their history of displacement. These narratives were also situated in debates about modernity and secularism, piety and religion, visions of the past and future, gender and class, and home and diaspora.

The following chapters focus on the life stories of five Iraqis who grappled with defining Iraqi selfhood amid the ongoing destruction of their homeland and the increasing polarization of the Iraqi community in London along sectarian and ethnic lines. Their reminiscences were rooted in the political structures they inhabited, as well as social sensibilities and generational differences. The older generation (chapters 1 and 2), whose members came of age in the 1940s and 1950s, played an important role in the anticolonial struggle in Iraq and shaped Iraqi memory of that time as an era defined by progressive and revolutionary ideals in which Iraqi subjects were revolutionary agents who were involved in a struggle to bring about social equality, women's rights, and national independence. These prevailing narratives of selfhood and reminiscences of the past were marked by shifts in the understanding of Iraqiness among the younger generation (chapters 3 and 4), whose members came of age in exile and were haunted by their parents' stories about Iraq. While the efforts of the younger generation to carve out an Iraqi subjectivity were informed by attempts to define notions of home and belonging around a place they barely remembered, they also reflected changes in the Iraqi political landscape, which had come to be defined by rising piety and aversion to political activism. Iraqi subjectivity became associated with a religious discourse that perceived Iraq as a place of holy religious sites and religious experiences that dated back to the seventh century. Yet another narrative and notion of subjectivity then began to challenge the prevailing discourse about the past and the religious counter-discourses. This narrative revolved around the endurance and suffering of the Iraqis who had remained in Iraq (chapter 5). The community in London came to perceive those who had lived through Saddam Hussein's authoritarian regime, the Iran-Iraq War, the Gulf War, the sanction years, and the U.S. occupation as Iraqis who had lived the quintessential Iraqi experience.

## Imperial Entanglements

This book sheds light on how Britain's and the United States' interventions in Iraq have shaped Iraqis' life trajectories and experiences of exile. While British colonial rule in Iraq has received wide scholarly attention, the role the United States has played in the country since the early 1960s has been mainly limited to studies of the occupation in 2003. Therefore, the book aims to write Iraqis back into the imperial history of particularly the United States. The histories of Iraq and the United States are deeply intertwined. On the one hand, the United States has had a direct impact on political developments in Iraq and the lives of Iraqis through its policies supporting regime changes and the perpetuation of war. On the other hand, Iraq has been essential to U.S. economic interests. Iraqi arms purchases bolstered the military-industrial complex in the United States, and stable access to Middle East oil secured U.S. dominance in the global economy. I employ the concept of imperial encounter to shed light on how the United States and Iraq, countries usually seen to occupy different worlds, are entangled.[5] This concept of the encounter decenters the nation-state and emphasizes global connections. A mere focus on the nation-state to understand histories of violence and displacement conceals the role of Western imperial powers in shaping affairs in Third World countries. The framework of the encounter demonstrates that Iraq and the United States are no longer separate entities, but are entangled in an unequal power relation that has reconfigured the lives of Iraqis. Scholars have advised against approaching the United States as an entity confined to its territorial boundaries; rather, we must examine the relationship between U.S. imperialism and other countries and U.S. efforts to produce subjects beyond its national boundaries through neoliberal policies.[6]

Rather than merely neoliberal policies, however, Iraqis have experienced the U.S. empire through political and military interventions. As a military empire, the United States has asserted its right to threaten and employ violence in order to protect its interests and allies, promote its values, and safeguard the world from what it regards as evil forces.[7] In this framework, U.S. militarism is presented as a gift to other nations, taking the forms of military aid, sales of weapons, training of troops, and the establishment of bases.[8] In Iraq, U.S. military involvement entailed military interventions in three wars and an occupation, the sale of arms to allies, economic aid to Hussein's regime in the 1980s, training of the Iraqi army and police after the invasion, and the establishment of bases in the Gulf. But it also involved the backing of coups, the support of authoritarian regimes, and the imposition of economic sanctions. The United States framed its support of Hussein's regime in the 1980s as protecting its national interests in the region, its imposition of the sanctions in the 1990s as aiming to disarm Iraq of weapons of mass destruction and protect allies in the region, and its invasion of Iraq in 2003 as delivering U.S. values—namely, freedom and democracy—to the Iraqi people.

In terms of U.S. imperial interventions in the world, Iraq is not an exceptional case. Scholars have begun to historicize the debate on U.S. imperialism and to situate the occupation of Iraq and Afghanistan within the imperial legacy of the Unites States.[9] Thus, the War on Terror after 9/11 can be seen as part and parcel of a long history of U.S. expansion and global domination.[10] Wars and military occupation were foundational to the United States in that genocidal violence was central to the establishment of the United States as a settler-colonial state, as well as to its political and economic hegemony. A permanent state of war, as far as the United States is concerned, thus represents a historical continuum of conquest, cleansing of new frontiers, and control of territories abroad.[11] In this narrative, U.S. interventions in Latin America, the Middle East, and Southeast Asia, as well as its establishment of military bases around the world and imposition of neoliberal reforms, are part of this foundational imperial violence.[12]

This approach to empire emphasizes connections between settler colonialism, racism, economic hegemony, and political interventions. Thus, the decades-long intervention of the United States in Iraq can be seen as part of a continuum of different imperial formations throughout the world. U.S. empire can no longer be seen as a singular event or a relic of the past. Rather, it has persisted throughout the centuries, brought various peoples into its orbit, and left individual lives in ruins.[13] This effort to see connections and assemblages in events that appear to be separate and disconnected raises some questions: How can we write the history of Iraq as part of U.S. imperial history? And how can we relate imperial formations in Iraq to those in other parts of the world, such as the Philippines, Cambodia, Vietnam, Guatemala, Honduras, and Samoa, and to marginalized groups within the United States?

Ann Stoler sheds light on a "U.S. imperial script: that Samoa is not related to the Philippines is not related to Nicaragua is not related to Iraq."[14] She introduces the term *disassemblage* to "identify how things get cut off from one another in our conceptualizations. What prevents people, relations, and things from being seen as proximate, implicated, and dependent?"[15] Neutral terms have been used to camouflage and disconnect imperialist ambitions: the occupation of Native American land has been seen as an expansion, not colonization; the undermining of Latin American independence movements is presented as wars against European colonial powers, rather than the thwarting of slaves' and creole pioneers' struggles for freedom; and military intervention abroad is cast as efforts to bring democracy and freedom to the rest of the world.[16]

The U.S. rhetoric of national security and protection of world peace, moreover, has been embedded in the desire to secure access to natural resources. Toby Jones asserts that American militarism in the Middle East, often justified as a way to combat terrorism, rogue states, weapons of mass destruction, and geopolitical insecurity, is also about control over the region's energy resources, particularly oil.[17] Jones proposes that scholars of U.S. empire focus on this intertwining of energy and security in U.S. foreign policy to understand how their infrastructures have been built into each other, and to what effect.[18] The efforts of the United States to secure access to oil have thrust Iraq and the region into an endless cycle of violence, which has led to the death and displacement of millions of Iraqis.

Iraq's oil reserves and geopolitical location have shaped colonial and imperial interests in the country since the early twentieth century. Britain's invasion of Iraq during World War I was partly motivated by its efforts to have access to the oilfields in Mosul.[19] Iraq officially gained its independence in 1932, but it remained under de facto British control. This status quo changed with the overthrow of the monarchy in 1958. The 1958 Revolution was a pivotal moment for Iraq's relations with imperial powers. While the fall of the monarchy led to the departure of the British, it also brought Iraq into the orbit of the United States more directly. The establishment of Iraq as a republic and the efforts of different Iraqi politicians to control the country's oil heralded the beginning of U.S. interventions in Iraq. After the first Iraqi president, Abdul Karim Qasim, nationalized the oilfields that the Iraq Petroleum Company—a British company—had not developed, the Kennedy administration came to see Qasim as a threat to U.S. interests and began to look for opposition groups that would overthrow him.[20] U.S. intelligence agencies saw an ally in the Baʿth Party, an anti-imperialist, socialist, and Arab nationalist party established in Iraq in 1947.[21] On February 8, 1963, backed by the CIA, the Baʿth Party staged a coup d'état that toppled Qasim. The coup began with a slaughter of Iraqi communists (the police and National Guard relying on lists provided by U.S. intelligence sources to hunt them down).[22] Between seven thousand and ten thousand communists were imprisoned and tortured.[23] Thousands were killed.[24]

The question of the nationalization of Iraqi oil fields remained a contentious issue for different U.S. administrations in the 1960s and early 1970s, with the latter offering or withholding military support to different Iraqi governments in their operations against the Kurds, depending on their oil policies.[25] In the late 1970s, Saddam Hussein's emergence as the undisputed leader of Iraq and the revolution in Iran together brought a major shift in U.S.-Iraq relations. In 1979, the Islamic Revolution in Iran overthrew Shah Mohammad Reza Pahlavi, a close ally of the United States, and the ensuing U.S. embassy crisis in Tehran prompted the United States to look for other allies in the region. Iraq was seen as a countervailing force to the new regime in Iran. At the time, Zbigniew Brzezinski, President Jimmy Carter's national security advisor, stated in a television interview that "we see no fundamental incompatibility of interests between the United States and Iraq," and added that "we do not feel that American-Iraqi relations need to be frozen in antagonism."[26] Shortly after the Islamic Revolution, Iraq invaded Iran, starting the Iran-Iraq War. The documents on the role of the Carter administration in giving Iraq the green light to invade Iran remain classified.[27] However, in the early 1980s, the United States began to support Iraq in its war effort. A major breakthrough in U.S.-Iraqi relations occurred in 1983 when Donald Rumsfeld, a special envoy for the Reagan administration at the time, met with Saddam Hussein to offer military and economic aid to Iraq. As a result of this meeting, the United States took Iraq off the list of State Sponsors of Terrorism, restored diplomatic relations, and provided Iraq with dual-use (military and civilian) goods.[28] The United States granted Iraq millions of dollars in trade credits, and U.S. farmers found a new market in Iraq. Moreover, the United States sold weapons to Iraq through Egypt, Jordan, Kuwait, and Saudi Arabia. It also encouraged European countries—in particular, Italy and France—to sell weapons to Hussein. Western governments, especially West Germany, even provided Iraq with chemical weapons.[29] In the meantime, the Ronald Reagan administration dismissed Hussein's brutality as a "stereotype" and pointed out signs of moderation that the regime was showing.[30]

During the "Tanker War," from 1984 to 1985, the United States began to engage actively on the side of Iraq. This phase of the war began when Iraq attacked Iran's oil installations and Iran retaliated by attacking ships in the Gulf that were doing business with Iraq. Western governments—namely, the

United States, Britain, and France—increased their presence in the Gulf. U.S. forces clashed with Iranian naval units, destroyed Iran's naval capacity in 1988, and shot down a civilian Iranian plane.[31] In addition to military support, the United States defended Iraq at the United Nations against Iran's accusation that Iraq had used chemical weapons on its soldiers, and it provided Iraq with satellite intelligence of Iranian troops' locations.[32] Realizing it was involved in a war not only with Iraq but also with Western powers, particularly the United States, Iran accepted a UN-brokered cease-fire.

Having diminished the power of Iran, Saddam Hussein turned his attention to Kurdistan, where an insurgency against his regime had erupted. The military operation culminated in the regime's use of chemical weapons against the Kurds, which led to the destruction of 80 percent of all the Kurdish villages and the death of somewhere between one hundred thousand and two hundred thousand people.[33] The U.S. Senate passed a bill calling for economic sanctions against Iraq in response to its use of chemical weapons. The Reagan administration, however, opposed the bill. Secretary of State George Shultz said that the attacks on the Kurds "were abhorrent and unjustifiable," but one of his deputies thought that the use of sanctions was "premature," while another official claimed that the United States needed "solid, businesslike relations, with Iraq."[34] By 1988, Iraq had become "the twelfth largest overall market for American agricultural exports," while the United States had become a major importer of Iraqi oil.[35] In addition, the United States kept providing Iraq with dual-use technologies. Any sanctions on Iraq would mean that U.S. companies would lose billions of dollars in contracts. The U.S. Chamber of Commerce urged the House Foreign Affairs Committee chairman to "set aside the emotions of the moment," and "ponder the economic costs of sanctions against Iraq."[36] The U.S. Iraq Business Forum—made up of major oil companies like Amoco, Mobil, and Exxon; defense contractors like Lockheed Martin; and other Fortune 500 companies, including AT&T and General Motors—led the anti-sanctions lobbying.[37]

Iraq had borrowed heavily to fund its war with Iran, and by the war's end, it was $40 billion in debt to Kuwait. Meanwhile, Kuwait had increased its oil production, which brought down prices and therefore Iraq's revenues. Iraq objected and refused to pay its debt. Instead, in the summer of 1990, Iraq invaded Kuwait, marking another shift in U.S.-Iraq relations, this time toward a policy of "dual containment" of both Iran and Iraq."[38] Following the invasion of Kuwait, the United States formed an international alliance to drive Iraq out of Kuwait. The military operations that followed, known as Operation Desert Storm, had a devastating impact on Iraq. A massive bombing campaign, which took place over forty-three days in 1991, caused an estimated $232 billion in damage.[39] The heavy bombardment targeted military installments but also led to a massive breakdown of infrastructure, including water and sewage treatment, agricultural production and food distribution, health care, communications, and power generation.[40] Four months after the war, Iraq had managed to restore electricity to only about a quarter of its prewar level.

The defeat of the Iraqi army was followed by uprisings in the north and south against Saddam Hussein's regime. Motivated by President George H. W. Bush's call upon the Iraqi people to overthrow the regime, people in Basra, Amara, Nasiriyya, Najaf, and Karbala rose up and managed to control large areas by the end of February 1991. At the same time, the Kurds rose against the regime in the north, and Peshmerga forces—Kurdish military groups—were in control of most of Kurdistan by the end of March. However, the United States and its allies did not provide the rebels with any support, fearing the fragmentation of Iraq and the formation of a Shi'i state beholden to Iran.[41] At the time, General Colin Powell, then chair of the Joint Chiefs of Staff, asserted that "for the previous ten years, Iran not Iraq had been our Persian Gulf nemesis. We wanted Iraq to continue as a threat and a counterweight to Iran."[42]

Soon afterward, the regime turned its attention to the uprising in the north. The Republican Guard was deployed and "hit back, capturing Kirkuk, driving into the rebel-held areas and inflicting heavy casualties on the Kurds."[43] The campaign against the Kurds raised fears of chemical attacks, and thousands of people fled to Iran and Turkey. As many as two million people "were on the move within the space of a few days, leading to the disintegration of the rebel forces."[44]

The fates of the Kurds and the Shi'is diverged after the failure of the uprisings. The United Nations, backed by the United States and Britain, set up a "safe haven" in Kurdistan, which granted the Kurds de facto autonomy from Baghdad. However, the south remained under the control of Hussein. A month after the failed uprisings, a former French foreign minister, Claude Cheysson, reflected, "Though it is horrible to say so, fortunately Saddam Hussein was there to crush the [Shi'i] uprising in the south. Otherwise it would have triggered a new tide of Islamic fundamentalism in Iran and across the Gulf."[45] Reeling from a devastating military campaign and failed uprisings, Iraqis had to contend with a degraded environment, a ruthless regime, and the continuation of harsh sanctions. Though Iraq withdrew from Kuwait in 1991, the United Nations would not lift the sanctions until Iraq disarmed, which Hussein refused to do, and this had a devastating impact on the Iraqi people. Families struggling to make ends meet had to sell their possessions, including furniture, cars, jewelry, clothing, electronic goods, and part of their houses, such as doors and windows.[46] In addition, the sanctions led to an increase in crime, theft, and prostitution. The basic monthly rations distributed by the Iraqi government prevented mass starvation in the country, but they did not limit malnutrition. It is estimated that at least five hundred thousand children died between 1990 and 2003 due to malnutrition and lack of basic services.[47] When asked by a journalist about the price of half a million Iraqi children for the sanctions, Madeleine Albright, the secretary of the state in the Bill Clinton administration, famously replied that "the price is worth it."[48] This catastrophe was brought about by policies adopted by the United States and Britain, in particular, which included restricting imports of food and goods into a country that was heavily dependent on foreign products, the undermining of the sale of oil in exchange for food, and the destruction of public infrastructure during the war.[49] Joy Gordon called the sanction years, from 1990 to 2003, an invisible war waged mainly by the United States and Britain through their efforts to stifle any attempts to lift the sanctions by members in the United Nations.

The election of President George W. Bush in 2001 and the appointment of neoconservatives in his administration brought about another shift in U.S. policy.[50] Since the late 1990s, neoconservatives had agitated for regime change in Iraq. September 11 provided an opportunity to sell the war to the U.S. public and internationally under the pretext of alleged links between Iraq and al-Qaeda, of saving Iraqis from Saddam Hussein's brutality, and of disarming Iraq. On March 19, 2003, the United States began its "shock and awe" military operation against Iraq, which ended on May 1, 2003. The military operation quickly achieved its purpose of overthrowing the Hussein regime.

Following the invasion, however, the situation in Iraq deteriorated immediately. Looting and destruction of state institutions ensued, while the

U.S. military protected only the Ministry of Oil. The U.S. occupation of Iraq and the measures taken by the Coalition Provisional Authority—such as the institutionalization of a sectarian quota system, the alienation of Sunnis, the disbanding of the army, the de-Ba'athification order, and the failure to protect Iraqi borders—fueled an insurgency in the country and led to rampant sectarian violence. Suicide bombings, car bombs, and explosions became daily occurrences. In addition, the U.S. military employed brute force to deal with the violence and the attacks on its troops. The leaked pictures of abused and brutalized prisoners at the notorious Abu Ghraib prison epitomized the U.S. military's use of extreme violence against Iraqis.[51] The estimated number of Iraqis killed due to the civil war and the U.S. occupation through 2018 is around 182,000.[52] Three and a half to five million Iraqis were either internally displaced or arrived as refugees in Jordan and Syria.[53] The devastation caused by the violence and the occupation were accompanied by a total collapse of basic services, such as water and electricity. The U.S. occupation of Iraq and the sectarian politics of successive Iraqi governments eventually led to the rise of the Islamic State, which controlled large swaths of Iraq in 2014 until its defeat in 2017.[54]

## Imperial Violence and the Politics of Erasure

Toby Jones situates the U.S. invasion of Iraq within a longer history of U.S. policy in the region. He looks at it as "the latest stage of American militarism in the Middle East. While more considerable in scale, duration, and devastation than previous military misadventures in the region, the Iraq War was the outgrowth of several decades of strategic thinking and policy making about oil."[55] Jones warns against the argument that September 11 was the catalyst for change in U.S. policy in the region, pointing out that this argument fails to consider that "oil and oil producers have long been militarized, the role oil has played in regional confrontation for almost four decades, and the connections between the most recent confrontation with Iraq and those of the past."[56] The U.S. strategic policy focuses on keeping "oil prices stable (not low), and keeping pro-U.S. regimes in power, rather than direct imperial control over oil."[57] To achieve these strategic goals, the United States militarized the region to maintain a fragile balance of power. The U.S. notion of security in the Gulf "was based almost entirely on the ability of oil producers to purchase the machines of war."[58] The arms race among the Gulf states was a large boon for the military-industrial complex in the United States. Between 1975 and 1979, Iran, Iraq, and Saudi Arabia made "one-quarter of all global arms purchases."[59] However, militarization exacerbated "existing instabilities and hastened an era of regional conflict."[60]

Jones approaches the Iran-Iraq War in terms of this U.S. policy of militarization of oil in the region. Though the U.S. oil policy was not responsible for Saddam Hussein's decision to invade Iran, the arms race and the militarization of the region emboldened Hussein to make the move. After the start of the war, "U.S. policy makers came to see a continuation of the war as a useful way to bog down two of the region's most highly militarized regimes and to stave-off short-term threats to the regional order and the political economy of oil."[61] Likewise, in 1990, Saddam Hussein pursued a military solution to Iraq's debt to Kuwait and to the latter's increase of its oil production. The invasion of Kuwait furthered the militarization of the region, and the mobilization of U.S. troops in that conflict was the largest since the Vietnam War.[62] In this framework, the United States' decision to pursue a policy of regime change in Iraq in 2003 was "the high-water mark of direct American militarism in the region"[63] Jones suggests we see the period not as a series of wars but as "a single long war, one in which pursuing regional security and protecting oil and American-friendly oil producers has been the principal strategic rationale."[64]

The United States' interventions in Iraq since 1958 not only thrust the country into a cycle of violence and perpetual wars, but also exacerbated ethnic and sectarian tensions. The brutal campaign against the lower-class Kurds and Shiites of the Iraqi Communist Party in 1963 by the upper-middle-class Sunni Arabs in the Ba'th Party represented an ethnic, sectarian, and class conflict.[65] Likewise, the United States' support of Kurds in the 1970s to destabilize Iraq—and its suspension of that support when relations with Baghdad improved—aggravated ethnic tensions in the country. In the 1980s, not only did the United States provide Iraq with dual-use technologies, it turned a blind eye to Hussein's use of chemical weapons against the Kurds and Iranian soldiers. Moreover, the decision of the United States to allow Saddam Hussein's forces to put down the rebellion in the south in 1991 polarized Iraq along sectarian lines when the rebels came to see that Hussein targeted them as Shi'is first and foremost. After 2003, the institutionalization of a sectarian quota system by the Coalition Provisional Authority, in which ethnic and sectarian identities became legal markers linked to access to power and privileges at the expense of a national identity, further destabilized the country. The United States' dismantlement of the Iraqi state to introduce neoliberal policies in the country, as well as its failure to protect Iraqi borders, fueled an insurgency that brought Iraq to the brink of a civil war.

However, U.S. officials and pundits read the authoritarian rule of Saddam Hussein and the sectarian violence that erupted in 2003 in Iraq as internal Iraqi affairs—manifestations of Oriental despotism and primordial hatred—rather than as events that have been entangled in national and imperial power dynamics. The U.S. imperial script, which disaggregates places and camouflages events, is based on a politics of concealment and culturalist interpretations. Erasing the history of the role of the United States in Iraq is part of the process of imperial formations, which are predicated upon simplified dominant discourses of events. The main discourse in the United States about what went wrong in Iraq has focused on intrinsic sectarian divisions and timeless characteristics of Iraqis. Interestingly, in 2007, a manual written for the American servicemembers in Iraq during World War II was republished; it included a new foreword by Lieutenant Coronel John A. Nagl, who had served in Iraq in 2003 and had contributed to *The U.S. Army/Marine Corps Counterinsurgency Field Manual*. To Nagl, the manual, written in 1943, is illuminating, since some of the guidance it contains is "timeless" and "eerie to anyone who has fought in Iraq recently." What Nagl finds fascinating and true about the manual is the figure of the tall man "in the flowing robes" who is a first-class fighter, "highly skilled in guerrilla warfare."[66] The book tells readers that if this figure is their friend, then he will be a staunch ally; however, if he is their enemy, they better be careful. The image of Iraqis as Arab fighters who existed throughout history is linked to another piece of advice in the manual that catches Nagl's attention, namely, the nomadic nature of the Iraq society. He laments the fact that had more consideration been shown to Sunni sheikhs who head tribes, the U.S. military could have prevented "the fervent insurgency" against its troops.[67] Not only did this narrative erase any role the United States played in Iraq affairs, it also presented Iraqis mainly as violent fighters who could not reconcile their differences.

This narrative was also reproduced by some academics. Fouad Ajami, who was one of the premier experts on the Middle East and an avid proponent of the U.S. invasion in 2003, ponders why Iraqis failed to accept "the foreigner's gift," namely the U.S. liberation of Iraq. He states that Saddam Hussein "has not resolved the ethnic and sectarian feuds of the country; he had suppressed them ... here too the tombstone would be rolled back, and from the grave there would spring the old atavisms awaiting release and satisfaction."[68] This statement reflects the dominant perception of Iraqi society in the wake of the U.S. invasion as a place consisting of three antagonistic groups: Sunnis, Shi'is, and Kurds. That Iraqis failed to accept the gift of freedom handed to them by U.S. liberators is attributed to the resilience of transhistorical primordial categories.

A striking feature of the military, academic, and journalistic writings on Iraq published after 2003 was the absence of the term *Iraqis*. In the foreword of the 1943 manual, Nagl refers to the inhabitants of Iraq often as "people" and sometimes as "insurgents." Though the manual itself uses the term *Iraqis*, Nagl employs the term only once in his foreword. This erasure of *Iraqis* is often repeated in newspapers articles written during the U.S. occupation of Iraq. Instead of *Iraqis*, the reader often encounters the terms *Sunnis*, *Shi'is*, and *Kurds*. The dominance of Orientalist tropes that depict Iraqis mainly in terms of religion and ethnicity implies the absence of national feelings among Iraqis and the artificiality of Iraq as a nation-state. Calls for the division of Iraq into three states—for the Sunnis in the center of Iraq, the Kurds in the north, and the Shi'is in the south—were predicated upon the premise that Iraqis could not coexist together as a nation. Writing for the *New York Times* in 2003, Leslie Gelb critiques President Bush's decision to transfer power to Iraqis, which overlooked the difficulties of governing a country composed of three distinct ethnic and sectarian communities.[69] Gelb argues that dividing Iraq into three states would "correct the historical defect" and ultimately serve U.S. interests. A divided Iraq would weaken the "the troublesome and domineering Sunnis" and enable the United States to get out of a costly war it was not winning. Violence after 2003 in Iraq emerges as an intrinsic phenomenon, linked to sectarian affiliations. Implied in narratives of sectarian upheaval is the suggestion that Hussein's use of violence was the only means to keep the country unified.

While Iraqis emerge as ahistorical figures who could not outgrow their divisions, the depiction of bloodshed perpetrated by Saddam Hussein's regime centers around the concept of spectacular violence and moral failings. Writing on the eve of the U.S. invasion of Iraq, John Burns sees the impending military operations as an opportunity to get access to "the darkest recesses of Iraqi life."[70] He depicts Saddam Hussein as a tyrant who "plunged this country into a bloodbath of medieval proportions, and exported some of that terror to his neighbors." Likewise, Erica Good provides another example of spectacular violence in describing prisons in Iraq under Hussein's reign: "The objects unearthed at Iraqi prisons, palaces and safe houses speak of brutality and indulgence. A gold machine gun. A cable used to deliver electric shocks to ears and genitals. Fantasy paintings of snakes, monsters and unclad women."[71] Good links Hussein's paranoia and aggression to the psychopathology of his early childhood. The violence committed by Hussein emerges as the product of personal moral failings.

But accounting for violence as a cultural phenomenon that has persisted throughout history erases the imperial and national entanglements that shaped political events and exacerbated ethnic and sectarian tensions in Iraq. Using these encounters as a framework for thinking about violence in Iraq as the confluence of national and imperial formations sheds light on the structural conditions.[72] Rather than seeing sectarian and ethnic identities as contemporary phenomena that are produced, reinforced, or otherwise transformed and weakened in historical contexts, the mainstream discourse on Iraq in the United States puts forward a timeless and culturalist interpretation of violence. The U.S. occupation of Iraq, coupled with its attendant deployment of sectarianism as a political technology, thus has foreclosed the possibility of nonsectarian modes of seeing or critiquing political life in Iraq.

These representations of Iraq raised heated debates among Iraqis in London over the nature of the Iraqi society and the turn of events after 2003. Through their reflections on their lives in Iraq and relationships in diaspora, Iraqis I met in London contested these essentialist depictions and provided alternative accounts of their country. Their narratives speak to the vibrant political and social landscapes that existed until the rise of Saddam Hussein to power in 1979 and the shifts in political projects and aspirations throughout the twentieth century. Through their chronicling of life in Iraq and diaspora, aiming to carve out Iraqi subjectivities informed by national and imperial events, Iraqis in London sought to write themselves back into an imperial history and challenge the politics of erasure—whether through literal violence or simplistic narratives—that they have endured for decades.

## Subject Formation

Just as Iraqi history has been entangled in national and imperial events, my London-based interlocutors' efforts to carve out an Iraqi subjectivity have been historically contingent processes that involved different colonial and imperial powers, disciplinary national institutions, and personal circumstances and experiences.[73] Different social and political constellations—including the state, family and community, colonial and imperial realities, and market logics—constitute the individual as a subject through social control. However, governmentality is not the only venue through which a subject is produced. Through inhabiting different political and social spaces, which also intersect with class and gender, subjects have the opportunity to reflect on their circumstances and fashion a self based on their experiences. Just as historically contingent settings constitute individuals as subjects, people themselves can carve a sense of selfhood through their narratives and attempts to make sense of their positions in the present and imagined future.

Colonial and imperial relations have played a major role in defining Iraqis' sense of selfhood, whether in the past or in the present.[74] For older Iraqis who came of age under British colonial rule in Iraq, the solution to end colonial realities and to do away with the pro-British and feudal Iraqi government was through anticolonial struggle. By organizing in the underground Iraqi Communist Party and participating in protests against treaties that the British officials imposed on Iraq and against social inequality, young Iraqis at the time saw themselves as revolutionaries who were engaged in a struggle to bring about radical transformations in Iraq that would constitute a total rupture with the status quo. As such, the British presence in Iraq shaped consciousness of oneself as a revolutionary subject inhabiting a historical moment that swept Third World countries with anticolonial spirit.

Unlike in Egypt and India, the British in Iraq did not aim to produce Iraqi subjects through regulation of the individual body or techniques of social control. Rather, they resorted to aerial bombardment, servitude, and corporal punishment as means to control and discipline the population.⁷⁵ They also engaged in heated debates with Iraqi officials and educators over reforming the educational system, the family, and the citizenship law. The British thought of development as the ability to access Iraq's natural resources, especially oil, and to develop the country according to native lines. British officials in Iraq were against the expansion of the public school system, fearing that over-education would produce subjects engaged in political agitation and unwilling to do manual labor. Iraqi nationalists, by contrast, saw the school and the family as arenas of social reform and economic development, which aimed to produce new Iraqi subjects worthy of sovereignty.⁷⁶ They particularly saw that educating young women would produce modern mothers who were capable of raising healthy citizens. However, the family and the school did not become sites to produce docile and governable subjects. Rather, they emerged as hubs for revolutionary action and imagination. Older Iraqis spoke of progressive and nationalist parents and brothers who from a young age made them aware of social inequality in the Iraqi society and of anticolonial struggle worldwide. Once they went to secondary schools, they were further exposed to communist and nationalist trends that advocated for political freedom, women's liberation, and social justice, all of which fueled their political and social activism.

As colonial policies shaped Iraqis' consciousness as revolutionary subjects, they also produced legal precarity for a certain segment of the population. In 1924, the British drafted the first Iraqi Nationality Law, which divided the population into authentic Iraqis (namely residents of Ottoman Iraq who held the Ottoman nationality) and inauthentic Iraqis (namely residents of Ottoman Iraq who opted for the Persian nationality under the Ottomans in order to avoid military service). This law and the subsequent amendments had a far-reaching impact decades later when the Baʻth regime in the early 1970s and 1980s used the law to deport thousands of so-called Iraqis of Iranian origin to Iran. It rendered certain Iraqis as second-class citizens who could be subject to denaturalization during times of crisis. Moreover, deported Iraqis who arrived in Iran became "unwelcome guests" when the Iran-Iraq War erupted, and many then moved to London in order to find a home and build a future defined by legal stability and social mobility. The years of exile the Iraqi deportees endured in Iran and the United Kingdom prompted them to fashion a multifaceted Iraqi self that was at once rooted in notions of Iraqi nationhood, British multiculturalism, Shi'i Islam, and diasporic connections. As such, colonial afterlives, represented by the nationality laws, continued to shape Iraqis' lives decades after the departure of the British from Iraq.

In addition to colonial relations, class, gender, and religious sensibilities also played a role in shaping how my interlocutors perceived themselves and other Iraqis. When older Iraqis reminisced about the "good old days" as a time of political mobilization, social vibrancy, and cultural renaissance, they often spoke about the experience of middle-class Baghdadis whose families could afford to send both their sons and daughters to school and college and who had the means to participate in the intellectual and artistic scene in the capital. This imagination of the vibrant past sidelined the experiences of the majority of Iraqis, who lived in abject poverty under the monarchy. When the poor figured into these narratives, they were presented as people in need of social intervention—through education and medical care—to refashion them as healthy citizens who could leave behind their backward traditions and participate in the development of the country. As such, the revolutionary project that aimed to produce modern subjects dedicated to national liberation and progress was also disciplinary in its outlook toward the poor. These notions of the self were rooted in debates on modernity, tradition, and religion. Iraqis who participated in the anticolonial struggle and endorsed communist ideals saw themselves as modern and progressive subjects who were doing away with tradition—such as the subordination of women and outmoded religious practices—and imagining a utopian future of sovereignty and equality. Moreover, this construction of the self as a revolutionary subject was gendered to a great extent in that the status of women became the marker of the modernity of the nation and the self. The debate over women's access to legal and political rights became a heated issue over national liberation and the role of women in contributing to the building of a modern state in Iraq.[77]

While the idea of Iraqis as revolutionaries became a prevailing discourse in diaspora, it began to be challenged by another discourse of the self, namely the construction of Iraqis as pious selves. With the rise of religiosity in diaspora since the 1990s, some of the younger Iraqis in London began to identify themselves as modern pious Muslims, whose idea of selfhood combined notions of religiosity, nationhood, and modernity. Rather than a hub for revolutionary ideas, Iraq emerges as a land of holy cities and Shi'i religious history that dates back to the seventh century. However, this discourse of the self constituted a rupture with religious practices of the past. Young religious Iraqis in London saw themselves as different from their parents, who practiced religion out of habit, rather than a true understanding based on the reading of religious texts. They saw this form of religiosity as modern in its outlook in that it aimed to break away from a traditional approach that entailed the blind following of religious scholars. This modern pious self was combined with a strong sense of attachment to Iraq as a nation-state because families had instilled nationalistic feelings in the youth through recurrent reminiscences of Iraq as a place of prosperity and social vibrancy. While this was a class-based discourse in its yearning for "the golden age of Iraq," it was also gendered in that historical religious women emerged as figures to emulate in facing a life defined by exile and diaspora. Religious women who played a major role in historical events in the past and had formidable religious knowledge—especially Prophet Mohammed's daughter and granddaughter—became role models for young religious women, who could not relate to communist women with their negative attitude toward religion.

The imagination of oneself as a revolutionary or a pious Muslim took place against the backdrop of exile and displacement, as well as the fragmentation of Iraq brought about by the U.S. intervention in Iraq for decades. The chronic conditions of dispossession under which Iraqis in Iraq and diaspora lived prompted questions of what is politically possible and what matters most in the making and unmaking of the self.[78] After decades of exile and viewing from afar the wars and violence raging in their homeland, Iraqis in London grappled with what it means to be an Iraqi. The response of Iraqis to this status quo no longer consisted in anti-imperial struggle against the United States. The failure of the postcolonial project of freedom and prosperity and the inability to imagine alternative futures after decades of authoritarianism and war prompted Iraqis in London to perceive Iraqis who arrived in London after 2003 through a narrative of endurance. The Iraqi subject after 2003 was no longer a revolutionary who dreamed of a radical break with the realities of colonialism and inequality through anticolonial struggle, nor was this subject the pious Muslim who believed that a religious project could be the solution to the situation in Iraq. Rather, U.S. imperialism had produced

Iraqis as enduring subjects who persisted under conditions of dispossession. To Iraqis who had arrived in London in the late 1970s and early 1990s, it was the Iraqis who had stayed in Iraq throughout Saddam Hussein's reign and who had been displaced after the U.S. occupation, who had persisted and suffered through decades of wars and sanctions, that emerged as the authentic Iraqis. It was the ability to endure and linger under precarious conditions of imperial and national violence, economic deprivation, and legal uncertainty that engendered a new sensibility of what it means to be an Iraqi. Providing an account of oneself became a survival technique that aimed to combat the politics of erasure. Whereas the U.S. imperial project was embedded in the denial of Iraqis' humanity, Iraqis found different ways to form themselves as subjects in order to survive and give meaning to their lives.[79]

This notion of the enduring subject was also classed and gendered. The narrative of endurance not only focused on the experiences of newly exiled Iraqis who had lived under Hussein's regime and U.S. occupation, but also provided a critique of middle-class sensibilities of both the revolutionary and religious discourses of the self. In this narrative, the monarchy and British colonial presence no longer emerged as a revolutionary time of high hopes, political vibrancy, and literary renaissance. Rather, it was resignified as a period of destitution and abject poverty for people who lived in the south or the slums of Baghdad. Iraqis in London who could not relate to the life of middle-class Baghdadis saw fellow Iraqis whose parents struggled to make ends meet under the monarchy as the authentic Iraqis whose experience reflected the struggle of the downtrodden majority of Iraqis. Moreover, the fact that the younger generation had lived through hardships and wars furthered the connection between authenticity, political subjectivity, and economic deprivation. In addition, this discourse of the enduring subject was gendered, in that it was Iraqi women who held the families together during the time of poverty under the monarchy and the sanctions in the 1990s and who took over professional positions to keep the state running when men were sent to war or disappeared in prisons after Saddam Hussein's consolidation of power in 1979. In this framework, the more one had suffered and endured during different eras, the more one was an Iraqi. As such, the figure of the enduring Iraqi woman especially from the lower or lower-middle class became the quintessential Iraqi, as men had failed to provide for the family.

Throughout the span of my fieldwork in London (2006–2019), I was struck by the efforts of Iraqis to carve out political subjectivities and to provide an alternative account of events in Iraq. These debates took place against the backdrop of the desire to show that Iraqis were true nationalists who felt a strong attachment to Iraq and that the salience of sectarian affiliations after 2003 marked a shift in the political landscape in Iraq and forms of self-making. As such, these narratives speak to the fact that subject formation was shaped by colonial rule; imperial interventions; anticolonial struggle; familial and state practices; and gendered, classed, and religious sensibilities. Moreover, the efforts to construct an Iraqi self took place in the context of a diasporic existence brought about by the U.S. interventions in Iraq since the late 1950s until the present.

## Diasporic Trajectories

The United States' interventions in Iraq—including its support of Saddam Hussein's regime and prolonging of wars and occupation—have led to the exodus of thousands of Iraqis from the country and the prolongation of their exile. Iraq does not have a history of economic emigration.[80] Rather, beginning in the first half of the twentieth century, Iraqis began to leave mainly for political reasons.[81] The Arab nature of the Iraqi state raised fears of discrimination and persecution among minorities in the country. The early migrants from the country belonged to religious minorities (such as Chaldeans, Armenians, Assyrians, and Jews) and to ethnic groups (such as Kurds and Turkomans).[82] These migrants formed Iraqi enclaves in the United States, Europe, and Australia. The first Iraqis to arrive in London were Iraqi Jews who were forced out of Iraq by the government and managed to go to London, rather than Israel, in the early 1950s. Following the fall of the monarchy in Iraq in 1958, elite urban Arab families associated with the monarchy also arrived in the United Kingdom. In the early 1960s, these small communities were joined by Iraqi Assyrians. They began to leave for London due to their military association with the British.[83] These communities formed Iraqi enclaves in London that numbered only a few thousand.[84]

It was not until the rise to power of Saddam Hussein in 1979 that Iraqi communities of considerable size began to emerge in Europe, the Middle East, and the United States. The first wave of Iraqis coming to the United

Kingdom arrived in the late 1970s following the rise of Hussein to power. The early 1990s saw the flight of thousands of Iraqis from Iraq and the consolidation of Iraqi communities in Detroit, London, Damascus, and Amman. The Gulf War of 1991, the failure of the uprisings against Saddam Hussein's regime in the north and the south, and the harsh UN-imposed economic sanctions from 1990 until the fall of Hussein's regime in 2003 led to a massive wave of arrivals of Iraqis to the United Kingdom, especially after the British government's decision to grant asylum to Iraqis in the aftermath of the 1991 Gulf War. The largest Iraqi community abroad (until 2003) was most likely in the United Kingdom, which had more than three hundred thousand Iraqis.[85] During my first phase of fieldwork (2006–2008), the Iraqi ambassador to London put the number of Iraqis in the United Kingdom at four hundred thousand, the majority of which resided in London.

The fact that many Iraqis preferred to settle in the United Kingdom following their displacement from Iraq speaks to the colonial ties between the two countries. Despite anticolonial sentiment and joy over the departure of the British from Iraq in 1958, many Iraqis still perceived Britain as a desirable place. Well-to-do families sent their children to study in the United Kingdom, and middle-class families took summer vacations in London. Iraqis who arrived in Britain at the end of the 1970s and early 1980s, therefore, had established networks in the country, which they mobilized to find jobs, start new businesses, and attain legal status. Britain appealed to people who fled Iraq following the Gulf War of 1991 because of this existing Iraqi community and the perception that Britain would be a safe haven that would provide opportunities for their children. Iraqis preferred to settle in London, in particular, because they saw it as a cosmopolitan city that harbored different migrant communities. The city also provided a platform for a different form of political engagement that was not necessarily associated with British politics. London thus became a venue that enabled Iraqis to maintain friendships with their fellow Iraqis, pursue Iraqi religious activities without fear of persecution, and engage in political activism to bring about regime change in Iraq.

Unlike established diasporas that maintain material connections to their homelands,[86] Iraq was largely closed off to its diaspora in London during Saddam Hussein's reign. It is in this sense that I argue that the Iraqi community in London was in exile prior to the fall of the regime. Their experiences were informed by "a condition of enforced absence"[87] and an inability to maintain direct transnational connections with Iraq. In the 1980s, visits to and from Iraq were impossible due to a ban on leaving the country and to the fear of persecution.[88] State employees read letters mailed in and out of the country to detect criticism of the regime and the exchange of vital information. Telephone calls had to be carried out through state operators, took hours to get through (if at all), and were recorded. Radio and television stations and newspapers were strictly controlled by the state, served as propaganda tools for the regime, and circulated only within Iraq. In the 1990s, while the internet and cell phones provided technological breakthroughs and changed communication patterns between other diasporic communities and their homelands, these devices were not allowed in Iraq.

Despite this experience of exile, Iraqis in London were able to forge a long-distance nationalism and form diasporic connections with other Iraqi communities abroad that served as conduits to contact family and friends in Iraq. Thus, while their homeland was closed to Iraqis in London prior to 2003, they retained ties through their family, friendships, and engagements with exilic opposition groups. They also enjoyed cultural productions about Iraq, idealistic reminiscences of "the good old days," and news from Iraq.[89] They kept Iraq alive in their memories and the memories of their children through nostalgic recollections and through literary and artistic productions. Meanwhile, they also lobbied the U.S. and British governments for regime change in Iraq in 2003.

The UN-imposed sanctions on Iraq, which ended flights to and from the country, as well as the partial scrapping of the ban on leaving Iraq in the 1990s, led to the emergence of Amman, Jordan, as an important center of communication. Iraqis who were unable to secure visas to Europe, the United States, and other Middle Eastern countries settled in Jordan, where visa requirements were less complicated. Other Iraqis made short trips to Jordan to meet relatives and friends who lived abroad. As such, Amman emerged as a meeting place for Iraqis from all over the world. This opened up the national sphere for the Iraqi community in London by proxy. Iraqis in London traveled to Amman to see relatives and friends and get a firsthand account of the situation in Iraq. The harsh conditions created by the sanctions wiped out people's savings and led to staggering inflation in the country, so Iraqis in London had to support relatives back home. Because transferring money to Iraq directly was not allowed, they circumvented restrictions by sending money to Iraq through friends and relatives in Amman.

Together, these developments consolidated a sense of long-distance nationalism and engendered diasporic connections between different Iraqi communities. Despite the emergence of these diasporic connections between Amman and London, Iraqis in London still perceived of their experience in exilic terms. When speaking of their lives in London prior to the fall of Saddam Hussein's regime, Iraqis I met used the term *exile* (*ghurba*) to stress the pain of not being able to visit Iraq for decades and their sense of enforced absence. Moreover, these transnational connections remained limited in scale, since Hussein's regime imposed high exit fees for leaving the country and banned certain groups from leaving at all, such as doctors, professors, and people with graduate degrees. Thus, the removal of Hussein from power assumed heightened importance within the exiled community. For many, their hopes of redemption and "return" hung on this moment.

The U.S. invasion of Iraq both opened and foreclosed possibilities for the Iraqi community in London. For example, regime change opened new channels of communication. After the fall of Saddam Hussein, dozens of newspapers were published in the country, both in print and online, and new satellite television stations were established that could reach Iraqi diasporic communities all over the world. Iraqis abroad and inside Iraq wrote articles for websites that became hubs for diasporic exchange. Cell phones were also introduced into Iraq, and calling families and friends became a daily occurrence. More importantly, Iraqis could visit Iraq. Indeed, most of the Iraqis I met in London had visited Baghdad at least once after 2003.

However, the U.S. invasion also foreclosed possibilities, most prominently by undermining the imagination of Iraq as a progressive, prosperous country. Iraqis watched the spiraling sectarian violence and felt a sense of disappointment and bewilderment, realizing that the utopian past they yearned for no longer existed. Visits to Iraq only furthered this sense of disenchantment and internal alienation, as Iraqis found themselves in a country they could not recognize and among people they could not relate to. In this sense, I argue, Iraqi exiles in London had to live with the realization that they were no longer exiles waiting to return home. Instead, they had become Iraqis in the United

Kingdom, and London was transformed from a stopping place on their journey back to the old country into a permanent home. The United Kingdom was, of course, a de facto home to Iraqis who had lived there for decades and acquired British citizenship, but they still imagined that a return would be possible after regime change in Iraq. The turn of events after 2003, however, solidified the reality that Britain was the place where they would spend the rest of their lives after all. This realization reconfigured the spatial imagination of the future. The future went from being in Iraq to being in London.

Despite this reconfiguration of the notions of home and the future, in their inability to find closure, Iraqis remained long-distance nationalists who dwelled upon Iraq and the past to a great extent. During my conversations with them, they spent most of their time speaking about their former lives in Iraq, rather than their experiences in Britain. Their reflections on their life trajectories were marked by the absence of Britain. My persistent questions about incidents of discrimination or exclusion, or of difficulties getting indefinite leave to remain (ILR) status or attain British citizenship, resulted in hasty comments that they had always felt respected and safe in Britain and that they had no trouble with the police or security agents, unlike in Iraq. As such, Iraqis perceived their experiences in the United Kingdom through the prism of their encounters with Saddam Hussein's security apparatus and in relation to the realities of fear and death they had lived through in Iraq. Their frame of reference was not incidents of discrimination in Britain but rather the arbitrary threats to their lives in Iraq. That the British government granted them asylum and citizenship, provided those who did not have assets in the country with housing and stipends, and did not harass them stood in stark contrast to the treatment Hussein's regime had meted out to them. Thus, if in the following chapters London appears on the margins, it is because my interlocutors did not want to dwell on their experiences in Britain. It was Iraq that consumed their attention.

## The Wound That Never Heals

Iraqis in London are haunted by events in Iraq and by concerns for loved ones in the country. The fact that the situation in Iraq keeps deteriorating means that most feel they cannot find closure. I spent many hours with my interlocutors during the peak of sectarian violence (between 2006 and 2008), watching news about explosions and suicide bombings and listening to their conversations while they called relatives and friends in Iraq to make sure they were safe. I continuously got updates from them about news from Iraq on my phone. During my interviews, they expressed disbelief at the turn of events and reminisced about how the past had been defined by prosperity and stability. As one of them told me, Iraq was "an open wound" that was always on her mind. The image of the open wound signals the inability to find closure and the constant pain she felt from the destruction of her homeland and the loss of relatives and friends. Iraqis in London not only grappled with the fact that their country had been thrust into violence and that citizens in Iraq lived in danger and without access to basic services, they also continued to mourn friends and relatives lost during the first Ba'th coup of 1963 and lamented the consequences of Saddam Hussein's reign and the wars that had spanned almost four decades.

Sigmund Freud called mourning "the reaction to the loss of a loved person, or to the loss of some abstract."[90] While mourning, a person is able to work through grief and find closure once the lost object or ideal is let go. Melancholia, by contrast, is "mourning without end. It entails an incorporation of the lost person or ideal as a means to keep it alive and thus suggests that the past—that is, the lost past—remains persistently present."[91] To Freud, the "complex of melancholia behaves like an open wound."[92] The decades of violence Iraqis lived through left them with unanswered questions about the fate of loved ones. While Iraqi communists dealt with their trauma of imprisonment and hiding during the first Ba'th coup of 1963, they also wondered about friends and relatives who died while being tortured. Iraqis who were deported to Iran in the early 1980s were tormented by the fate of their young male relatives who were separated from them upon deportation. I met many deported Iraqis who had family members that had been arrested in the early 1980s and never heard from again. After the fall of Hussein's regime in 2003, they discovered that these family members were killed in the late 1980s and buried in mass graves. However, there was no information about how they had died or where they were buried. Family members of communists and Da'wa Party members in the late 1970s and early 1980s, as well as family members of people who participated in the uprisings in the 1991, also struggled with the inability to find answers about the fate of their relatives.

The pictures of mass graves that were discovered after the fall of the regime in 2003 haunted Iraqis who had lost family members and friends, reopening wounds that had never really healed. This constant mourning and inability to find closure gave rise to what I call a discourse of graded suffering. Iraqis who knew the fate of their lost relatives and had buried them were considered fortunate; they, at least, had managed to find closure and move on. Moreover, the ongoing violence in Iraq and loss of friends and relatives perpetuated the cycle of mourning and the inability to let go of lost people.

However, Iraqis were not only mourning the loss of friends and relatives. They also mourned the destruction of their homeland. David Scott's reading of Freud's essay on mourning and melancholia puts the loss of political ideals at the center of melancholic feelings.[93] The loss of political ideals is on a par with the loss of loved ones, and mourning turns into melancholia because of the mourner's inability to let go of the lost object. Iraqis experienced the ongoing destruction of Iraq as a personal and tragic loss. What intensifies this sense of loss and inability to achieve closure is the fact that Iraq has suffered through ceaseless violence for at least four decades. The spiraling violence in Iraq makes people obsessive about following the news from the country and reinforces a sense of melancholia. Mourning the lost ideals of "the good old days" is unending.

This unrelenting mourning engenders nostalgia. Kathleen Stewart writes that nostalgia is a "longing for what is lacking in a changed present . . . a yearning for what is now unattainable, simply because of the irreversibility of time."[94] In other words, nostalgia is a cultural practice that provides a moral critique of the present. For Iraqis in London, the present, defined by the U.S. occupation of Iraq and sectarian violence, had become unbearable. The past gained saliency vis-à-vis the present and a forestalled future. Unlike the present, the past held the prospect of a promising future, where justice, democracy, security, and prosperity might prevail. The configuration of the past vis-à-vis the present was also marked by classed, gendered, political, and religious sensibilities. While the communists thought of the 1950s as the "good old days" when anticolonial struggle and the women's liberation movement dominated the scene, Iraqis from lower-middle-class backgrounds thought of the 1970s, a period defined by prosperity and economic reforms following the rise of oil prices, as the golden age. Sadly, after rampant sectarian violence and the government's absolute failure to provide basic services to its citizens after 2003, Iraqis in London began to idealize Saddam Hussein's reign as a time when violence was committed only behind closed doors and electricity was not often cut. These shifting nostalgic narratives reflect how acts of remembrance are always informed by the conditions of the present. Thus, trying to make sense of the bleak present became an integral part of daily life for Iraqis in London.

## Writing/Narrating Home

Storytelling defined my fieldwork. My Iraqi interlocutors in London eloquently told stories about their lives and experiences in Iraq and about their efforts to define home and selfhood. In doing so, they were trying to make sense of the present and reflect on the past. Storytelling, to them, became a way to reconnect to their homeland, to guard against the erasure of their past, and to carve out an Iraqi subjectivity against fragmentation and wars. The idea that anthropology is embedded in storytelling and that its challenge is how to render these stories has been crucial to my use of life stories to offer a more nuanced picture of Iraqis' aspirations and losses. Rather than selecting snippets from a large pool of interviews that would fit my analysis, I share the life stories of five Iraqis to provide uninterrupted narratives of their evolving perceptions of their lives as well as their positions at political moments that shaped their trajectories. Moreover, these life stories reveal emerging and shifting discourses on home, the past, and Iraqi subjectivity within the Iraqi community in London.

Storytelling, narratives, and testimonies have emerged as a technique of empowerment and bearing witness for Black and Chicana feminists concerned about the mainstream representation of women like themselves whose histories and realities were erased and misrepresented. Employing the binary of oppressor/oppressed, bell hooks argues that as "subjects, people have the right to define their own reality, establish their own identities, name their history. As objects, one's reality is defined by others, one's identity created by others, one's history named only in ways that define one's relationship to those who are subject."[95] As such, for oppressed people to become subjects and engage in liberatory projects, resistance to mainstream myths about them entails "identifying themselves as subjects, by defining their reality, shaping their new identity, naming their history, telling their story."[96] To hooks, marginalized groups—whether white women, Black women, gay groups, or ethnic minorities—had their experiences written for them by white men or people with power. Reclaiming one's voice by providing a narrative of oneself and one's reality is a fundamental issue for marginalized people.[97] Likewise, Patricia Hill Collins reflects on how stereotypical representation of Black women as welfare mothers or prostitutes was part and parcel of their oppression.[98]

Many people of color find that providing an account of themselves allows them to combat stereotypes and reductionist understandings, so much so that this form of storytelling sometimes can become a way of life.[99] According to Jewel Amoah, people of color not only find a means to confront stereotypes through storytelling but also manage to carve "their own sphere of theorized existence."[100] Storytelling thus provides an alternative account of their experiences that lays bare the systems of power and oppression in which they exist, while also allowing them to share their experiences with each other and build networks of solidarity. To Amoah, narrative is a method of criticism because "it gives a voice to the silenced and thereby is a tool of liberation."[101] But narrative is also a form of resistance to the politics of erasure and a method of reclaiming one's humanity amid structures of power that aim to destroy and deny their existence. In such cases, narrative "is both the theory *and* the practice."[102]

Faced with daily news about sectarian violence in Iraq and simplistic media representations, Iraqis in London aimed to provide alternative accounts of their history and experiences through narratives and life stories. For them, the efforts to carve out an Iraqi subjectivity rooted in historical events and structures of power were meant to resist the politics of erasure that rendered them as faceless statistics and the mainstream portrayal of them as sectarian subjects. Reclaiming their voices through storytelling enabled Iraqis to claim authorship of their narratives and to shed light on their daily struggles and interpretations of events.

The five life stories of Iraqi Londoners that anchor this book intersected with my own life story and experiences in Iraq. During the span of my fieldwork, I became a storyteller to my interlocutors in London, as they were as curious about my story as I was about theirs. Narrating my life story thus became part of the ritual of my fieldwork. More importantly, my life story was a way to gain the trust of my interlocutors. During the 1980s, Saddam Hussein's agents operated freely in London and sent reports back to Baghdad. Though the British government expelled these agents after the invasion of Kuwait in 1990, Iraqi Londoners still distrusted new faces in the community. After 2003, Iraqis were concerned that the new arrivals might be Hussein loyalists, so establishing that I was not a loyalist was an important aspect of my fieldwork. In order to gain people's trust, I had to talk about my background and experiences in Iraq—in particular, the death of my parents and sister due to Hussein's persecution. Iraqis in London decided to share their stories with me because they identified with me on some level. To the communists, I was the daughter of comrades, since both of my parents were communists. Religious people warmed up to me, though they disapproved of my lack of religiosity, because my father hailed from Najaf, a holy Shi'i city in southern Iraq. For others, it was my story about losing my family that they connected with, because "I understood what suffering meant." The young generation who grew up under Hussein's regime shared with me how their parents instilled caution and fear in them from a young age in the 1980s and how the sanctions in the 1990s exposed them to financial hardships. Given that the intersections of my life story with the various narratives of my interlocutors were such an integral part of my fieldwork, I have included parts of my story between each chapter of this book. Through these narrations, I, like the Iraqi Londoners, am also carving out an Iraqi political subjectivity informed by war and violence and a notion of home that is defined by fear and dissonance with the stories I heard from my parents about the "good old days."

## The Chapters

The first two chapters document the early waves of displacement that accompanied the rise to power of Saddam Hussein and the emergence of London as host to an Iraqi community. Chapter 1 traces how British colonial rule in Iraq inspired anticolonial movements in the 1940s and 1950s, which engendered forms of political and cultural vibrancy in the country. I focus on the life story of Hanan, an Iraqi communist woman whose idealizations of the past, when the Iraqi Communist Party dominated the political scene, constitute a dominant discourse about the late 1940s until the early 1960s that has shaped Iraqi memory for generations. This discourse valorized the experiences of middle-class Iraqis from Baghdad, perceived progressive Iraqi women as a marker of modernity, and disavowed the experiences of religious people and the downtrodden. It chronicles how Iraqis came to inhabit a postcolonial present that was defined by disenchantment and nostalgia, which provided a moral critique of the present, and that was sutured to the notion of a unified modern Iraq that stood in contrast to the sectarian fragmentation of the Iraqi body politic both in Iraq and in diaspora.

While Hanan carved an Iraqi political subjectivity through reminiscences, Khalil (chapter 2) fashioned an Iraqi self through continuous political activism, which aimed to critique the mythologized communist past as well as the current state of political dialogue in Iraq and in diaspora. Khalil aimed to create a more democratic political sphere that would include people from different political and religious backgrounds. This chapter provides a glimpse into the silences and erasures of the prevailing discourse of the past and chronicles the emergence of a diasporic political sphere in London that opposed the reign of Saddam Hussein and sought regime change in Iraq through establishing contacts with U.S. and British intelligence agencies. This same sectarian discourse championed by Iraqis in London became the premise for political organization in Iraq after the U.S. occupation in 2003. In the midst of two competing narratives—namely, the communist narrative of the past and the sectarian discourse of the present—Khalil aimed to create an alternative political sphere through continuous political activism that perceived the notion of democracy as a platform to change political discourse and practices in Iraq and in diaspora.

The recollections of Hanan and Khalil center on their engagement with the colonial realities of 1950s Iraq, the postcolonial quagmires that followed the first and second Ba'thist coups, and the rise of Saddam Hussein to power. Alternatively, the life stories of my next two interlocutors deal with how a younger generation—born under Ba'thist rule and Hussein's reign and growing up in exile—envisioned the past and the future and attempted to carve out their own Iraqi subjectivity defined by the absence of political activism. Chapters 3 and 4 deal with the second wave of arrivals of Iraqis in London following the loss of hope for returning to Iraq after the consolidation of Hussein's power in the 1980s and 1990s. They indicate the shifts from the discourse of the secular past to a new emphasis on religion: on Iraq as a place of holy shrines and on London as a center for Iraqi religious organizations. Chapter 3 focuses on a young man named Ali, whose life story is marked by religious paths and secular longings. The chapter examines transnational religious networks that religious people mobilized during moments of persecution to build communities of solidarity abroad. Iraqi subjectivity is informed here by a sense of belonging to a community of believers and by a sense that one could find such a community in London. However, this religious subjectivity and efforts to imagine home did not entail disavowing the dominant discourse. Amid the rise of sectarianism and divisions within the Iraqi community in London, Ali imagined the 1950s—a time when the "real Iraq" existed—as providing an alternative to the fragmented present.

While Ali's narrative was connected to the political activism of religious scholars, the life story of Hadjar (chapter 4) speaks to experiences of devout Shi'i Iraqis whose sense of belonging revolved around pilgrimage to holy cities in Iraq and the personal cultivation of a pious self. Growing up in exile in Iran and London, Hadjar unsettled the prevailing discourse of the 1950s in her efforts to construct a religious subjectivity through travels and diasporic routes. Informed by her elder sisters' reminiscences of Iraq as a time of prosperity and by a yearning to fashion a religious self, Hadjar embarked on journeys to find her roots through routes. She shows how the U.S. occupation of Iraq opened the national sphere of Iraq to the younger generation and reconfigured notions of home and subjectivity through diasporic circuits.

Chapter 5 chronicles the displacement of Rasha from Iraq following the U.S. occupation. It examines the rise of a discourse on Iraqi subjectivity among Iraqis in London that linked authenticity with suffering and endurance. This notion of authenticity was tied not to life experiences informed by Baghdadi middle-class aspirations, but to a life of persecution and war under Hussein's regime. Rasha was seen as an authentic Iraqi because her family hailed from the south and lived in destitution under the monarchy, an area representing the "true Iraq" due to decades of marginalization and injustice. But Rasha was also perceived as an authentic Iraqi because she experienced the full reign of Saddam Hussein and lived through the Iran-Iraq War, the Gulf War, the sanctions years, and the U.S. occupation. She represented a link to events Iraqis in London had not experienced. This notion of authenticity indicates an emerging shift among the community in London. The perception of Iraqis who had lived through the 1950s as citizens who experienced the "real" Iraq was changing to a concept of citizenship associated with suffering and the endurance of hardships since the monarchy. This notion of authentic citizenship was clearly gendered: the community perceived Rasha as a strong Iraqi woman who lived through hardships but remained unwavering in the face of uncertainty and difficulties. The discourse on the enduring Iraqi self draws attention to new forms of sensibilities about subjectivity and belonging, which are marked by different classed, gendered, and generational experiences.

# CHILDHOOD STORIES

The past loomed large when I was growing up under Saddam Hussein's regime. My mother reminisced about the social and political landscape under the monarchy (1921–1958) quite often, and she would contrast that landscape with the status quo under Hussein's reign. These reminiscences were sometimes nostalgic, sometimes contradictory. On the one hand, they revolved around the social and political vibrancy that dominated the Iraqi street between the late 1940s and early 1960s. On the other hand, they touched on the abject poverty in Iraqi society and the persecution and precarity that her family endured due to its political activism. My parents belonged to a generation that was deeply attuned to anticolonial struggles and social inequalities. They each joined the Iraqi Communist Party (ICP) at an early age, in the late 1940s or early 1950s. My mother, especially, talked about her clandestine activism—since the ICP was banned under the monarchy—and the protests in which she participated in 1948 and 1952 against different Iraqi governments, which were seen as corrupt and beholden to British interests in Iraq.

My mother talked about how Al-Wathba—or "The Leap," a series of protests in 1948 against the Portsmouth Treaty, which tied Iraq closely to Britain and grew to include different sectors of the society—defined her political outlook. She was only thirteen at the time, and she marched with middle school, high school, and college students to protest the treaty. She remembered details about where the march started and ended, how the police opened fire on the protesters, and how the massive protests led to the resignation of the prime minister. My mother cherished the memories of Al-Wathba for the anticolonial momentum and sense of camaraderie it engendered. She felt she was part of a political event in which the Iraqi people, rather than a colonial power or state, would shape the future of Iraq. The Iraqi people rose against—leaped against—the colonial status quo and forced the government to fold and annul the treaty.

I am more familiar with the history of my mother's family, especially her and her father's activism. My mother often spoke about how the monarchy persecuted her father due to his critical articles on the ruling class as well as his close contacts with the Iraqi Communist Party. My grandfather had a big influence on his children, in particular my mother, who joined the ICP at the age of sixteen. Predictably, my grandfather's political views landed him in jail many times. As a result, he was often fired from his position as an Arabic teacher in public schools, and my grandmother, who was an uneducated housewife, had to make ends meet. I grew up with stories of my grandmother and one of her children making strenuous trips to a notorious prison in southern Iraq when my grandfather had been sentenced to a year in jail; of my grandmother burning my grandfather's papers, ICP pamphlets, or Marxist literature in the house following each arrest to avoid further incrimination or interrogation; and of my mother taking extra caution when she went to secretly held meetings or distributed ICP publications. The power of the secret police was not to be taken lightly. While my mother was never arrested under the monarchy, she failed to obtain "the certificate of good behavior" issued by the Office of General Security, which was required to attend a university or college. Like many young Iraqi communists who failed to secure this document, she went to Egypt to pursue her bachelor's degree. It was there that she met my father, who also had had to go to Cairo for his undergraduate degree, and fell in love with him.

Under Hussein's regime, my mother narrated these stories with a tinge of nostalgia. While she criticized the monarchy's persecution of political opponents and the abject poverty that affected a large segment of Iraqi society, she emphasized that the ruling elites showed respect and restraint toward political dissidents. She talked about how the policemen who arrested my grandfather were very polite and apologized to him and his family for arresting him, emphasizing that they were only following orders; how her political activism did not affect the ability of her siblings to secure "the certificate of good behavior" or chances to go to universities; how friends did not stop visiting them after the arrest of my grandfather; and how my grandfather could easily find teaching jobs in Jewish schools in Baghdad when the government fired him from the public schools. The fact that the family had not been socially shunned or collectively punished under the monarchy assumed a new significance when Hussein's reign began.

The fall of the monarchy in 1958 was a time of great happiness for my mother. There is a picture of her in a newspaper hugging an Iraqi friend as they heard the news while in Egypt. My mother looked young and full of hope, her face beaming, as if her dreams had just come true. Indeed, the fall of the monarchy was a moment that vindicated the will of the people and their desire to get rid of British colonial domination and an oppressive feudal system. Many believed that only a promising future could follow. To my parents and other Iraqi students, the fall of the monarchy meant that they could return to Iraq to complete their degrees and get involved in building up their country. Of course, these dreams never materialized. Political life in Iraq after the monarchy came to be defined by a bitter rivalry between communists and Arab nationalists. Anxious about the prospects of oil nationalization, the United States grew determined to overthrow the Iraqi government under the pretext of combating communism in Iraq. So began the country's descent into an era of postcolonial chaos.

I am less certain about my father's political development, but I think he was exposed to Marxist ideas and joined the Iraqi Communist Party while still in school. I do not know my father's family, the majority of whom lived in Najaf, in the south of Iraq. By the time I was born, my father was not on speaking terms with his siblings, who lived in Baghdad. His sister, once an ardent communist, later became a loyalist of the Ba'th regime and worked for the intelligence agency under Hussein's rule. My father's siblings were divided over her loyalty to the regime, and my father eventually ended all contact with them, a decision that seemed to relieve his brothers and sisters. Indeed, by the 1970s, having a communist or a dissident in one's family had consequences for everyone, even distant relatives. A person could not study specific topics at university—such as journalism, education, and physical education—if she had a fourth cousin who was a communist or a member of a banned religious party. People lost jobs or ended up in jail because of the activism of their relatives. For my paternal uncles and aunts, not having a relationship with my father was welcomed. It proved to the regime that they did not share my father's political views.

I am assuming my father's connections with the ICP persisted, because he was a staunch supporter of the party until his death in 1982. My mother, however, became disillusioned in the early 1960s and left the party. She never explained why, but she often mentioned her disappointment with some party members who were driven by personal interests rather than principles. Yet she firmly believed that communism as a theory was laudable and that things only went wrong in practice. Her comrades, understandably, disagreed with her and accused her of being a bourgeois sellout. She knew she could not stay in Iraq after she ended her relations with the party. Ironically, her only option was to go to the Soviet Union, which offered hundreds of fellowships to Iraqis interested in studying in the USSR. My mother received a fellowship and chose to do a PhD in Russian literature. In many ways, her decision to sever all ties with the ICP saved her from a bleak fate, for she left Iraq in 1962, a year before the first CIA-backed Ba'th coup. The CIA provided the leaders of the coup with lists of thousands of ICP members. This short-lived coup started with a brutal campaign against communists, many of whom were subsequently imprisoned, raped, tortured, or executed. My father was tortured and sentenced to one year in jail. My mother and grandfather were spared because they were abroad, but my mother could not return to Iraq after finishing her PhD in 1969. Following the second Ba'th coup, in 1968, she was banned from entering the country because of her political history. Despite the ominous political situation, she wanted to return. She waited for a year and then secured permission to come back when the Ba'th regime relaxed its persecution of communists for a while. She felt that Iraq was the place where she belonged and held on to a hope that the Ba'th regime would soon collapse.

( CHAPTER 1 )

# EMANCIPATION AND REVOLUTION

On a mild August afternoon in 2007, I was walking toward a council hall in West London to attend a talk organized by the Iraqi Women's League (IWL). I expected to see a big building, like other council halls I had been to, but I found myself inside a small building that consisted of a minimally furnished room. There were only three rows of chairs, which would accommodate twenty-four people, and a table at the front. The walls were bare, and the fact that the room did not get much natural light intensified its bareness. As I sat down and looked at the small audience, I saw the familiar faces of Iraqi communists whom I always encountered when I attended events organized by the Iraqi Communist Party (ICP) and its affiliate, the IWL. The majority of the attendees were older people in their sixties and above. I was the only young person in the room. This talk, like most events held by the ICP and IWL, stood in stark contrast to events organized by Iraqi religious groups in London. Religious events always drew big crowds from different age groups and were held either in big buildings owned by the organization or in huge rented council halls. The atmosphere at religious events, moreover, was always lively and animated, unlike with this quiet elderly audience. As I looked around, I felt a tinge of sadness. I could only imagine how bustling and well attended the events and meetings held by the ICP must have been in its heyday between the late 1940s and early 1960s. The attendees today looked sad, dispirited, and ragged, even though their clothes were not old. They seemed to belong to a different era and to uncomfortably inhabit the present.

The IWL was hosting Hanan, who was delivering a talk on the Iraqi Personal Status Code of 1959. I was curious to listen to what Hanan would say, given that I had interviewed her many times. Hanan was a robust, tall woman in her mid-seventies who had a strong presence when she spoke. She belonged to a generation of leftist Iraqi feminists who became more active and organized in their fight for women's rights beginning in the early 1950s. She was also still a staunch communist, who believed that the ICP was the only political party in Iraq that had people's best interests at heart and always made sacrifices for the sake of the downtrodden. During our long interviews, Hanan spoke passionately and nostalgically about the past. Her memories revolved around the anticolonial struggle against the British and the Iraqi monarchy in the 1940s and 1950s, which culminated in the 1958 revolution that toppled the monarchy and forced the British to leave Iraq. She also vehemently expressed her profound disappointment with the present situation. The rise of religiosity and sectarianism among Iraqis in Iraq and in diaspora left her baffled and angry. More importantly, she was appalled at the turn of events in post-Saddam Iraq. Hanan had imagined that the long-awaited moment of Saddam Hussein's removal would be a moment of exhilaration and would bring stability to Iraq. Instead, it resulted in further destruction and violence as well as the occupation of Iraq by the U.S. military. Sometimes Hanan broke my heart when she spoke about her generation's hardships and dreams. During our conversations, she struggled to make sense of the present and to convince herself that all was not lost.

As the event started, Hanan began to speak in a steady, confident voice about the Personal Status Code and about the IWL's role in drafting one of the most progressive laws in the Middle East in the late 1950s, which protected women's rights in matters such as marriage, divorce, child custody, and inheritance. Hanan spoke proudly about the law and saw it as an achievement of communist women's struggles and demands. Based on a progressive interpretation of both Sunni and Shi'i Islamic laws, the Personal Status Code unified family regulations, appointed state-trained judges to secular courts, and introduced civil rulings on equal inheritance for both men and women. Hanan also spoke furiously about a current proposal to annul the law. The law came under a serious attack following the fall of Saddam Hussein's regime in 2003. A conservative Islamist member of the U.S.-appointed Iraqi Governing Council proposed its annulment and the adoption of strict Islamic laws. The proposal raised fears among Iraqi women that the new law would put the legal age of marriage for girls at nine, strip women of the right to ask for divorce, and give preference to men over the custody of children. Following protests from women's organizations, the proposal for a new law was scrapped. But in 2005, the law became one of the main contentious issues in a newly proposed constitution for Iraq, which effectively relegated personal status matters to religious courts. At the time of the talk, the fate of the Personal Status Code was still unclear. Hanan's talk emphasized its importance and warned of setbacks for women's rights if it were revoked.

As I listened to Hanan, I could sometimes anticipate what she was going to say. During our interviews and in other talks she had delivered, she would often discuss the Personal Status Code in great detail. As Hanan finished talking about the potential repercussions if the law were revoked, she began to drift and talk about "the good old days"—namely, the late 1940s through the early 1960s. She reminisced about a time when progressive, secular thought dominated the Iraqi public sphere and when religion and identity politics were tenuous. She recalled how her generation thought their political visions would shape the future in accordance with their progressive and revolutionary ideals. After Hanan finished speaking, the attendees shared their own stories about the past and deplored the status quo in diaspora and Iraq. Her talk provided this dwindling communist community with an opportunity to get together, discuss the achievements of the past, and vent about their disappointment with the present. In responding to the conditions of war, sanctions, and authoritarianism in Iraq, all exacerbated by U.S. interventions, testimonies about an idealized past were central to the construction of the self as a leftist, secular subject. In telling and retelling these stories, Iraqi communists carved out a dominant discourse, particularly about the 1950s, that allowed Iraqis in London to recall that decade as a time of social and political vibrancy. Though Hanan and her comrades stood on the margins of the present, they shaped Iraqi historical memory by reproducing their idealized narratives about the past. Nostalgic remembrances became political acts that provided a moral critique of the present and stitched together a notion of a unified modern Iraq in the face of the fragmented Iraqi body politic, both in Iraq and in diaspora, that sectarianism, war, and the U.S. occupation had made the reality.

These narratives about the idealized past vis-à-vis the bleak present also reflect how different players—the state, the family, and colonial and imperial powers—have shaped notions of selfhood and have been entangled in debates about modernity, gender, and class. The anticolonial sentiments that filled the streets of Iraq in the first half of the twentieth century produced Iraqis as revolutionary subjects who thought of themselves as agents of history, bringing about political independence, social justice, and gender reforms through their activism. Revolutionary Iraqis looked forward to the future and aimed to break with the past. They thought of time as unfolding in a progressive, linear way, whereby the traditional past would give way to the revolutionary present, and the present would produce the utopian future. Rather than agents of social control and disciplinary technologies, as imagined by Iraqi educators, schools and families emerged as important provocateurs, fueling radical political consciousness and debates on reforms among the youth. The construction of the self as a revolutionary subject who was leaving behind the backward traditions and championing progress was also gendered and classed to a great extent. The status of women—particularly with regard to education, the veil, polygamy, and seclusion—became a marker of the modernity of the nation-state and the self. In this framework, the modern Iraqi subject was someone who championed women's liberation and rights. This progressive self was also classed, in that the dominant discourse about social and intellectual vibrancy in Iraq spoke only to the experiences of middle-class Baghdadis; it marginalized the lived realities of the downtrodden.

While British colonial rule had instigated anticolonial sensibilities and a belief in a utopian future, the U.S. intervention in Iraq foreclosed the possibility of such a future through its support of an authoritarian regime, the prolongation of wars, and its invasion of the country. After the fall of Saddam Hussein's regime and the U.S. occupation, the optimistic revolutionary Iraqi subject was no more, replaced by a disillusioned and nostalgic exile who was unable to find closure due to the ongoing violence in Iraq. This Iraqi subject inhabited a stalled present and looked toward a diminished future, experiencing time as an impasse, whereby the anticolonial past gave in to a postcolonial nightmare. Unable to look forward to the future anymore, the nostalgic subject found the past, rather than the future, utopian. This nostalgic self was in the thrall of melancholia over lost ideals and haunted by the absence of alternatives to the contemporary imperial reality with its chronic conditions of dispossession and violence. In this narrative, the past emerged as a refuge from the present and the irreversibility of time. Moreover, the disappointment with the turn of events in Iraq after 2003 rehashed debates about modernity and religion, and gender and class. The new religious ruling elites in Iraq were the antithesis of secular and revolutionary Iraqis: they were "backward" people and the "riffraff" who were not concerned about gender equality, social justice, or political stability. They represented a diversion from modernity and a regress into obsolete tradition.

## A Prelude to the Revolution

Politically, Hanan came of age after World War II, when Iraq was a monarchy closely controlled by the British and ruled by a Sunni elite class that excluded the majority of the population from meaningful participation in government.[1] A vibrant public sphere defined by demands for social equality, national independence, and anticolonial struggle dominated the Iraqi street. Diverse political ideologies—including Marxism, socialism, social democracy, and Arab nationalism—began to emerge and gain momentum.[2] At the time, people debated the social and political conditions in the country, and oppositional political thought circulated through communist cells, reading clubs, literary salons, newspapers, cafés, and labor and student organizations.[3] A defining feature of this public sphere was a progressive discourse that developed around notions of political independence, economic prosperity, social justice, democracy, and women's rights. Notably absent was discussion of religion.[4] By the late 1940s, the underground Iraqi Communist Party, established in 1934, emerged as a pivotal political platform in the country and played a major role in politics despite state repression and censorship. Unlike other political parties in the country, the Communist Party's inclusive agenda appealed to people from different socioeconomic, ethnic, and religious backgrounds.

In the early 1940s, Hanan was vaguely aware that Iraq was under British mandate, but it was her upbringing and family background that shaped her political views, particularly on women's rights. Hanan grew up in a middle-class home with what she described as an enlightened father who saw women's education as essential to the advancement of society and criticized female seclusion, the veil, and polygamy. Her father, who was an officer in the army, took it for granted that his two daughters would go to school and receive the same level of education as his sons. In this regard, he was influenced by nineteenth-century Egyptian and contemporary Iraqi male reformers—in particular, Qasim Amin and the Iraqi poets Jamil Sidqi al-Zahawi and Maʿruf al-Rusafi—who advocated the education of women and the end of seclusion. Hanan's mother was also a role model. She belonged to the first generation of women in Iraq to attend school and college in the early twentieth century. After graduation, she worked as a teacher until she got married. Hanan's parents instilled in her the idea that she would go to school and have a career rather than get married at an early age. Moreover, at an early age her parents' heated debate about the veil informed her association of the veil with backwardness. The debate at home revolved around her father's desire that his wife "take off the rag," according to Hanan, since it indicated "backwardness and lack of modernity," but her mother was concerned with social norms. After the family moved to Baghdad, her mother decided to take off the veil.

Hanan experienced the family as a space to form new notions of selfhood. On the one hand, her parents sought to instill new gender norms in her and her sister through education and unveiling. The idea of a new woman who would enjoy independence due to her education and would contribute to the development of her country through work after finishing college marked a departure from the traditional woman who stayed home and was dedicated to the upbringing of children solely. On the other hand, the family, represented by Hanan's elder brothers, emerged as an arena of revolutionary ideas revolving around anticolonial struggle and the fight for social justice. Hanan's communist-leaning brothers encouraged her to read anticolonial books and journals about popular demands for independence in countries in the Third World. This politicization at a young age led to the formation of radical sensibilities that constituted a break with the school curriculum's disciplinary project of producing docile and governable subjects.[5]

In addition to her upbringing, Hanan's social and political experience in the late 1940s, after her family moved to Baghdad, defined her political outlook and activism for decades to come—in particular, her anti-imperial sentiments and her advocacy of social justice. Hanan grew up in a Baghdad defined by stark social inequality and visible poverty. In their efforts to secure the acquiescence of the peasants, the British consolidated the power of tribal leaders and landlords by giving them land tenure. This policy had been in place since the establishment of the Iraqi state in 1921.[6] It eventually left the majority of peasants landless, living in abject poverty and debt.[7] Destitution and indebtedness led to the massive influx of migrants into Baghdad from the countryside in the south.[8] The migrants built the *sarifas* (shantytowns) on parcels of wasteland, which consisted of clusters of one-room huts made of reeds and mats and covered with mud in the winter.[9] The *sarifa* dwellers lived in close proximity to middle-class and wealthy neighborhoods; thus, they were not hidden from sight.[10] But under the monarchy, no tangible steps were taken to improve their living conditions.[11] These slums loom large in the memories of Baghdadis who became politicized and advocated for just social policies under the monarchy. Indeed, the conditions in the *sarifas* deepened Hanan's awareness of the inequality and injustice prevalent in Iraqi society, and her political activism in the coming years would focus on improving the living conditions there, particularly for women.

However, it was at school that Hanan became most politicized. She belonged to a generation of high school and college students who were inspired by communist ideas, opposed British colonialism, and lived and breathed politics from an early age. Hanan's first taste of political activism took place in 1948, when she was only fifteen years old. At the time, the Iraqi government was negotiating the renewal of the Anglo-Iraqi Treaty of 1930 with the British. The proposed treaty, the Portsmouth Treaty,[12] did not differ in essence from the Anglo-Iraqi Treaty and still tied Iraq closely to Britain.[13] When the details of the new treaty became known, a series of protests broke out against it in Baghdad. Known as Al-Wathba (the Leap), these protests were spearheaded by high school and college students and buttressed by workers, *sarifa* dwellers, lawyers, doctors, and women. When Hanan spoke about her participation in the protests, her face lit up and her voice became animated:

> I was in high school when the demonstrations broke out in 1948. My siblings and I participated in them. All the students in my school marched from

Adhamiyya to Bab al-Muʿddam. We passed by the Law School and continued marching with the law students. Then we reached the Medical School, where we all gathered and protested. Workers and poor people joined us as well. Women took part in the demonstration also. They sometimes marched along with men, and they walked as a group at other times. They also tried to protect men from the police by standing between them and the police. We shouted "Give Bread to the People," and "Long Live the Unity of Workers and Students." The demonstrations scared the regime, and it ordered the police to open fire on us. Many people fell, including the brother of Muhammad Mahdi al-Jawahiri, Jaʿfar.[14] Al-Jawahiri wrote a poem eulogizing his brother and read it to the demonstrators. The protests forced the government to abolish the Portsmouth Treaty and to resign. The people's will prevailed during those days. We managed to force our will on the government then. These were amazing days, unlike nowadays. We had high hopes.

During our long interviews, Hanan reminisced about Al-Wathba many times. She recalled in minute detail where the demonstrations started, how high school students joined forces with college students, and how the police opened fire on them. Their ability to take to the streets, to defy the government, and to mobilize thousands of people galvanized Hanan's generation; they could see the impact of their political power in the streets. As Hanan and her peers came of age, they felt that they could shape the future of Iraq. Al-Wathba delineated the possibility of a different political and social future attained through people's struggles and demands. Moreover, it signaled that women could have a role in bringing about political transformation. During the protests, women emerged as political players for the first time in modern Iraqi history. While these reminiscences constructed members of Hanan's generation—both men and women—as revolutionary subjects who embraced political struggle and progressive ideals, they also produced a notion of a unified nation. In her recollections, Hanan emphasized how people from different walks of life took part in the protests and how progressive political ideals brought people together and defined their political outlooks and aspirations. Through these reminiscences, Hanan was providing a critique of the fragmented present and delineating a past when national unity was a possibility.

Al-Wathba was a turning point in Hanan's political activism. Following the protests, she joined the communist-led Students Union, whose main responsibility was to mobilize students to protest and participate in demonstrations. While in college studying English literature, Hanan took part in the 1952 intifada (uprising), a series of grassroots movements led by students against the monarchy. Hanan's role in the protests attracted the attention of the leaders of the newly founded League for the Defense of Women's Rights, who invited her to join. The organization advocated women's suffrage, independence, social justice, and a democratic political system. Its immediate aim was to bring about social reforms that would improve the living conditions of both rural and urban women. The League, which was affiliated with the Iraqi Communist Party, appealed to Hanan, given its anti-imperialist overtones and concern with women's rights, particularly the eradication of illiteracy and the establishment of clinics for women. Hanan's duties with the League involved teaching women who lived in the *sarifas* how to read and write, informing them of their rights, and mobilizing them to take part in protests. While the League's social program was disciplinary in its outlook, in that it aimed to produce working and peasant women as healthy citizens capable of contributing to the development of society and of raising healthy children, it was also revolutionary in its aspiration. It saw the education and welfare of women as a first step toward their radicalization and their participation in anticolonial struggle.

While at college, Hanan began to read widely on social and political issues because the Students Union and the Iraqi Women's League focused on political mobilization and activism, rather than education. She was particularly influenced by the works of Naziha al-Dulaimi, an Iraqi feminist woman who was a founder of the League, and Salama Musa, a prominent Egyptian writer. Hanan found al-Dulaimi's book, *Al-Mar'a al-Iraqiyya* (Iraqi woman), illuminating in that it shed light on the lives of Iraqi women through a class analysis.[15] Al-Dulaimi saw that women of all classes were oppressed by marriage, an institution that treated them like possessions, and that peasant women as a class bore a double burden, since they were victims of male and tribal domination as well as class oppression.[16] In addition, she linked the problems facing Iraqi women to Iraq's lack of genuine independence under the monarchy. She believed that women's liberation would follow the liberation of Iraq from the yoke of colonialism and that women's subordination would come to an end once the socioeconomic order associated with imperialism was overthrown.[17] Al-Dulaimi opposed "gradual modernization," which was advocated by women activists associated with the ruling elites in Iraq, and called for a radical change that would do away with the whole political system in Iraq and put the country on the path toward modernity, including political independence, social justice, women's liberation, and technological progress.[18] Hanan found this class analysis, with its anti-imperial overtones, especially appealing, since it linked the issues of women to the wider political realities in Iraq and saw questions of sovereignty and women's liberation as constitutive of each other.

In addition, Hanan told me that she was influenced by the works of Salama Musa, a social critic who agitated for social change to replace existing social institutions with new ones.[19] Musa criticized the Christian and Islamic institutions for being traditional and called for the separation of church and state, limiting the role of the church to religious matters. He advocated for a renaissance based on the incorporation of Western values of progress, socialism, and science. He was also concerned about the valorization of the past, including religious ceremonies and texts, and urged his compatriots to look toward the future instead.[20] Musa's ideas, particularly his association of religion with traditions that should be left behind, shaped Hanan's views on religion and secularism, in particular her association of religion with backward conventions. She was also taken by Musa's calls for women's economic independence, which would free them from having to marry out for economic reasons. His call for socialism and the end of private property, as well as his critique of the landed class in Egypt as a hindrance to progress, resonated with Hanan's sense of justice and equality. To Hanan, Musa's thought was a guiding spirit of modernism.

During these years of activism, Hanan had to be careful. The League's revolutionary and anti-imperialist agenda made it suspect in the eyes of the government, which refused to grant the organization a permit to operate publicly. Going underground, the League came under state scrutiny; however, the government did not pursue its members the way it did members of the banned ICP. The League's focus on social problems made it less threatening.

After Hanan finished college, she joined the Iraqi Communist Party, whose popularity increased after Al-Wathba, due to the role it played in mobilizing students and workers.[21] The party's demands for social and economic reforms, national independence, and Kurdish rights appealed to Hanan. In addition, the communists saw women as having the same political, social, and economic rights as men. The party also emphasized egalitarian politics and inclusive nationalism, which resonated with Hanan, who saw the other major political trend in Iraq, Arab nationalism, as not speaking to people's demands and concerns. The Arab nationalists' view that Iraq should be seen as one part of a larger Arab nation was exclusionary, limiting governmental positions to Sunni Arabs and alienating the majority of the population—including Kurds, Shi'is, Jews, and other minorities—from the nation. Though Arab nationalists harbored anticolonial sentiments, they could not speak to the aspirations and well-being of all Iraqis, in her opinion, since they mostly belonged to the urban middle class and were associated with the ruling elites. To her, the Iraqi Communist Party, with its anti-sectarian rhetoric, emphasis on class struggle, and revolutionary overtones, could transform Iraq's social and political status quo. The party's slogan, "A Free Homeland and a Happy People," promised a utopia where equality and independence would prevail. In her opinion, political reforms could not come from an Iraqi government that was tied to the British. Rather, they could only be brought about through the political activism of dedicated political subjects who would transform the social and political spheres of the country.

Joining the Iraqi Communist Party shaped Hanan's life in another way. It was during one of the party's educational meetings for its members that Hanan met her future husband, Raed. Like Hanan, Raed was a staunch communist who dreamed of a revolution of the masses. The couple fell in love and got married by the mid-1950s. Hanan's decision to get married as soon as she met Raed reflected the social constraints that faced women at the time. Though women took part in protests and demonstrations and joined political parties, they still were expected to act according to social norms, which dictated that a woman did not date; once she met a man, she was to marry. When I asked Hanan if politically active women of her generation faced pressure to adhere to norms of propriety, she told me that no one prevented her from having a boyfriend, for instance. She was quick to add,

"We prevented ourselves [from breaking social norms]. People's respect for us mattered a lot. We did not do anything that people would not approve of socially. We shunned any action that would raise questions about our behavior." The modern Iraqi woman could go unveiled, be politically active, and have a career; however, people around her—including her family—expected her to guard her reputation (and that of the family) by adhering to proper behavior.

## A Revolutionary Moment

Hanan, like most of the communists of her generation, was consumed by the idea of an imminent revolution that promised a utopian future. Her outlook and activism were attuned to a future that would constitute a total rupture with the social injustices and colonial realities of the present. Hanan observed the wave of national-level socialist movements that were sweeping the Third World and hoped for the overthrow of the monarchy and the ousting of the British from Iraq. The revolution in Iraq, however, did not take place through popular mobilization. Rather, the Free Officers—a group of nationalist military men who were aggravated by the Eisenhower Doctrine, which offered military and economic aid to Arab countries that resisted communism, including Iraq—staged a coup d'état that toppled the monarchy on July 14, 1958. Many Iraqis greeted the news of the coup with a sense of euphoria. As soon as Abd al-Salam Aref, a leader of the coup, read Proclamation No. 1 and declared the establishment of the Republic of Iraq, one hundred thousand Iraqis[22] took to the streets in Baghdad to show their support of the revolution.[23] Hanan was among them:

> On July 12, the ICP circulated leaflets among its members that they should expect big events to take place within the coming days. The party had all its members on alert. In the morning of July 14, we were living in Waziriyya and my eldest daughter was one year old. We were sleeping on the roof, and my daughter woke up early and I took her inside the house. Then I heard the sound of cannons, and the house shook. I thought to myself, "There is a revolution." My husband came down from the roof. I took my daughter to my mother's, and we took to the streets. What an indescribable day. Indescribable. No one stayed home. Everyone was in the street cheering for the revolution. I don't think I'll ever see a day like that again. We left everything

and took to the streets. We were in the streets till the morning. The streets didn't quiet down. Some disgusting things took place, like the dragging of corpses.[24] However, in the midst of such events, we didn't pay attention or condemn these acts. The people were angry.

To Hanan, as well as to the majority of Iraqis at the time, the coup was not an attempt to replace one government with another. Rather, it was a revolutionary event that drastically transformed the political scene in Iraq. Iraq ceased to be a monarchy tied to the British; it was now a republic. Moreover, news of the coup engendered massive demonstrations hailing the fall of the monarchy. Hanan became caught up in these demonstrations, and she saw history unfold before her. She once told me that July 14, 1958, was the most important day in her life. Hanan did not consider usual life milestones—such as the birth of her first child or the death of her parents—as defining moments. It was this political moment that defined her life. Despite the passage of time, Hanan relived the revolutionary era through her telling and retelling of its major events. Her words alone cannot fully capture the enthusiasm I heard in her voice. While reflecting on the demonstrations, her voice quivered with the burst of hope she experienced at the time. It was Hanan's embodiment of these memories that conveyed the revolutionary momentum she inhabited. Decades later, she still relished these memories and the feeling of being in the midst of history.

Hanan's memories of the first Iraqi republic revolved around hopes for alternative futures. She reflected in great detail on the political and social reforms under the rule of the first Iraqi president, Abdul Karim Qasim. The social and economic policies enacted between 1958 and 1963 were unprecedented and brought about tangible differences in society. The government expanded the education and health care systems and enacted progressive labor laws. They inaugurated comprehensive land reform a few months after the revolution, which diminished the political power of large landowners, imposed limits on individual holdings, and redistributed land to landless peasants. The government also commissioned the construction of al-Thawara City, a low-cost housing complex for *sarifa* dwellers. It founded housing associations to enable professional people working for the government to buy land and build their houses or to buy government-built houses at a reasonable rate. The government also supported the progressive Personal Status Code of 1959, described above, and enacted Law 80 of 1961, which gave the state the right to reclaim oilfields not exploited by the British-tied Iraq Petroleum Company. This step curtailed the power of oil companies, which were seen as cheating Iraq out of profits necessary for national economic development.[25]

Hanan was ecstatic over these reforms. To her, they constituted revolutionary change that signaled the onset of a postcolonial utopia. She described this period as "a time of optimism," when she thought that her generation could "steer the situation in the direction we wanted." In her account, this generation was made up of revolutionaries who were driven by patriotic feelings and a desire to help fellow Iraqis. She remarked that "everyone was working for the interests of the people" and that "Iraq was becoming a paradise." Interestingly, Hanan saw these reforms as achievements brought about through the work of ordinary Iraqis, not simply measures enacted by the government. She minimized the role of the state in favor of political actors who were taking the lead in transforming the country. In this Marxist paradise of solidarity and camaraderie, Hanan understood history as unfolding in a progressive and revolutionary way, whereby the colonial past yielded to the postcolonial present, which in turn yielded to a utopian future. Change meant progress, and this was all tied to a communist political project that emphasized independence, national unity, and prosperity.

Hanan was not merely a bystander who appreciated the reforms of those years from afar. She played a major role in bringing about one of the most important reforms at the time: the Personal Status Code of 1959. Since its formation in 1952, the League for the Defense of Women's Rights, along with the government-affiliated Iraqi Women's Union, sought to address social challenges facing Iraqi women with regard to family laws. However, all efforts to bring about a progressive personal status law under the monarchy had failed.[26] After the revolution, the League for the Defense of Women's Rights—which was renamed the Iraqi Women's League—formed a committee tasked with looking into problems facing women. Hanan was part of the committee, which recommended the adoption of a personal status law that protected women's legal and family rights.[27] The efforts of these women activists culminated in the Personal Status Code of 1959. The law signaled a new state gender discourse that revolved around granting women legal rights.[28]

It required that women consent to marriage, outlawed forced marriage, set a minimum marriage age for women (eighteen, but sixteen in certain cases), restricted polygamy and divorce, granted rights to women to request divorce, and gave preference to maternal custody. The law also made a woman's testimony equal to a man's—as opposed to religious rulings, which considered the testimony of two women as equal to that of one man. Though these articles provided more security and rights for women, they did not meet the high expectations of women activists like Hanan. For instance, women involved in drafting the law wanted to have polygamy banned, but they could not do so without alienating more-traditional people and religious clerics. The area where the law posed a serious challenge to Islamic rules was inheritance. The new law did away with the Quranic prescription that a male inherits twice the share of a female; instead, it dictated that women inherit shares equal to those of men. Hanan was proud of this law and saw it as her generation's legacy, one that shaped the lives of Iraqi women for generations after her, since the law remained in effect despite some amendments under subsequent Iraqi governments.[29]

In addition to social and political reforms, Hanan also reminisced about the period as a time of cultural renaissance in Baghdad. The overthrow of the monarchy engendered a cultural revival, whereby writers and artists began to experiment with new forms of literary and artistic expressions, and various ideas about the future of Iraq and the role of intellectuals in shaping that future appeared in books, journals, and newspapers.[30] Hanan threw herself into the middle of this vibrant cultural space. She and her friends met in cafés to discuss the latest books they had read or exhibition they had gone to. They saw plays at the theater and listened to classical music at each other's houses. Hanan describes those days of social and political reform and cultural renaissance as a "golden age in Iraq," when "a bright future awaited Iraqis." These reflections about the vibrant past, which were narrated by middle-class Baghdadis, became the dominant discourse about life in Iraq in the 1950s and early 1960s that shaped Iraqi memory for generations.

## A Long Hiatus and Exile

Hanan's depiction of the revolutionary past as a utopia, however,[31] silenced another reality, namely, the reality of deep divisions and political disagreements that plagued the first Iraqi republic from its beginning until its last days in 1963. The reign of President Qasim came to be defined by a bitter conflict between the communists and Arab nationalists over whether Iraq should become part of a union with Egypt and Syria.[32] While Arab nationalists advocated the union, communists believed in an Iraqi territorial entity that included everyone—and not just Arabs—in the nation. In addition, people began to be disillusioned with Qasim's arbitrary rule and with the deepening economic decline in the country. Disaffection among the armed forces grew as well. Hanan did not make any references to these developments and the sense of disappointment felt by some Iraqis. The internal contradictions of progressive politics in Hanan's narrative were flattened to preserve a memory of the idealized past.

Moreover, the fall of the monarchy and the departure of the British, which posed a threat to the existing geopolitical order in the Middle East and the established political economy of oil, marked the beginning of the U.S. intervention in the Iraqi political scene.[33] The turning point in U.S. foreign policy toward Iraq was Iraq's nationalization of 99.5 percent of its oil resources in 1961.[34] Backed by the CIA, the Ba'th Party carried out a coup d'état against Qasim. One of the first proclamations issued by coup leaders targeted the communists, who were described as "the partners in crime of the enemy of God Qasim" and who sought "to sow confusion in the ranks of people."[35] The leaders of the coup also gave orders to the military, the police, and the National Guard "to annihilate anyone who disturbs the peace."[36] The police and the National Guard, relying on lists provided by U.S. intelligence sources, arrested, tortured, and sentenced to death thousands of communists.

As soon as the news of the coup broke out, Hanan feared for her life. She went into hiding at a relative's house to escape arrest and torture. While in hiding, she heard the news that her husband, brother, and brother-in-law—who were all communists—had been arrested and tortured. Hanan's brother and brother-in-law were sent on what came to be known as the Train of Death, which carried prisoners from Baghdad to a prison in the south in cargo trains, while her husband broke down under torture and informed on his comrades. Hanan also began to hear stories about friends of hers that had been tortured. She was particularly haunted by the story of Amal, one of her best friends; after Amal's husband died while being tortured, a security guard tied Amal to his corpse for three days. Following this ordeal, Amal was raped. Hanan also heard about the death of close comrades. She decided to stay in hiding lest she face a similar fate.

The Ba'th coup of 1963 failed after a few months, when a counter-coup removed the Ba'th regime from power. In the chaos of the second coup, Hanan's husband managed to escape prison and went into hiding. The new regime also pursued an anticommunist policy, and Hanan and her husband had to remain in hiding for two years. During this time, Hanan could only see her children from a distance. Her mother would bring her children to the relatives' house where Hanan was hiding out, but Hanan would only look at them from the window. She did not dare to go out and see them in case they happened to say something in public about her whereabouts. After two years, Hanan and her husband fled to Kuwait and lived there until the second Ba'th coup in 1968.

Following the coup in 1968, the new regime announced an amnesty. Communists who had fled the country were allowed to come back, and those who had been dismissed from their jobs, like Hanan, were reinstated. Hanan and her family returned to Iraq. However, her return posed a dilemma. The Iraqi Communist Party, whose leadership was dominated by men, told her if that if she decided to stay in the party, she had to leave her husband, since he had informed on his comrades. Hanan felt torn between her obligations as a mother and wife and her commitment to the party. The predicament Hanan found herself in speaks to the disparity between the egalitarian ideology of the party, which emphasized the equality of men and women, and the practices of the leaders, who still saw the action of Hanan's husband as having consequences for her future in the party. The political rigidity of men in the party reaffirmed patriarchal norms that saw a woman as a dependent of her husband who had to bear the repercussions of his actions despite her decades of political and feminist activism. In the end, she chose to leave the party for the sake of her children. Despite her progressive politics, Hanan still could not escape the social expectation that women be good wives who protect their families first and foremost.

Moreover, Hanan faced another reality when she returned to Iraq. The Ba'th Party's ascent to power in 1968 was marked by drastic changes in the political structures of the country. The new ruling class consisted mainly of Ba'th army officers who hailed from certain clans and families from the northwest. Ahmad Hasan al-Bakr was one of the main officers behind the 1968 coup, and he became president, prime minister, chairman of the Revolutionary Command Council, and the secretary-general of the Ba'th party. Shortly after assuming all these positions, he began eliminating both his allies and rivals and promoting his relatives, most notably Saddam Hussein. These political developments were a departure from the utopian future that Hanan had hoped—and worked—for.

During our conversations, Hanan did not like to dwell on the rest of the 1960s or the 1970s that much. Unlike her energized and detailed reminiscences on the monarchy and early days of Qasim's reign, her reflections on the latter period were terse, dispirited, and punctuated by silences. The silences in her historical account replicated the periods of her political inaction. During the rest of the 1960s and the 1970s, Hanan, who taught English in a high school, led a low-key life. While she did not experience direct harassment or threats, her husband was arrested a few times. However, by the mid-1970s, she began to feel uncomfortable with the increasing power of the Ba'th regime. In 1976, she decided to retire at an early age because of state pressure on her to join the Ba'th Party. Hanan was fortunate in that her husband was well off, which enabled her to retire early. He had worked in the private sector in Kuwait, and when he returned to Iraq in 1968, he opened a business.

In 1979, while vacationing in London for the summer, Hanan heard news of an escalation in the repression of communists. At the time, an already-powerful Saddam Hussein assumed power and became the president. His reign began with a cold-blooded purge of the Ba'th Party, the liquidation of the Iraqi Communist Party, the persecution of the Shi'i opposition and Kurdish movements, the expulsion of the so-called Iraqis of Iranian origin, and the elimination and silencing of anyone else who was perceived as a threat to his rule. When Hanan learned about the arrest and disappearance of close communist friends, she feared for her and her husband's lives and decided not to go back to Iraq.

At first, Hanan hoped that exile would be short-lived, but she was dismayed at the regime's ability to stay in power after all the brutalities it committed. She remembered a time when top government officials had to resign because the police opened fire on people during Al-Wathba of 1948. The fact that the regime continued to grow stronger and more brutal was incomprehensible. The outbreak of the Iran-Iraq War in 1980 was a further setback, dashing any hope of an immediate return to Iraq. From that point, Hanan began to wait for the fall of Saddam Hussein as the moment when she would be able to go back to Iraq. The fall of Hussein, moreover, assumed a redemptive quality; Hanan imagined that a regime change would mean that she could "go back to the Iraq I knew." Saddam Hussein became a barrier to the imagined golden age of the 1950s and early 1960s and to the possibility of reliving the political vibrancy that existed in Iraq at that time.[37]

While in London, Hanan did not have to look for a job. Her husband's business network again provided the family with a comfortable life. The fact that many of Hanan's friends who had fled Iraq in the late 1970s and early 1980s lived in London gave her a rich social life. She also remained in touch with Iraqi communists in London, though she did not get involved with the IWL or ICP directly.[38] Women from the IWL asked her to join the organization again, but she declined because she did not think they had a clear program or even enthusiasm. Instead of political activism, Hanan dedicated her time to social causes and community building. She became involved with the ICP-affiliated Iraqi Forum, which provided services to Iraqi refugees and organized cultural events—such as lectures on the political situation in Iraq, poetry readings, and art exhibitions—for the Iraqi community. She became instrumental in consolidating the forum and making it accessible to people by finding a new location in the center of London. Hanan's concern with the maintenance of community welfare and cultural continuity between London and Iraq also kept alive a particular imagined Iraq. The forum offered a venue to retain the past in the lives of Iraqis and thus to keep the idea of Iraq alive. The self-perception that Iraqi communists were concerned about the well-being of the community, rather than personal interests, was reinforced in these acts of solidarity.

The 1990s furthered Hanan's anguish and anxiety over Iraq and the future. Saddam Hussein's invasion of Kuwait in 1990 and the Gulf War of 1991 first raised hopes that the regime would fall, especially following the uprisings in the north and south of the country. However, the United States' decision to keep Saddam Hussein in power—for fear of another Shi'i government in the region—was a blow to that hope. This turn of events left Iraqis in

Iraq reeling under a dictatorial regime that grew stronger and more brutal, a war that resulted in most of the country's infrastructure destroyed, harsh economic sanctions that lasted until the fall of the regime in 2003, and a degraded ecological system. It also left Iraqis in London struggling with the fact that any return would be further delayed. They also worried about the ongoing—or increasing—suffering of loved ones in Iraq. The deteriorating situation in Iraq came to haunt Hanan, whose sense of guilt and privilege deepened during this period. She had a hard time coming to terms with the fact that while she lived a comfortable life in London, Iraqis in Iraq did not have enough food or uninterrupted access to water and electricity. As she once told me, she used to cry when she showered, thinking of all the Iraqis who did not have water to drink. The anguish Hanan felt over the situation in Iraq intensified her efforts to help Iraqis, such as holding fund-raisers to send medicines to Iraq and helping Iraqi refugees arriving in London in the early 1990s through the Iraqi Forum.[39] Through these acts of solidarity, Hanan aimed to maintain the possibility of the idealized past, a time when Iraqis were unified by their concerns about the future of their country and the well-being of their fellow citizens.

## Disillusionment

Hanan's life in exile was punctuated by imperial events that shaped the national sphere in Iraq. Because of the United States' role in prolonging the Iran-Iraq War (1980–1988), its decision to keep Saddam Hussein in power in 1991 and veto any efforts to lift the sanctions on the country, and finally its occupation of Iraq in 2003 and institutionalization of a sectarian quota system, the imagined possibility of an Iraq defined by stability and democracy grew more elusive every day. The decision of the United States to bring about regime change in Iraq through military action constituted a serious setback not only to the dreams of prosperity and peace but also to the visions of national sovereignty and independence. For Hanan's generation of communists, who were committed to anticolonial and anti-imperialist struggles, the invasion of Iraq furthered the sense of disillusionment with the postcolonial present.[40] Hanan, along with the Iraqi Communist Party, opposed the war. She and her comrades participated in the antiwar demonstrations in London, raising the slogan "No to Dictatorship. No to War." To Hanan, the war meant more suffering for the Iraqi people and more destruction of an already war-torn Iraq. Moreover, it would bring Iraq back under the yoke of direct imperialism.

Hanan watched news of the invasion obsessively. Despite her opposition to the invasion and her pain at seeing U.S. troops enter Baghdad, there was one scene that made her happy for a fleeting moment. On April 9, 2003, Hanan turned the television on and saw live coverage of a scene unfolding in Firdous Square, where a twelve-meter statue of Saddam Hussein stood. There was a group of Iraqi men who were trying to pull down the statue. While someone hooked a rope around its neck to bring it down, another man hammered at the marble base of the statue with little success. Shortly afterward, U.S. tanks reached the square. U.S. soldiers tied the rope around the statue to a tank, which pulled back slowly and brought down the statue. Hanan recalled that she felt "great joy" when she saw the fall of the statue; she read it as the fall of the regime. Her phone began to ring incessantly. Iraqi friends and relatives called her to congratulate her on the fall of the regime. She and some friends decided to go to the Iraqi embassy in London to celebrate the event. When they reached the embassy, they found a group of forty Iraqis there. They clapped and cheered for about an hour before they decided to go back home. During this time, Hanan imagined that regime change would entail a total rupture with the status quo and that progressive social and political transformations would follow. Utopian futures, reminiscent of the changes following the fall of the monarchy, again emerged as a possibility.

But when Hanan got home, she turned the television on and saw the news of looting of governmental institutions by Iraqis. The scenes of looting left her in shock. Like the fall of the monarchy, Hanan anticipated busy and bustling streets with people celebrating the fall of the regime. Instead, she saw looters gleefully and openly loading cars and carts with furniture and electronics taken from government ministries and offices. The looting indicated to Hanan that Iraqi society had changed during her long absence. When Hanan talked about that day, she emphasized that she was never disconnected from Iraq; even though she had been in exile for decades, she followed what was happening in the country closely. She thought she knew what years of wars and sanctions had done to the Iraqi people, but she was appalled to see an Iraq that was very different from what she imagined. She remarked that "Iraqis have become Ali Baba," referring to the story in the

Arabian Nights about Ali Baba and the Forty Thieves. Indeed, the metaphor of Iraqis turning into Ali Baba was common at the time. To Hanan, it seemed that Iraqi society had reverted to a premodern form of disorder, which stood in stark contrast to the modernizing hopes that marked her youth and that animated her activism while in exile.

The weeks and months following the U.S. occupation of Iraq furthered Hanan's disillusionment and undermined her hopes for alternative futures. The institutionalization of a sectarian quota system by the United States came as a shock to her. Hanan's perception of the past, shaped by her experiences in leftist and revolutionary politics in Iraq and in exile, made it difficult for her to understand political developments that differed so much from the future she had imagined for the country since the late 1950s. In her reminiscences of the past, Hanan was silent on political groups whose agenda focused on ethnic and religious sensibilities. During her detailed reminiscences about the past, Hanan did not mention that the first religious party in Iraq was established in 1959 or that Kurdish parties had posed a threat to Iraqi governments since the inception of the Iraqi state in 1921. She also thought little of the fact that the three major parties, which had constituted a serious threat to Hussein's reign from within Iraq since the late 1970s, were Kurdish and Shi'i parties, or the fact that the main Iraqi parties that operated in exile—particularly in London, Tehran, and Damascus—were religious and ethnic parties.[41] To Hanan, religious and ethnic groups, by definition, represent a form of backwardness, a radical departure from secular and leftist politics and a challenge to the notions of progressive change and a subjectivity informed by modernist aspiration. Hanan's discourse about an idealized revolutionary past silenced or dismissed these political developments. It was only after the fall of Saddam Hussein's regime that she could no longer disregard the rise of religious and ethnic parties as they came to dominate the political scene.

Moreover, the emergence of these political parties as major players in Iraqi politics forced Hanan to confront the rise of religiosity among Iraqis. While she dismissed the piety among Iraqis in London as the product of alienation from British society and a desire to carve out a distinct identity, she thought that the situation in Iraq would be different. However, the opening up of the national space to the Iraqi diaspora and the broadcast of images of veiled women and religious events in Iraq undermined Hanan's perception of

Iraqis as secular, modern subjects who embraced leftist politics. During our interviews, she spoke vehemently against religiosity and often equated it with ignorance, dismissing it as a phenomenon foreign to Iraqis:

> It is known that the Iraqi people are irreligious. What we are seeing now is strange. There are peoples—like the Egyptians, Yemenis, and Sudanese—who are religious by nature. But not Iraqis. We used to laugh at someone who prayed before. With the renaissance after the end of World War II and the dominance of liberational thought, people were busy with classical music, art, books, and social life. No one thought about religion. The Iraqi Communist Party didn't take a stand against religion. However, most of its members were enlightened. Things changed now. You can't stand against the religious trend. The Islamists are strong and more active. Look at their gatherings. They are always well attended, and a lot of young people attend them. Do you find anyone in her forties in our meetings? No. Everyone is from my generation. What is happening is strange. I always wonder: where did this ignorance and backwardness come from? We are moving backward, not forward.

Hanan belonged to a generation of secularist communists who saw their political project as a break with the past—with religion and tradition. She perceived Islam as intrinsically antiquated and observant Iraqis as inimical to modernity. Religion represented a regressive movement into the premodern past, while secularism was linked to enlightenment. Moreover, modernity became tied to nation building and the formation of progressive subjects dedicated to Iraq; religion, by contrast, became linked to the fragmentation of Iraq and to forms of selfhood that she saw as inimical to an inclusive Iraq. To Hanan, the rise of religiosity was disrupting the progressive march of time—in which the past yielded to the present and the present would yield to the utopian future. She came to experience the present, with its prolonged realities of wars and violence, as an impasse with no hopes for alternative futures. It especially pained Hanan to see the younger generations, including her comrades' children and her own grandchildren, flocking to religion. She had high hopes that the youth would take over and embrace the revolutionary ideals of her generation. Just as her generation of high school and college students had led the political struggle against the British and the monarchy, Hanan expected the young to now spearhead a progressive political movement that would transform the political and social scenes in Iraq. Her disappointment was "immense." Rather than espousing an alternative political project, the younger generation was "brainwashed." She emphasized that, given the current situation, both in Iraq and in diaspora, Iraqis would need decades and even centuries to catch up with the West.

Hanan's critique of religiosity and reminiscences about the past reflect her middle-class sensibilities. In describing her generation as vanguards of liberational and enlightened thought, Hanan was referring to middle-class communists who had access to high culture. The experiences of peasants, workers, and people who practiced religion did not factor into this imagination, even though the Iraqi Communist Party included people from different class, religious, and ethnic backgrounds. Her middle-class sensibilities were more apparent when Hanan talked about Iraqi politicians who held power at the present, especially Shi'i politicians. She described them as "the riffraff" (*shkulat*) who had "no taste, no thought, no ethics." Unlike her generation, which "looked forward to life" and "wanted the good life for everyone," Iraqi politicians at the present "loved death" and "did not think about life." Hanan equated manifestations of religiosity with an aversion to life and extolment of death. Rather than critiquing Iraqi politicians for their policies and divisive politics, Hanan scorned them for their lack of cultural capital. In her narrative, communists focused on the welfare of the individual and the nation, while the project of religious people was predicated upon the denial of life and the disintegration of the nation.

The political present disillusioned Hanan not only for its religious overtones, but also for the dominance of fanatical sectarianism. She thought that sectarianism was a new phenomenon that did not exist in the past. She dismissed it as a manifestation of outmoded thinking and as the product of the discourse employed by the U.S. administration in 2003 that depicted Iraq as a place inhabited by Sunnis, Shi'is, Kurds, and minorities. While Hanan often dwelled on the rise of sectarianism in the present, when venting her disappointment at the turn of events in contemporary Iraq and the fragmentation of the Iraqi community in London, she was noticeably silent on this issue in her recollections of the past. She asserted that sectarianism never existed in the past, that she never knew if her neighbors or classmates at school were Sunni, Shi'i, or Kurdish, and she valorized this lack of awareness about sects.

Knowledge of someone's sect was simply a marker of a premodern sensibility. Hanan's silence on the existence of sectarian affiliations in the past betrayed a deep-seated anxiety that the idea of the true Iraq as a unified collectivity and Iraqis as modern subjects was mistaken. Any admission that sectarian and ethnic sentiments might have carried weight in Iraqi society and or politics undermined the modernist project endorsed by communists. Hanan did not perceive sectarianism and ethnic politics as being a result of the political exclusion of a significant portion of Iraqi society—particular Shi'is and Kurds—from meaningful political participation in the state for most of the twentieth century; she did not see them connected to emergent Iraqi political projects, whether in the past or the present, that were a response to this history of exclusion.[42]

Hanan's disapproval of ethnic and sectarian identities as a manifestation of primitive thinking shrouded in silence her own ethnic background. When she dwelled on the past and the present, she always described herself as an Iraqi first and foremost. She never mentioned that she was a Kurd, even though she had a distinctively Kurdish last name. When I brought up her Kurdish background in our conversation, she described herself as a Kurdish Iraqi, rather than an Iraqi Kurd: she was an Iraqi first, Kurd second. To her, Kurdishness was a tenuous marker of identity that surfaced only when someone expressed anti-Kurdish sentiments. Hanan ascribed her lack of attachment to a Kurdish identity to the fact that she was brought up with a love for Iraq and that the Iraqi Communist Party did not differentiate between its members on the basis of their ethnic, religious, or sectarian affiliations. As Hanan reflected on her (lack of) ethnic affiliation, she was quick to assert that sectarian identities—namely, whether she was a Sunni or a Shi'i—did not matter to her at all because she was not religious. She saw any acknowledgment of these identities as a sign of backwardness.

Despite her disillusionment with the present, especially with the rise of religiosity and sectarianism, Hanan still hoped that she would find traces of the idealized past if she visited Iraq. While living in exile, Hanan was haunted by the prospect of never being able to visit Baghdad before she died. When Saddam Hussein's regime fell in 2003, she wanted to go to Iraq immediately, but her children dissuaded her because of the instability in the country. With the escalating violence in the following months and years, Hanan came to regret her decision not to visit Iraq when she had had the chance. In 2009, at the age of seventy-six, she decided she had to go to Iraq, and she managed to arrange a trip with the help of a friend who lived there. As the airplane landed, Hanan saw Baghdad for the first time in thirty years. She was overwhelmed with emotions and began to cry, unable to believe that she was finally in Baghdad. However, this emotional homecoming was followed by feelings of perplexity and loss.[43] Hanan expected to see Baghdad as she had left it: a clean, modern city. Instead, she found a neglected city she could not recognize and a people she could not relate to. It pained Hanan to see that Baghdad had become dirty, dusty, and divided by concrete walls. There were piles of trash everywhere, holes in the street, and vendors occupying the pavement selling flip-flops and cookware. She also thought that the inhabitants of Baghdad had changed—including in appearance. She ascribed this change to the fact that most Baghdadis had fled the country during Hussein's reign and that people from the countryside had taken over the city. Instead of an enchanted city, Hanan realized that time had passed and that the Baghdad she knew no longer existed. Her memories did not define the city anymore. She found herself a stranger in her own city, unable to safely walk the streets. She couldn't reach her house because it was blocked by concrete walls, and she couldn't recognize her parents' house.

## Perpetual Haunting

After the U.S. occupation of Iraq and the fall of Saddam Hussein's regime, not only did Hanan have to face the loss of political ideals and a superfluous existence, but she also had to recognize the deterioration of the situation in Iraq, which constantly haunted her:

> We got rid of Saddam, but things are going from bad to worse. Hundreds of victims die every day. Iraqis are dying like flies or ants. Those who are still alive are virtually dead. Can you call the life of an Iraqi a life? . . . Akh, Akh. I have an open wound in my heart. Iraq doesn't depart my thought or imagination. Some people blame me for listening to the news a lot. The first thing I do after I wake up is to turn on the television. I start with Iraqi channels and then move to the British ones. Iraq comes first. I'm here [in London], but my heart is there. I have no worries but Iraq. There are of course daily

worries—like when my brother was in hospital, but these are normal things. My biggest worry is Iraq.

The turn of events in post-Saddam Iraq represented the unthinkable to Hanan. Whenever I visited Hanan, she always had the television muted and turned to an Iraqi channel. She often switched between different Iraqi and British channels while speaking to see if there was news about explosions or suicide attacks in the country. One time, in 2007, there was a breaking news flash about an explosion in Baghdad. Hanan immediately raised the volume to find out about the location of the attack and the number of casualties. There was not much information other than that the explosion happened near the center of Baghdad. Hanan immediately switched from al-Iraqiyya, Iraq's official television channel, to Al-Baghdaddiyya to find more details of the attack, with no success. She then switched to the BBC. She kept switching back and forth between different channels desperately trying to get more information. As our gazes were fixed on the TV, a friend of Hanan called. The friend had a relative in Baghdad, who called Hanan's friend to assure her that his family was unhurt and to tell her about what he had heard about the attack. It turned out a car with explosives was parked near a busy market in Kadimiyya, and the death toll was expected to be high. The update from the friend disheartened Hanan, and her tone lost its usual vigor and excitement. Hanan's spirited reminiscences about the past were replaced with dejected anger at the turn of events in Iraq and dismay that the situation kept going from bad to worse. The fact that Iraq was always in the news following the U.S. invasion barred any reprieve from the unending cycle of violence. The constant coverage of violence unfolding in Iraq engendered anxiety over the well-being of the Iraqi people in general, of friends and relatives in particular. It also intensified concerns that stability and peace were no longer attainable.

Hanan's preoccupation with Iraq—whether in her fixation on the idealized past or current developments in Iraq—defined her daily life during the thirteen years I came to know her. As she put it, Iraq was an open wound in the heart that could not be healed. The pain of the ongoing war and destruction of her homeland was something she struggled with daily. The image of the open wound emphasized the intense and persistent pain Hanan felt. Iraq was not a distant memory that she thought of every now and then. Rather, it was a source of ongoing agony. Indeed, it was hard to miss the heartbreak Hanan felt when she spoke about Iraq. The tone of her voice oscillated between tender fondness for the past and heartfelt despair at the unending suffering of the Iraqi people in the present. Though Hanan had lived in London since the late 1970s, her heart was still in Iraq. On different occasions, Hanan emphasized that though she had a good and comfortable life in London and had no major personal worries, she was unhappy internally. To her, Iraq was her homeland and the place where she belonged. She once told me that Iraq was the most important thing to her—that she loved her family and children, but she loved Iraq more than anything else. She was perpetually haunted by the destruction of her country and the loss of alternative futures.

During my time with Hanan, she hardly spoke about the future. She no longer could imagine what the future of Iraq would look like. She had once imagined a future defined by progress, prosperity, democracy, and social equality. But the failure of the modernist communist project and the transformation of the Iraqi political and social scene after 2003 made it impossible for her to imagine alternative futures. Instead, she resorted to a vague notion of hope. When I first began interviewing Hanan in 2006, she hoped that the situation in Iraq would eventually improve—that the violence would have to come to an end sooner or later. When I met with her ten years later, she still talked of hope but also about her sense of despair. The fall of Mosul to the Islamic State in 2014 represented a serious setback to the stability of Iraq. It was such a shock to Hanan that she feared she would become paralyzed watching the news on television. She could not believe that a small group of fighters could take such a big city so easily and quickly and that the Iraqi army was in disarray. The unthinkable—that Iraq could still take a turn for the worse—became a reality. In her profound despair, she became haunted for the first time by the prospect that "Iraq was over."

When I interviewed Hanan in 2018, she still oscillated between hope and despair. Sometimes she said that she had no hope that the situation in Iraq would improve; at other times, she believed that the situation would inevitably take a different turn. She believed she had to fight against despair, to fight against the feeling that her generation's struggle was in vain. With the demise of alternative futures and the possibility of the disintegration of Iraq, clinging to hope became her only option. As she told me when I last saw her,

"Sometimes, I feel despair, and sometimes, I feel hope. You can't lose hope. If you lose hope, it is difficult. You can't let go of Iraq. You can't allow it to disappear from the map. This is our country."

In the summer of 2019, I interviewed Hanan for the last time. My visit this time was short, as Hanan was very terse, which was unlike her. She commented on the rampant corruption in the country and the impossibility of finding a way out of the situation in Iraq, given that most of the politicians had militias that would put an end to any effort to bring a change to the status quo. As we drank tea, she told me how Saddam Hussein's reign had actually been better, as there was at least a semblance of a state that managed to provide services and employment.

## A Photograph of the Past

Whenever I visited Hanan at her house to interview her, I was struck by how her living room had an inescapably Iraqi touch. Though the furniture was modern, most of the accessories revolved around Iraq. Paintings depicting Iraqi traditional scenes—such as peasant women in abayas and fields of palm trees—hung on the walls.[44] The bookcase was filled with Arabic books about the history of the Iraqi Communist Party (ICP) and its affiliate, the Iraqi Women's League (IWL), memoirs by Iraqi communists, and poetry books and novels by Iraqi authors. On the shelves there were also two replicas of the iconic Freedom Monument, which is located in the center of Baghdad and commemorates the achievements of the 1958 Revolution. The juxtaposition of different familial and political artifacts provided a glimpse of Hanan's world. Among the family pictures on the shelf behind the sofa where Hanan sat during our interviews, there was a photograph of young Iraqi women dressed in modern attire, including Hanan, marching in the streets of Baghdad in the early 1960s. The march was organized by the Iraqi Women's League in 1962 to commemorate the anniversary of the 1958 Revolution. This photograph always caught my eye while Hanan reminisced about the past. As I gazed at the photograph, an idealized picture of the past materialized in front of me. The picture constructed a neat narrative frequently rehearsed by a generation of Iraqi communists who came of age during World War II. It recalled a time when the Iraqi Communist Party and the Iraqi Women's League dominated the political scene in Iraq, voicing demands for genuine independence, social and political equality, and women's rights, as well as dreams about a revolution that would transform Iraqi society and politics.

The photograph also spoke of youth, class, and modernity. The iconic figure in this picture was the young, modern, middle-class woman who championed a progressive political agenda and played an important role in the Iraqi political scene, whether through taking part in demonstrations, educating peasant women, or advocating for reforms that would improve the status of women. The young Iraqi woman represented Iraqi modernity and progressive ideals. But this framing of the political past silenced a significant segment of the Iraqi society. As I looked at the picture, I wondered if working and peasant women, who historically took part in political demonstrations and protests advocating for Iraq's independence and social justice, participated in that march. The focus of the picture on modern women erased the presence of Iraqi women who did not fit that frame. The photograph, as such, reproduced Hanan's imagination of her generation as championing modernity and leaving behind "backwardness," particularly religion. In constructing the Iraqi self as a modern and progressive subject, the photograph, just as Hanan's testimonies about the past, reproduced a discourse about the 1950s and early 1960s as a time defined by secularism and anticolonial struggle that was prevalent among Iraqis in London. Though Hanan and her comrades found themselves politically irrelevant in the present with the rise of religiosity and sectarianism, they still shaped Iraqi historical memory through idealized narratives about the past.

Like Hanan's narrative, the picture was a statement on how colonial and imperial realities had shaped Iraqi subjectivity and memories. On the one hand, it depicted how the British presence in Iraq until the Revolution of 1958 engendered anticolonial and revolutionary sentiments. The demands for genuine independence and social equality that dominated the Iraqi landscape at the time produced Hanan and her comrades as revolutionary subjects dedicated to the welfare of the Iraqi people and the country. Moreover, the anticolonial sentiments and the social and political transformations in Iraq following the fall of the monarchy and the departure of the British from Iraq shaped Iraqi memory as well, in that depictions of the past by Hanan and her comrades became the dominating discourse about "the good old days" that remained prevalent in the present. In addition, this discourse on

Iraqi subjectivity was informed by classed and gendered sensibilities in that middle-class, educated, unveiled women became the symbols of Iraqi modernity. On the other hand, the picture depicted Hanan as a nostalgic subject, who yearned for a past that represented a rupture with the present. As such, the picture provided a critical statement on the political present and imperial realities. The postcolonial present—which came to be dominated by wars, violence, an authoritarian regime, and direct U.S. intervention in Iraqi affairs since 1963—resulted in displacement and prolonged exile for decades. With Hanan's TV also tuned to Iraqi channels that broadcast news about suicide bombings, sectarian violence, and atrocities committed by the U.S. soldiers in Iraq, the photograph on the shelf maintained an alternative image of Iraq, in which the possibility of a prosperous and independent Iraq was once an attainable reality.

# IN THE SHADOW OF FEAR

As a child, listening to accounts of the late 1940s and 1950s, I felt unlucky to have been born under Saddam Hussein's regime. I envied the carefree and happy attitude my parents seemed to have enjoyed in their youth. I also came to understand that it was pure chance that my parents had not disappeared or been killed in 1963. Growing up, I always feared that I could suddenly lose them. This fear began when I was around five years old. At that time, the Ba'th regime escalated their crackdown on dissident Iraqis. Despite my young age, I felt the growing fear and sense of caution in people around me. I knew that my parents were communists and opposed the regime. I also knew that my aunt's husband had been arrested, a fact that no one tried to hide. However, nobody informed me or my sister of the time my father had spent in jail. When he was arrested in 1978, my mother told us that he had gone abroad for a while. I remember waking up in the middle of the night to the sound of people talking in the house. I went down the steps to find my mother and her father, who lived with us, talking to my father. I understood then that my father had just been released from jail. I overheard him talking about how happy he was when he removed his blindfold and saw that the security guard had dropped him off by my sister's school in central Baghdad. He repeated that story many times that night, but he did not mention anything about his arrest. My sister's school symbolized familiarity, a connection with a world he recognized after the alienation he had experienced behind bars. This must have been in 1978. I remember his arrest and release in 1979 more vividly.

One evening in 1979, my father, who was a surgeon and had to attend to his private practice after finishing his rounds at the hospital, came home late as usual. He arrived shortly after my grandfather had fallen while moving my sister's bicycle from the middle of the garage. I remember being frightened and screaming, "Mama, grandpa fell." As my father was about to examine my grandfather's foot, the doorbell rang. Two men in civilian clothes—not military or police uniforms—came in and told my father that he needed to go with them. My father asked my mother to take my grandfather to the hospital the next day to have his foot X-rayed. Then, without making a fuss, and before he had the chance to eat the dinner my mother had prepared, he walked out with the men as we all watched in silence.

The next day, we found out that my grandfather had fractured a bone in his foot. He subsequently developed a clot and remained in the hospital until after my father was released from prison a few weeks later. I remember my mother, worried and heavy-hearted, telling my father upon his release about my grandfather's ailing condition. He passed away on July 11, 1979, only three weeks after his foot injury.

It was a difficult year for my family. In May, after disappearing for six months in the cells of the Iraqi intelligence agency (the Mukhabarat), the "revolutionary court" sentenced my maternal aunt's husband to twenty years in prison under the flimsy pretext of contacting foreign companies. Communist friends of my parents, apprehended around the time of my father's arrests, disappeared in prison. It was also around this time that my mother was fired from her job as a professor of Russian literature at Baghdad University because she refused to sign a document of allegiance to the Ba'th Party. As punishment, the regime transferred her to work in a cement factory in southern Iraq. My mother submitted her letter of resignation and stayed at home.

Sometimes, my parents spoke about these developments, especially the arrest of my aunt's husband and my mother's dismissal, in front of me and my sister. But often, they tried to keep us in the dark, for our safety and theirs. My parents started to censor themselves when teachers, on orders from the regime, began to ask young students about their parents' conversations at home in an attempt to track down political opponents. There were many stories of parents ending up in prison because their children repeated at school what they had heard at home. One of my earliest childhood memories is of me standing behind the closed door of the living room in our house, where my mother, aunt, and grandfather were talking. I wanted to sit with them, but my mother insisted that I leave. I knew that they wanted to talk about something serious and did not want me to hear what they had to say. My sister, who was two years older, was a calm person who minded her own business. I, by contrast, was very anxious and fearful. A conversation behind closed doors was not in the least reassuring to me. I remember my mother telling me, as she was walking me out of the living room, that it was better for me not to hear the conversation they were having in case I repeated any of it by accident in front of my teacher the following day. I promised her that I would not say a word at school, but she was relentless. As my mother closed the door, I pretended to walk away, but I only took a few steps and tried to listen to what they were saying. I do not remember the content of the conversation, but it must have revolved around my father and my aunt's husband, who were both in jail, or around rumors they had heard about the regime's brutality. Such whispered and secretive conversations made me constantly apprehensive. After that moment, I obsessed over the fate of my parents, and I suffered severe anxiety and stomachaches. My parents' efforts to reassure me were unsuccessful. Their vulnerability was too conspicuous, despite their apparent calm demeanor and composure.

In 1980, my family experienced a lull in their persecution. After serving the first two years of his sentence in the notorious Abu Ghraib prison, my aunt's husband was released by a personal order from Saddam Hussein. My uncle was a prominent architect, and Hussein decided to release him to have him supervise the rebuilding of parts of Baghdad for a conference of the Non-Aligned Movement. The decision to dismiss my mother from her job was rescinded, and she went back to her position at the university. My father was not re-arrested after his release in 1979. The respite from persecution, however, was not enough to mitigate my feelings of uncertainty. I knew that things could take a bad turn at any second.

Indeed, this lull did not last long. Throughout the 1980s, political pressure on my mother to cooperate with the regime intensified. There were bad days when she came under direct pressure and calm days when the regime seemed to forget about her. She sometimes received phone calls from newspaper editors asking her to write articles on Saddam Hussein, and she would decline, giving the excuse that she only wrote about literature. Members of General Security, which is an arm of the intelligence agency in Iraq, visited us at home a few times to inquire about her political beliefs and past political affiliations. At first, my mother acknowledged that she had been a communist, but friends advised her not to mention this fact. They argued that it was better to bury any information that could be used against her. These phone calls and visits made us very anxious. My mother always feared that the regime would further threaten her—or increase the pressure on her—in the future. Stories about opponents of the regime who had been threatened about cooperating alarmed us further. It pained my mother tremendously when she came across articles praising Saddam Hussein written by people who she knew were really against the regime, or when she saw an acquaintance applaud the regime on television. She was terrified at the possibility that, at any given point, she could be the next person to "fall" and cooperate with the regime.

The fact that my mother taught at a university meant that she was constantly in close contact with the regime, which kept a close eye on universities. Most departments—except for the departments of education, physical education, and journalism—were not limited to loyalists to the regime or the Ba'th Party. Professors were not legally forced to become members of the Ba'th Party, like schoolteachers were, though they were continuously urged to cooperate, and some of them did, either out of fear, coaxing, or coercion. Moreover, students who worked for the intelligence agency had a strong presence on campuses. They were called students "of special admission" (*qaboul khas*), and they were tasked with watching, and writing reports on, other students and professors. My mother was especially worried about these students since she feared they would fabricate reports or misrepresent what she would say in class. Some of these students also tried to use their enormous power to intimidate professors, either implicitly or explicitly, into giving them good grades. My mother was concerned that her integrity as a professor would be compromised if the chairperson or dean asked her to pass students despite their bad performance. Finally, these students were a source of rumors. They always related stories about the regime to my mother and other professors, such as news of a failed coup d'état or a military campaign against the Kurds. They sometimes complained about severe punishments for slight mistakes they made, as well as backstabbing among members of the intelligence agency. No one was sure if these stories and rumors were true or whether they were meant to elicit a (hopefully negative) reaction from the professors. Every time my mother returned home from work was a victory; I was relieved that she had survived yet another day unscathed.

My parents should have left Iraq in the late 1970s or early 1980s, when my aunt and her husband as well as a good number of their friends had left, before travel was banned in 1983. However, their experience under the monarchy shaped their visions of Iraq. That the regime could last after all the atrocities it committed and after invading Iran was unthinkable to them. They often reminisced about how Al-Wathba, in which they took part, forced the Iraqi government to resign in 1948. My parents fondly remembered it as an example of popular power, when the government had to give in to the will of the people and their demands, especially after the police shot dead several protesters. My parents firmly believed that Saddam Hussein's regime could not remain in power given its brutality. I remember my mother's dismay during the early days of the Iran-Iraq War. One day, as if she was trying to convince herself, she openly told me that the regime was going to fall very soon and that this was a war of attrition that the regime would not be able to survive. My parents failed to see that the unthinkable was becoming a reality, and therefore they didn't leave Iraq. They believed that the regime would soon collapse, so they should stay and weather the difficult years until that happened.

But the regime grew stronger every day, and this took a toll on my father in particular. During the last two years of his life, he became severely depressed and started drinking a lot. Unlike my mother, he rarely talked about the past. He mainly lamented the liquidation of the ICP in the late 1970s and the death and disappearance of some of his close friends. He sometimes banged his head against the wall as he talked about the fate of his friends. He often wished that he had died before witnessing these developments and talked about how the struggle of his generation was forestalled by the European- and U.S.-backed reign of Saddam Hussein. That his dreams were crushed became too much of a burden to bear. In late 1982, he had a stroke, and he passed away five days later. In retrospect, I believe that he suffered from survivor's guilt, but I was too young at the time to understand it. After I left Iraq in 1997, my aunt's husband—who had been arrested in 1978—told me that the regime had threatened my father, saying they would assault his wife and daughters if he refused to cooperate with them. It seems that my mother knew about this threat but decided not mention it to me or my sister.

( CHAPTER 2 )

# REVISIONIST POLITICS

On a cold winter day in 2006, I was standing in front of Acton Town station waiting for Khalil to come and pick me up. Thoughts were raging in my head. I tried to imagine what it would be like to see Khalil for the first time in twenty-seven years. Khalil was my father's best friend in Iraq. After he fled the country in 1979, following the increasing persecution of communists, our families lost touch. When I arrived in London in 2006 to start fieldwork, it did not occur to me to find him. But one day I was with Abu Warda, an Iraqi man who was my initial contact with Iraqis in London, when he received a phone call from a friend. I heard him say that he would contact "Dr. Khalil Tariq" about some forthcoming meeting in their group, the Coalition of Democracy in Iraq. As soon as Abu Warda ended the phone call, I asked him about Khalil and told him about our history. He immediately called Khalil. At first, he just talked to him about the group meeting, but then he said, "I have a surprise for you. Do you remember your friend, Muhammad Saleh Smeisim? Well, his daughter is here, and she would like to talk to you." When I picked up the phone and said hello, I began pacing, and I could hear my voice rising and my heart pounding. After a short conversation, Khalil invited me for tea at his house. As I waited for Khalil to pick me up, I kept thinking about our families' history and of how the meeting that day would have been different had my parents left Iraq in the late 1970s, as Khalil had. Though I met many communists in London who knew my parents, seeing

Khalil was different. He was a close friend of my parents and knew aspects of their political activism and lives that I only had had glimpses of.

As I was having these various thoughts, I saw a Mercedes-Benz pulling in. A man who looked Iraqi got out. I smiled and asked, "Uncle Khalil?"

"Yes," the man replied.

"How are you?"

We shook hands, and I got into the car. Khalil was in his mid- to late sixties at the time. His gray hair was thinning in the middle of his head. His pale green suit was an odd color but otherwise typical of suits worn by Iraqi men in London—basic with minimal finishes, but slightly baggy, which always gave me the impression that they were bought in the late 1980s, even though they were new. Khalil and I made small talk about the neighborhood.

After a short ride, we got to the house. His wife, Mary, received me with a big smile and a hug, unlike my formal handshake with Khalil. She was a warm and energetic woman. As soon as I stepped into the living room, I felt like I was in an Iraqi home. There were paintings of Iraq on the wall depicting palm trees, Iraqi women in traditional garments, and Iraqi boats (*balam*) in rivers. A Persian carpet covered the floor, and a glass-and-wood cupboard full of fine china stood against a wall. There were plants of different sizes on the windowsills and decorative clay pots on the shelf above the fireplace. The TV was turned to an Iraqi network but put on mute. After disappearing into the kitchen for a short while, Mary came back with tea in small Iraqi cups (*istikan*) and Iraqi pastries stuffed with dates and walnuts that she had baked. During our conversation, we updated each other on our lives over the past twenty-seven years. Mary, who used to be a pediatrician in Iraq, had had to quit her job to raise her two young daughters when they came to Britain in the late 1970s. Unlike many Iraqis, who could not find jobs in their profession in Britain because British employers did not recognize their Iraqi degrees, Khalil, who was a heart surgeon, managed to continue his career in his new home country because he had obtained his medical degree in Britain after he fled Iraq following the 1963 coup.

Khalil lit a cigarette and mentioned that he began to smoke in 1963, when he went into hiding during the Ba'th coup. His mother brought him cigarettes to kill time because he could not listen to the radio for fear that the neighbors might suspect someone was hiding. This remark led to a conversation about Khalil's relationship with the Iraqi Communist Party. I thought that Khalil was still a communist, but he told me that he resigned from the party in 1977 due to his disagreement with the party's alliance with the Ba'thists in the 1970s. He shared with me that he and my father did not approve of the National Patriotic Front alliance with the Ba'thists. They thought that leaders in the Iraqi Communist Party were naive to believe that the Ba'thists were interested in a genuine alliance and failed to see that the alliance was a ruse on the part of the Ba'thists to find out information about members of the party. They also thought the ICP could not challenge orders from the USSR, which was in favor of the alliance following the strengthening of relations between the Iraqi Ba'thist regime and the USSR. To protest the alliance, Khalil resigned from the party. After he submitted his resignation, he came to our house to tell my parents of his resignation. Approving of Khalil's stand, my mother, who was long critical of the ICP, told my father, "This is the difference between a courageous and non-courageous person." But my father refused to resign. Khalil told me he corrected my mother: "I told her, 'Muhammad's views of the party are like the views held by nuns towards God. The party is sacred to Muhammad.' We laughed at this." To Khalil, the alliance proved fatal to the ICP, since it gave the Ba'thists access to the organization and membership of the party, an access that enabled them to liquidate the party by the end of the 1970s through the arrest and elimination of a considerable number of its members. When the onslaught of communists began in 1978, Khalil decided to flee Iraq and settle in the United Kingdom.

When he arrived in London in the late 1980s after living for a decade in Wales, Khalil found himself amid an exilic Iraqi political scene that he could not relate to. Though he kept in touch with other Iraqi communists who had fled Iraq, he did not try to join the party, which operated mainly in London after its liquidation in Iraq. He thought the party lacked a clear agenda and did not make efforts to reckon with its past. He also grew uncomfortable with the sectarian discourse dominant among the exilic opposition in London, which envisioned a sectarian quota system for government positions in post-Saddam Iraq. To create an alternative political space, Khalil got involved in politics again in the early 1990s. Along with a group of liberal Iraqis in London, he formed the Coalition of Democracy in Iraq in an attempt to build an Iraqi political niche that revolved around the idea of a secular and democratic Iraq.

As I listened to Khalil, I realized that I had come across an ex-communist whose reflection on the political struggles in the 1950s and early 1960s interrogated the nostalgic discourse held by the majority of communists in London about the idealized past. Unsatisfied with the exilic political scene in London, he attempted to find a political space that provided an alternative to the communist project of the past as well as the sectarian and ethnic project of the present. Khalil's experience with the exilic political sphere also sheds light on how the London-based Iraqi politicians reshaped the political discourse and landscape in Iraq after 2003. I asked Khalil if I could interview him, and he readily agreed. Thus, the visit to Khalil and Mary, which was meant to connect me with people from my past, turned out to be an opportunity to find alternative narratives about Iraq's past and present.

During our extensive conversations and interviews, Khalil always offered a trajectory of how his political thought, as well as his notion of selfhood, evolved over the decades. As a young man, Khalil was a revolutionary subject who got involved in the anticolonial struggle against the British and believed that the communist political project promised gender and social equality and political independence. However, his political involvement with the Iraqi Communist Party throughout the decades made him more reflective about its leaders' actions and policies. Eventually he left the party and chose a political ideology that emphasized democracy as a solution to the problems in Iraq. While Hanan was a nostalgic subject who had been carried out on the revolutionary tide and still clung to an idealized account of the past, Khalil was a reflective subject who dwelled upon his political experience in the past.[1] To him, political realities were mired in contradictions and erasures, and political activism necessitated a reckoning with the inconsistencies between ideals and practices in order to forge a path toward stability and prosperity. In this framework, political activism is no longer limited to anticolonial struggle in the past; rather, it is an ongoing, reflective career that evolves over time. It was during moments of his ongoing political activism—such as his participation in clandestine meetings and demonstrations in the past, or forming an organization dedicated to democracy in diaspora and in Iraq after 2003—that Khalil produced himself as an Iraqi subject dedicated to the welfare of all

Iraqis, the acceptance of difference, and the building of alternative futures. As such, this Iraqi self was still progressive and nationalist in its outlook in that while it championed social justice, it also aimed to build an inclusive sense of belonging amid divisions and fragmentation. However, to be an Iraqi subject was to be able to reckon with the past in order to avoid idealizing it and to learn from mistakes in order to bring about an alternative future built upon dialogue and compromise.

Khalil's narratives about selfhood and political thought were gendered and classed. Just as Hanan imagined herself to represent a modern Iraqi woman who espoused gender equality, Khalil saw himself as the antithesis of traditional men who believed that women should dedicate their lives to their husbands and children. The new Iraqi man joined the Iraqi modern woman in her struggle for equality and marched beside her in demonstrations and protests against the British and the monarchy. After he got politically engaged in the early 1990s in London, Khalil was concerned with the dwindling role women played in the exilic opposition. Still, the question of women's rights did not preoccupy him extensively. After 2003, the pressing question to Khalil became the integrity of Iraq; all other issues, including gender equality, become secondary to preserving Iraq as a unified nation-state. In addition, Khalil expressed middle-classed and urban sensibilities vis-à-vis other Iraqis. He saw the rural areas at present in Iraq as hindering the emergence of a civil state, since peasants were more attached to their land and families than to government institutions. To Khalil, the accumulation of wealth in cities facilitated the flourishing of diverse intellectual and cultural activities, which in turn had led to the rise of the civil state in places like the United Kingdom. In this scenario, the peasants emerge as people devoid of national feelings toward Iraq, while urban dwellers—particularly those in the middle class, given their access to intellectual and cultural activities—become nation builders dedicated to the fostering of a democratic and civil state.

Khalil's life story intersected with Hanan's narrative to a certain extent. They both constructed a sense of selfhood based on anticolonial struggle and progressive ideals in the past and their middle-class and urban sensibilities. While the British presence in Iraq had thrust them into a revolutionary tide that was sweeping the Third World in the 1950s, the United States' intervention in Iraq exposed them to two phases of exile. The first phase was after the

Ba'th coup in 1963, and the second came after the rise of Saddam Hussein to power in 1979, with the United States supporting him throughout the 1980s and keeping him in power after the Gulf War of 1991. Khalil and Hanan were both haunted by the turn of events in Iraq since the late 1970s. However, their political trajectories and views diverged considerably as well. For Hanan, the failure of the postcolonial project and the fact that her political activism ended due to her husband's action led her to idealize the past as a means to provide an alternative narrative to the bleak present. Khalil, however, attentive to the contradictions in the communist political project and invested in political critique as a form of reckoning with the past, continued to strive for a unified Iraqi space through his work with the Iraqi opposition in exile. He always managed to keep a distance between himself and events; as such, he was always the dispassionate politician who constantly analyzed political events. The political was always personal to Hanan, whose voice oscillated between revolutionary hopes and disenchantment. Khalil, by contrast, always spoke in the same even tone about political events. While Hanan was the passionate radical, Khalil was the realist who defied the idealized narrative of the past and the sectarian discourse of the present.

## Counter-Narratives of the Past

The 1950s and early 1960s have been mythologized among the majority of Iraqi communists as a time of social and political vibrancy—a time when the future still held promise. These nostalgic reminiscences, in turn, shape contemporary memory among non-monarchist Iraqis in London, who perceive that period as the antithesis of the sectarian and fragmented present. However, this romanticization of the past and the discourse of progress are fraught with silences, erasures, and contradictions. In Khalil's narrative, by contrast, the revolutionary past was mired in the murky reality of political divisions, power struggles, and a lack of clarity. Khalil's reflections critiqued the Iraqi Communist Party and its role in events that "gambled with the fate of the country" and sometimes pushed it to the verge of civil war, as he told me. Yet, to him, that time was still defined by a sense of camaraderie, now missing in the political present, and by secular political ideologies that sidelined sectarian affiliations. Despite his critique of the past, Khalil cherished the memories of his classmates and comrades relating to him as a communist, rather than as a Christian, since religion did not shape his sense of selfhood.

Khalil was a few years younger than Hanan and too young to remember Al-Wathba. However, his life experience and introduction to politics intersected with Hanan's narrative of her politicization at an early age in Baghdad to some extent. Unlike Hanan, whose parents were not involved in politics, Khalil's political awareness started at home in Mosul. His maternal uncles were leftists, though they never joined the Iraqi Communist Party. One of his uncles was arrested on charges of circulating communist pamphlets, and Khalil's mother explained to him that his uncle was arrested because he advocated an ideology that aimed to end poverty and inequality in Iraq. Indeed, his mother played an important role in shaping his political views. Though she had only finished primary school, and now had many children to take care of, she was an avid reader who regularly sent him to the public library to borrow books that promoted progressive ideologies, social justice, women's rights, and patriotism. Like Hanan, it was his family's move to Baghdad from Mosul in 1950 that shaped Khalil's political outlook. Khalil's father was a successful merchant, and Khalil grew up in a middle-class neighborhood in Mosul. There, he rarely came in touch with people from the lower or rural classes. And unlike Baghdad, Mosul was a conservative city, where the division between classes and between urban and rural dwellers was deeply entrenched. The family's move to Baghdad exposed Khalil to fervent political activism and made him aware of the stark social inequalities in Iraq. At the age of eleven, when Khalil saw the *sarifas* built adjacent to middle-class neighborhoods in Baghdad, he understood what his uncles meant when they talked about inequalities and injustices in Iraqi society.

Despite his family's influence and his exposure to scenes of abject poverty, like Hanan, it was only at school that Khalil became politically active. Khalil was only thirteen years old when the 1952 intifada broke out in Baghdad. Though he was too young to participate in the demonstrations, he became aware of the different political trends in the country—in particular, communism and the Arab nationalism advocated by the Ba'th Party, which had some presence in the early days of the protests under the name the League of Nationalist Youth. Following the intifada, Khalil began to read the literature circulated by the ICP and the Ba'th Party avidly. He thought that the

Baʻth Party's notion of socialism and emphasis on Islam and Arab unity were vague. He leaned more toward the Iraqi Communist Party, with its fight for the downtrodden and for social justice. The ICP's emphasis on women's rights and efforts to help both urban and rural women resonated with Khalil, who saw himself as an advocate of women's rights and as the antithesis of traditional men. To him, progressive men believed women should have access to equal education and the same legal rights as men. Just as Hanan saw herself as representing the modern, progressive woman, Khalil perceived himself a progressive man who advocated for gender equality.

In high school, Khalil formally joined the ICP. However, his relationship with the party came to an end quickly when his organizer—his liaison with the party—was arrested and severed his relationship with the party. After enrolling in college in 1956, Khalil took part in the uprising that broke out in Baghdad and other cities during the Suez Crisis in Egypt. Egyptian president Gamal Abd Nasser nationalized the Suez Canal, and in response, Britain, France, and Israel waged war on Egypt. Professors and students in Baghdad, incensed by the show of imperial force and admiring Nasser for nationalizing the Suez Canal, demonstrated in support of Egypt. The Iraqi government used security forces to quickly put down the demonstrations. Khalil's role in the uprising of 1956 drew the attention of the communists, who contacted him and asked him to join the party. Khalil then ran for the Student Union as a communist, and he was elected both by communists and Baʻthists, since he was on good terms with both groups. He was tasked with supervising eight committees and the organization of comrades in the Faculty of Medicine, Dentistry, and Pharmacology. Like Hanan, he aspired to see radical change in Iraq through political activism, which would represent a rupture with existing social and political inequalities and colonialism. He and his comrades held literacy classes in factories, open to both men and women, and visited poor people in the *sarifas* to provide medical care. However, unlike Hanan, he perceived the murky reality of politics at the time. Though Khalil enjoyed the political momentum, particularly the sense of camaraderie, he was wary of the leadership of the Iraqi Communist Party. He thought the base of the ICP was inspiring in its commitment to the downtrodden, but its leaders were divided over who should lead the party, and they disregarded the main focus of the party, which was supposed to be the welfare of the people.

Khalil's misgivings about the Iraqi Communist Party came to the forefront during the 1958 Revolution. Unlike Hanan, Khalil did not experience the revolution as a time of hope and possibility for alternative futures. On the contrary, he felt disenchanted and fearful of the future:

> On the eve of the revolution, we received orders from the Iraqi Communist Party to be on alert. When the revolution took place on July 14, I took to the streets. The atmosphere was strange. I felt there was an absence of a unifying political slogan. I couldn't find a slogan I could shout and rally people around it. There was only the slogan that Arabs and Kurds are brethren. There was no slogan for a unified national front. There was lack of clarity. People shouted: "Down with the Monarchy and Long Live the Republic." The Iraqi Communist Party did not have any slogans. However, the demonstrations were unbelievable. Tremendous. I didn't go to the palace. I crossed the bridge and saw the corpse of the regent dangling. I got disgusted and went back home.

To Khalil, the revolution did not materialize the utopian future defined by the end of a feudal regime and the ousting of the British. He thought the 1958 Revolution lacked political vision. The following months and years brought about radical social and economic reforms, but this did not appease Khalil's fears, particularly of the Iraqi Communist Party's policies. The Iraqi street became polarized between the communists and Arab nationalists as represented by the Ba'th Party and the Nasserists (supporters of the Egyptian president, Abd Nasser). Street demonstrations came to define life in Baghdad, with various groups vying to command the streets and advocate for their case with Qasim.[2] The pro-Qasim demonstrations and counterdemonstrations intensified the sense of crisis for Khalil. He thought that the ICP enjoyed enormous momentum at the level of the street following the fall of the monarchy—though it was not authorized to operate openly—but it lacked a clear vision toward Qasim or the future. While the leaders of the party fought over who would lead the party, the base was left to the impulsive reactions of its members.

While Hanan was silent on the major political events that took place between 1958 and 1963, given her romantic view of the past, Khalil's reminiscences about political events at the time delineated a sense of constant crisis in the country partly brought about by the Iraqi Communist Party's policies.

Khalil considered the Mosul massacre of 1959 another instance of the party's failure to estimate the seriousness of the situation and act accordingly. The economic reforms brought about by the Qasim regime and the weakening position of Arab nationalists in the army and government left landowners and military leaders organizing for political change. Landowners and Arab nationalist officers in Mosul, led by Abd Awahhab al-Shawaf, coordinating with some army officers in Baghdad, began to plot a coup against Qasim in early 1959. When Qasim learned about the coup, he allowed the communists to go to Mosul to put it down.[3]

Khalil was against holding a rally in Mosul. He knew that "Mosul was a conservative society and that the rally would intensify the crisis." When his organizer at the ICP ordered him to go to Mosul to take part in the rally, he refused. His fears were realized when the rally led to bloody clashes between the communists and the Arab nationalists and threatened the civil peace in Mosul. The conflict also aggravated ethnic and religious tensions in the country.[4] Ethnic, religious, and class divisions coincided with political alignments, with Kurds fighting Arabs, Assyrian and Aramean Christians fighting Arab Muslims, Arab clans fighting other Arab clans, peasants fighting landowners, soldiers fighting their officers in the Fifth Brigade, and the poor fighting the rich.[5] During the violence in Mosul, which lasted four days, the communists held a "people's court" and had summary trials of the coup plotters, followed by summary executions.[6] They hung the dead bodies from lampposts or dragged them in the streets. After five days, Qasim finally sent two battalions to restore order in the city. According to Khalil:

> The massacre of Mosul showed the ICP's lack of appreciation of the seriousness of the situation. It drove Mosul to the verge of a civil war and reflected the lack of education among communists. I was always critical of the party's emphasis on political mobilization at the expense of educating its members with communist literature and of delineating a clear agenda for future political struggle. The summary trials and executions in Mosul showed that members of the party had a shallow understanding of the concept of people's courts. They read something and implemented it in a naive way without any thinking about the ramifications of their action. Their [communists'] action aggravated political divisions within the country.

While Hanan was silent on the tensions between Qasim and the communists, Khalil reflected on the ICP's lack of a clear position toward Qasim. In the summer of 1959, after putting down the coup against him, the Baghdad bureau of the Iraqi Communist Party decided to remove Qasim from power. The party ordered Khalil and his comrades to take to the streets with the slogan "Let the Communist Party take power" and to bring weapons if they had them. Members of the party took to the streets while its leaders met to decide the fate of Qasim. In the end, they decided not to topple Qasim and sent a message to its members to withdraw from the streets. Khalil believed that if the leaders of the party were against Qasim, they should have joined the national democrats, who demanded fair elections and the formation of a government run by a civilian, not a general. However, their lack of a clear position, which was complicated by conflicting orders from the USSR, contributed to the instability in the country.

The 1963 CIA-backed coup brought about the first phase of exile for Khalil, who was arrested and jailed for a month as soon as the coup broke out. When he was released after his case was referred to a court, he went into hiding. He was sentenced to eight years in prison in absentia on charges of instigating sedition. Meanwhile, his family found someone who worked at the office in charge of issuing passports. They managed to acquire a forged passport for him, and he left for Beirut and from there went to Prague to join other Iraqi communists who were exiled by the coup. In Prague, the Iraqi Communist Party put him in charge of the Iraqi student organizations abroad. In 1968, he went to Britain to become the head of the ICP branch in the United Kingdom. At the same time, Khalil decided to specialize in cardiovascular surgery and to become a fellow in the British Cardiovascular Society. He thought that having a career would enable him to be critical of the ICP, since he would not be dependent on the party for his livelihood. Shortly after arriving in Britain, the ICP ordered him to return to Iraq and to dedicate his time fully to the party. Following advice from a leftist friend from Baghdad, Khalil refused to give up his studies and return to Iraq. In retaliation, the party demoted him to a member of a cell and stripped him of his responsibility as a head of the ICP branch in Britain. From that moment, Khalil dedicated himself to school and his career, and he had little contact with the ICP.

In 1973, Khalil gave up his position as a cardiologist in a hospital in Manchester, to the disappointment of his superior, and went back to Iraq. He decided to return because he felt more "in [his] element in the Iraqi society" and because he thought that he "had a role to play in Iraq" as a politician. Another reason for Khalil's return was the National Patriotic Front that the Iraqi Communist Party signed with the Ba'th regime in 1972 under the auspices of the USSR. In 1973, the general-secretary of the ICP and Iraqi president Ahmed Hasan al-Bakr signed the National Action Charter to delineate common socialist goals. The Ba'th regime legally recognized the ICP and allowed it to publish and organize openly. But the revival of the activities of the ICP in trade unions, students' and women's organizations, and peasant associations did not go unchallenged by Ba'thist members. Moreover, because of the open structure of the ICP, the Ba'th regime gained access to the party's membership rolls and organization.[7] Khalil opposed the National Front and thought that the Ba'thists were not serious about any meaningful alliance with the communists. He thought that by returning to Iraq, he could change the position of the communist party. He believed that the ICP had two options: reject the National Front and maintain the reputation of the party by going underground, or join the alliance with the understanding that the party would have to follow the orders of the Ba'th Party, which was the de facto leader of the National Front. Khalil tried to change the direction of the party by participating in its internal election and challenging its leadership. However, he lost, and he found himself powerless vis-à-vis his comrades, whose practices conflicted with communist ideals:

> I hated the Iraqi communists' hypocrisy and flattery of the Ba'thists. I was disgusted by their behavior. The Ba'thists executed the sons of al-Nahar family, and at night members of the ICP toasted the Ba'thists at a party in the Bulgarian embassy in Baghdad. When I raised this issue with the ICP and asked why they did not protest, they told me that "the sons of al-Nahar aren't communists. They quit the Party. We submitted a protest." What protest! You were toasting the Ba'th and its leadership that was ruling the country. Where is the revolutionary feeling? Where is the revolutionary solidarity? I didn't shut up. I resigned. The communists circulate a rumor that I resigned because I didn't want to sacrifice my clinic for the sake of the party.

Though Khalil resigned from the party, he remained on good terms with some communists, especially those who shared his critique of the party's policies. By the late 1970s, leaders of the ICP began to realize that the National Front was a ruse and that the Baʻthists were only using them to identify the party's membership. The onslaught against communists that began in 1978 was facilitated partly by the detailed information the Baʻth Party had been able to gather on the ICP. In 1979, Khalil was detained for a few hours by the security forces because of his past affiliation with the communists, and many of his communist friends disappeared or were killed. After he was released, he decided that he could not live in Iraq anymore, and he left for Britain.

## Exilic Politics

Khalil arrived in London in the late 1980s as the British capital was emerging as a center for the Iraqi diaspora and for the Iraqi opposition in exile. Interestingly, Khalil's tone changed when he reflected on the history and activities of the opposition. He no longer narrated political events through a personal experience, but rather provided a dispassionate, historical narrative about the political circumstances that led to the rise of different political visions since the late 1970s until the present. Given that there was no extensive literature about the opposition in exile—particularly Shiʻi and Kurdish parties—he hoped to give me some context of how political shifts in Iraq in the late 1970s gained momentum in exile. Unlike Hanan, who was keen on providing passionate, grand narratives about anticolonial struggle and revolutionary reforms, Khalil was more interested in the details that would reveal how different political projects—focused on ethnic and religious mobilization—began to displace secular parties, particularly the Iraqi Communist Party.

### *A Fledging Exilic Scene in the 1980s*

The rise of Saddam Hussein to power in 1979 signaled the end of political vibrancy in Iraq and shifted political activism to Iraqi diasporic centers abroad, especially London, Damascus, and Tehran. While Tehran and Damascus, whose governments were against the Iraqi regime, encouraged and harbored Iraqi exilic groups in the early 1980s, London did not emerge as a major center for the opposition until the 1990s, when the British government expelled Hussein's agents in London following the invasion of Kuwait. During the

1980s, Khalil focused on building his medical practice as a surgeon and did not get involved in politics directly. However, he kept in touch with some Iraqi communists and Arab nationalists and began to cultivate relations with two Iraqi groups, namely the Shi'i Islamists and Kurds.

Following the liquidation of the Iraqi Communist Party and moderate voices within the Ba'th Party, Hussein's regime failed to end the threat of two groups: the Shi'is and the Kurds. While Shi'i religious scholars established religious groups and parties in the late 1950s to combat the challenge to their power and interests posed by the spread of communism and the reforms that were implemented after the fall of the monarchy, Shi'i parties did not emerge as a major player in the Iraqi political scene until the 1970s. The Islamic Revolution in Iran in 1979 inspired Shi'i groups in Iraq. Rather than limiting their political activism to clandestine educational activism, Shi'i groups adopted urban guerrilla warfare in order to challenge Hussein's regime.[8] The most influential Iraqi Shi'i party at the time was the Islamic Da'wa (Call) Party, which called for the establishment of an Islamic government. The Hussein regime retaliated against the activism of the party by executing its leader, Grand Ayatollah Muhammad Baqir al-Sadr, and rounding up and executing thousands of Da'wa members and sympathizers.[9] The brutality with which the regime dealt with members of the party and politically active Shi'is led to an exodus to Iran. The arrival in Iran of Iraqi Shi'is, who advocated a different political agenda, led to an effort to unify these different groups under one organization. In 1982, the Supreme Council for the Islamic Revolution in Iraq (SCIRI) was established in Iran. Though the council was meant to act as an umbrella group, it quickly became associated with Muhammad Baqir al-Hakim.[10] The Iranian government supported the SCIRI and advocated the doctrine of *velayat-e-faqih* (rule of the jurisconsult or chief cleric, which was the official Iranian Islamic republican doctrine) as a formula for Iraq as well. This stance alienated many Shi'i Iraqi groups, in particular the Da'wa Party.[11] In the 1980s, the Da'wa Party and SCIRI, in addition to centers affiliated with religious scholars from well-known ulama families—such as the Kho'i Foundation and the Ahl al-Bait Center—began to have a presence in London, and they played an important role among the opposition groups in London.

In addition to Shi'i groups, the Kurds also challenged Hussein's regime. Under the monarchy and Qasim's reign, the Kurds' relationship with Baghdad was fraught. There were several military actions following failed negotiations, since Iraqi governments never took serious steps to recognize Kurdish demands for autonomy and self-determination. Under the second Ba'th regime, the relationship between Baghdad and the Kurds deteriorated drastically. In May 1971, Saddam Hussein took charge of the Ba'th-Kurdish committee, and it became clear that Kurds would not be granted the rights promised in the Manifesto of March 1970. Fighting broke out between the Iraqi regime and Kurdish forces, who were supported by Iran and the United States. The involvement of Iran in the conflict between the Kurds and the Iraqi regime threatened to escalate into a war between Iran and Iraq, which neither country wanted. Secret negotiations began between the two countries, which ended with an agreement whereby Iraq conceded some of Shatt al-Arab to Iran, and Iran and the United States agreed to stop its support of the Kurds. The Algiers Agreement between Iraq and Iran led to the collapse of the Kurdish revolt. Kurdish fighters—known as Peshmerga—accepted amnesty, while Mulla Mustafa Barzani, who was the leader of the Kurdish Democratic Party (KDP), fled to Iran along with 150,000 civilian refugees.[12] The divisions within the KDP led to the split of the party between the Barzanis and Jalal Talabani, who formed the Patriot Union of Kurdistan (PUK). Members of the PUK, who were critical of Barzani's tribal leadership, advocated nationalist and socialist principles.[13] Following the collapse of the Kurdish revolt and the disintegration of the KDP, the Iraqi regime began a campaign of resettling Kurdish communities at the Turkish and Iranian borders near major towns and relocating others to southern Iraq, near the Arab Shi'i population. Around half a million Kurds were displaced from their villages.[14] Moreover, the regime encouraged Arab families to settle in the north to change the demographics of the area. This collective punishment meted out to the Kurds led to the flight of thousands. Some of them arrived in London, where they established a presence for the Patriot Union of Kurdistan and the Kurdish Democratic Party.

Following the liquidation of the Iraqi Communist Party in Iraq, a large number of communists fled to London. There, they established a strong presence through the establishment of the Iraqi Forum. Moreover, some Arab nationalists and Ba'thists who opposed Hussein's regime fled to Britain. In London, Khalil began to keep in touch with Kurdish and Shi'i groups, as well as secular figures, who formed the nucleus of the fledgling opposition to Hussein's regime. However, he was not involved in political activism. In 1989, Khalil decided to get involved in politics again. Along with other liberal Iraqis in London, he formed the Coalition of Democracy in Iraq:

> One of the factors that pushed us to establish the Coalition of Democracy in Iraq was an article published in the magazine *Al-Youm al-Sabi'*, which used to come out in Paris. The magazine published the minutes of the meeting held by the Ba'th leadership of Iraq about democracy. Taha Yasin Ramadan [a close associate of Saddam Hussein] said that "we have democracy in Iraq unrivaled in the world. We have three million Ba'thists. Each one has a wife, father, mother, and children. This means three times three; this means we have nine million proponents of the regime. This is the best democracy in the world." No one replied to this claim. We said this talk is unacceptable. We have to form a committee that nourishes democratic meetings and democratic ideas. We formed the coalition, and we held our first conference after the invasion of Kuwait. We began to hold an annual conference since then. Groups from different political backgrounds in the opposition—both Islamist and non-Islamists, such as the Da'wa Party, the Supreme Council for the Islamic Revolution in Iraq, the Iraqi Communist Party, the Kurds, Sayyid Bahr al-Ulloum from Ahl al-Bait Center—made speeches at our conferences.

Khalil and his friends envisioned the Coalition of Democracy in Iraq as a rallying group that would include Iraqis from across the political spectrum who were invested in building a democratic Iraq. The question of carving an inclusive space in exile that brought together diverse groups—such as Islamists, secularists, Kurds, communists, and Arab nationalists—was an urgent issue for the members of the coalition in the early 1990s. The members were concerned by the fragmented nature of Iraqi community in London and the sectarian discourse endorsed by the opposition groups in exile. The main issue that preoccupied members of the coalition was how to create a democratic space in Iraq that would recognize the aspirations of religious and Kurdish groups, who were historically alienated from the state, while at the same time preserving the rights of people who did not subscribe to these communal discourses and ensure the integrity of Iraq as a nation-state. As a young man,

Khalil thought that "the lack of dialogue and compromise" between communists and Arab nationalists in the 1950s and 1960s was "unnecessary and detrimental to national cohesion." Decades later, he still thought that the establishment of an inclusive national sphere in exile, based on dialogue and compromise, would circumvent the ideological rigidity of the past. Unlike Hanan, Khalil realized that the Iraqi political scene was changing and was defined by a new political project, particularly among the Shi'is and Kurds, that was based on a religious and ethnic discourse. While Hanan distanced herself from religious Iraqis, Khalil cultivated relations with religious political figures. He thought that the establishment of a genuinely democratic and plural Iraq would succeed in representing the aspirations of different groups.

### *A Flourishing Exilic Opposition in the 1990s*

This nascent Iraqi opposition scene in London—which comprised different religious, ethnic, and secular groups—was transformed in the early 1990s. The fall of the Soviet Union led to the exodus of Iraqi communists from the Communist Bloc, and their arrival in Britain as refugees, especially after they realized that a return to Iraq was no longer possible after the Gulf War of 1991. The invasion of Kuwait led to a rupture in relations between Saddam Hussein's regime and Western countries. In an attempt to isolate the Iraqi regime, Western governments cut relations with Baghdad and imposed sanctions. At the same time, the British government expelled Hussein's agents from Britain and opened channels of communications with the Iraqi opposition. The ousting of Hussein's agents and the improving relations with the British government provided opposition groups with the freedom to operate openly. London emerged as an important center for the opposition against Hussein's regime in exile.

Moreover, the Gulf War of 1991 and the failure of the uprisings in the north and the south had far-reaching implications for the Iraqi community in London. While the Kurds and the Shia posed a serious challenge to Hussein's reign in the late 1970s and throughout the 1980s, they also emerged as a serious power that threatened to topple the regime following the defeat of the Iraqi army in the Gulf War. President George H. W. Bush's call upon the Iraqi people to overthrow the regime inspired people in Basra, Amara, Nasiriyya, Najaf, and Karbala to rise up, and they took control of large areas by the end of February. Meanwhile, the Kurds' Peshmerga forces captured most of Kurdistan by the end of March. However, the United States and its allies, fearing Iraq would splinter and that a new Shi'i state would form, refused to support the rebels.[15] Shortly after that, Hussein's regime managed to brutally put down the uprisings in the south and the north, which led to the displacement of thousands of Iraqis.

A mass exodus of Iraqis followed the failed uprisings and joined the exilic Iraqi communities in London, especially when the British government granted asylum to thousands of Iraqis—mainly Kurds and Shi'is—on a humanitarian basis. Along with members of the community who arrived in the late 1970s and early 1980s, the new arrivals bolstered the Iraqi opposition in exile and worked toward regime change in Iraq. Two major umbrella groups emerged at the time: the Iraq National Congress (INC), led by Ahmed Chalabi,[16] and the Iraqi National Accord (INA), led by Iyad Allawi.[17] The former comprised different political groups, such as the KDP and PUK, the Da'wa Party, and SCIRI, while the latter consisted of a group of reformed Ba'thists and Arab nationalists who opposed Hussein's regime. The two groups had serious differences—due, in part, to the rivalry between Chalabi and Allawi and the latter's distaste for Islamist-leaning groups who had close contacts with Iran. Along with the communists and members of the Coalition of Democracy in Iraq, these exilic groups advocated different political ideologies and projects, including militant Islamism, moderate liberal Islam, Arab and Kurdish nationalism, liberalism, and Marxism. Despite major differences in imagining the future of Iraq, they were unified in their desire to see a regime change. This exilic political sphere was masculine to a great extent in that men constituted the majority of membership in parties, groups, and conferences. Unlike the past, when men and women marched together in demonstrations and advocated for gender equality, women barely had a voice in this political sphere. The issue of gender equality was sidelined by the focus on regime change and grappling over power.

In addition, unlike mainstream political parties in the 1950s, which were against Western intervention in Iraqi affairs, most of these exilic groups opened channels of communication, particularly with U.S. and British intelligence agencies and the U.S. State Department, and lobbied the U.S. government to bring about a regime change in Iraq. For instance, while Chalabi cultivated close relations with the United States and used his access to media outlets to agitate for regime change in Iraq, Allawi was in touch with the British MI6. Kurdish and Shi'i figures also established contact with different U.S. administrations. Moreover, these opposition groups began to organize conferences, with the support of the United States, to work toward regime change in Iraq and to envision a post-Hussein Iraq. According to Khalil:

> The first conference for the opposition was held in Vienna in early 1992. It was decided that another conference would be held in Iraq later in the year, in Salahuddin, which was under Kurdish control. The opposition didn't have a clear agenda beyond general ideas about regime change. The general trend was Sunni, Shi'i, and Kurd. The Salahuddin Conference was held on a sectarian basis. Iran played an important role in the development of this trend since 1991. The conference was delayed for two days so that participants coming from Iran in buses would increase the number of Shi'is and exceed the numbers of Sunnis and Kurds. The discourse at the conference was sectarian and it continued to be so since then.

The Salahuddin Conference—which was boycotted by Iyad Allawi's Iraqi National Accord—saw the emergence of the Iraq National Congress (INC) as an umbrella for different opposition groups, including Islamist and Kurdish groups. As such, it marked a shift in the Iraqi political scene in that a sectarian discourse, rather than secular ideologies, carried the day. The executive bodies of INC were distributed according to sectarian, religious, and ethnic affiliations. The leadership council, for instance, had a Sunni, Shi'i, and Kurd.[18] Mainstream opposition groups—namely the Kurds and the Shi'is—reckoned that since its being established, the Iraqi state had been dominated by Sunni Arabs who had marginalized their aspirations and interests, and now it was time for them to assume power in the country. What concerned Khalil was the fact that the Iraqi political sphere would be dominated by groups who were furthering the interests of people who belonged to their sect or ethnicity rather than the interests of the Iraqi people as a whole. He aspired to carve out a political space that was defined by inclusivity and consensus around political issues, just as the Iraqi Communist

Party had brought people from different background together over issues of social justice and political independence in the past. The internal divisions within the opposition—such as the power struggle between Chalabi and Allawi and the division among Shi'i and Kurdish groups—increased Khalil's anxiety that the welfare of the Iraqi people and that the construction of an Iraq representative of different perspectives and backgrounds would be the first casualty of the fragmented nature of the opposition. Khalil grew weary of the opposition in the 1990s, and he sent a memorandum to the U.S. State Department warning it against relying on Iraqi exiles in their efforts to seek regime change in Iraq.

Haunted by the division within the opposition and its sectarian discourse, Khalil aimed to create dialogue and compromise among the different groups through his writing and work with the Coalition of Democracy in Iraq. He thought that the opposition "needed a clear agenda shared by all parties regardless of their programs and political organization." That agenda—which he wanted to be concise and devoid of particulars that would result in divisions—needed to focus on the ability of the Iraqi people to gain its freedom and to have an opinion on the nature and form of the constitution and government they wanted. One of the important concerns for Khalil was his conviction that it was the Iraqi people inside Iraq, rather than Iraqis abroad, who did not experience daily violence and hardship, who should decide their own future. The discourse of colonialism, Zionism, and obscurantism adopted by some opposition groups, as well as the decision of others to boycott this or that group because its members were not religious enough or collaborated with Western governments were matters of luxury, in Khalil's opinion, that did not serve the immediate needs of the Iraqi people. Khalil thought the contemporary political moment in the 1990s signaled a shift from the radical politics of the past, which perceived national liberation as the main catalyst for activism. He believed that Iraqis should coordinate with and seek help from Arab, regional, and international powers in their efforts to remove Hussein from power. He envisioned the establishment of a genuine national front that comprised the diverse Iraqi groups as the solution to the establishment of an inclusive and democratic Iraq. A national front would entail compromise and the precedence of national interests over the interests of individual parties, but parties would not have to disappear;

they would only have to cooperate and coordinate to achieve solidarity and the common good.

*The Neoconservative Turn in the Late 1990s and the Invasion*
In the late 1990s, the Iraq National Congress, represented by Ahmed Chalabi, secured a victory in its efforts to get the Clinton administration committed to a policy of regime change in Iraq. After failing to have access to high-ranking officials in the U.S. State Department, Chalabi began to establish contacts with the neoconservatives, who were agitating to see Hussein removed from power. Of all the Iraqi opposition groups, the INC and Chalabi were seen as sympathetic to the neoconservatives' plans for Iraq.[19] Chalabi worked with U.S. congressional staffers to write the Iraq Liberation Act (ILA).[20] Signed by Bill Clinton in 1998, the act stated that "It should be the policy of the United States to support efforts to remove the regime headed by Saddam Hussein from power in Iraq and to promote the emergence of a democratic government to replace that regime."[21] The ILA also provided funding for the opposition.[22] It recognized seven opposition groups: the INC, the INA, the KDP, the PUK, SCIRI, the Islamic Movement of Kurdistan, and the Constitutional Monarchy Movement. Yet, despite the announcement of the ILA, the Clinton administration remained equivocal about bringing about regime change in Baghdad.

The election of George W. Bush in 2001, the rise of neoconservatives in the new administration, and the failure of the United Nations to uphold the sanctions imposed on Iraq and to resume weapons inspection combined to reorganize U.S. policy. The new administration perceived Iraq as a threat and worked toward a plan of regime change—by unilateral means, if necessary.[23] The September 11 attack and the "War on Terror" that ensued sealed the fate of Saddam Hussein. Members of the Bush administration saw the War on Terror as having long-term implications, beyond the immediate overthrow of al-Qaeda, in that it could be employed to reshape the international order according to U.S. interests.[24] The United States turned its attention to regimes that were seen as hostile to its interests and were suspected of developing chemical, biological, or nuclear weapons.[25] The case against Iraq was built on the claim that it was developing weapons of mass destruction. The INC became instrumental in promoting this vision by planting defectors who claimed that Iraq had weapons of mass destruction.²⁶ The truth of these allegations could not be verified since Iraq did not allow UN weapons inspectors inside the country. On March 17, George Bush gave a forty-eight-hour ultimatum to Saddam Hussein to leave Iraq. Two days later, Operation Iraqi Freedom began, and the invasion of Iraq proceeded.

Khalil had an ambivalent view of the U.S. occupation of Iraq. He firmly believed that regime change in the country would not happen without international intervention, and he saw the United States as a powerful player in Iraqi affairs that could topple Saddam Hussein's regime. Thus, like the majority of Iraqis I met in London, Khalil supported the invasion. However, he had misgivings about the intentions of the U.S. administration. He was particularly concerned with the Bush administration's close relations with the Iraqi opposition, which endorsed the sectarian discourse, and with its reluctance to engage with Iraqi groups who opposed this discourse. When the U.S. troops entered Baghdad and toppled Saddam Hussein's statue, Khalil did not feel any joy, unlike Hanan. Regime change left him with questions about the role of the United States in Iraq, in particular the U.S. plans to withdraw troops, and what a post-Hussein Iraq would look like. When the Bush administration expressed no intentions to leave Iraq, Khalil came to see the United States as an occupying force bent on furthering its own interests at the expense of Iraqis' welfare. Moreover, he was disenchanted when the Coalition Provisional Authority (CPA), founded by the United States to govern Iraq, established the Iraqi Governing Council (IGC). The CPA—with its stereotypical understanding of Iraq as a place inhabited by Sunnis, Shi'is, and Kurds—endorsed the opposition's sectarian vision of Iraq and allocated positions within the IGC according to communal affiliations.²⁷

Khalil felt alienated from this political scene and believed that the opposition in London participated in furthering divisions in Iraq. One-third of the twenty-five members of the IGC were London-based exiles.²⁸ Other Iraqis in London assumed other positions in Iraq, including ministries and diplomatic missions. Khalil's alienation and disappointment intensified when he went back to Iraq:

> I went to Baghdad in 2005 to see if it is possible to hold a conference by the Coalition of Democracy in Iraq, in Baghdad. Dr. Nouman Mustafa, who

lived in London prior to 2003, told me, "Why didn't you come to Iraq earlier? We could have given you a seat in the parliament." I asked him, "On which ticket would you have given me this position?" He said, "We wanted Christians." I told him, "Never in my life have I got involved in politics on a Christian ticket. I work as an Iraqi." He laughed and said, "I know." When I was active in my youth, both Ba'thists and communists elected me as a deputy of the Students Union. No one said, "he is a Christian." And now, they told me I should participate as a Christian. I'm not upset that I didn't get a position. My purpose is to serve Iraq. All my life, I worked to serve Iraq. The difference between me and others is that I didn't lose the compass. I had my profession and I didn't have to change my political views because I needed a position. I always had my practice while I was politically active.

Given his alienation from the divisive political landscape in post-Hussein Iraq, Khalil dedicated more time to political work, especially after his retirement. He thought that an alternative political scene, which provided a critique of the sectarian realities brought about by the policies of U.S. officials and Iraqi politicians was more necessary than ever before.

## Toward a Secular, Democratic Future

Khalil and members of the Coalition of Democracy in Iraq aimed to cultivate a space of dialogue and democratic thought among different Iraqi parties, whether they were in London or in Iraq. They thought the current Iraqi political sphere lacked hegemonic ideologies, such as Arab nationalism or communism, as well as charismatic ideologues. In the past, ideologues managed to mobilize the Iraqi street and set the tone of political debate in the country for decades. While Sati Al-Husri, the director of education, wrote extensively on Arab nationalism, Yusuf Salman Yusuf (known as Fahd), the secretary of the Iraqi Communist Party, set a communist agenda and made the ICP a contending force on the Iraqi street, and Sayyid Muhammad Baqir al-Sadr rallied the youth to an Islamist revivalist agenda and critiqued Marxism as an economic theory. Khalil was critical of the political activism at the present and perceived the political scene as more fragmented, corrupt, devoid of political priorities, and lacking in political clarity than in the past. Through his writing and his instrumental role in the Coalition of Democracy in Iraq, he aimed to set an agenda that would provide solutions to the current predicament in Iraq and unify Iraqis over a shared vision of the future.

While his past activism was rooted in notions of struggle and defiance (*nidal* and *tahadi*), Khalil was now more attentive to the necessity of "political work" (*'amal siyyassi*) that aimed at building democratic institutions. The hiatus from political engagement between 1979 and 1989 gave him time to reflect on the postcolonial predicament in Iraq and his experience in the United Kingdom. He came to see that the main obstacle to the development of democracy in Iraq in the past was the lack of consensus among party leadership between, on the one hand, the struggle for total independence and overthrow of direct and indirect colonial rule and, on the other hand, the advocacy for the building of democratic state institutions and civil and political organizations. Informed by his experience in the United Kingdom, Khalil envisioned that the current political moment necessitated a different type of political engagement. Like most Iraqis in London, he reiterated that he never encountered any problems with the British government for his political activity. He believed that the fact that Britain had democratic institutions provided him the freedom to pursue a political career without repercussions, unlike in Iraq. However, to Khalil, this shift in his political view did not constitute a radical rupture in his political thought; he had always been dedicated to the idea of progress for Iraq and the welfare of its people.

Like Hanan, Khalil was concerned about the turn of events in Iraq after the fall of Hussein. The spiraling violence, the reorganization of the political scene according to sectarian quotas, the rampant corruption, the displacement of millions of Iraqis both inside and outside Iraq, and the failure of the state to provide basic services to the people—such as electricity, trash collection, and infrastructure rebuilding—confirmed his conviction that Iraq was in need of a secular democratic government. He wrote articles that aimed to introduce rudimentary ideas about these notions to the Iraqi public. He believed that Iraqi politicians had misconceptions about the notions of democracy and secularism because they equated democracy with the rule of the majority and secularism with atheism. He believed that the nature of the Iraqi state, which relied on tribes and was unable to weaken the power of the religious establishment, would not allow for the emergence of democracy. In his opinion, historically, Iraq did not have a powerful middle class that would play a strong role in politics. Unlike Europe, where the middle class managed to have a say in politics through the payment of taxes, Iraq was a rentier state, where the government relied on its monopoly of natural resources as a source of revenues and did not need to negotiate with the middle class about the rule of the country. While a weak middle class that was excluded from the sphere of decision-making curtailed the emergence of democracy in Iraq, the state also relied on tribes in its control of the country. Following the fall of Hussein, the religious establishment—represented by different Shi'i parties—rose to power because Hussein's regime had failed to weaken it. The establishment of the sectarian quota system after 2003 led to the weakening of the notion of citizenship and the strengthening of parochial and communal identities and interests.

Unlike Hanan, Khalil did not perceive the failure of the religious establishment to build a stable and democratic government as a symptom of its backwardness and ignorance. Rather than a classist understanding, he thought of the problem in political terms. He believed that the good people in the establishment who had Iraq's best interests at heart did not have a chance to lead. Rather, the Iraqi political scene was dominated by corrupt politicians who cared only about "pillage and plunder," regardless of their political and religious backgrounds. The solution to this predicament, in Khalil's view, was the establishment of a "civil state" (*dawla madaniyya*), which, like many Iraqi liberals, he envisioned in liberal terms. To him, the civil state was only a topic of debate in Arab and Muslim countries; it was no longer debated in the rest of the world because it had already been established there long ago. Given the lack of contemporary research on the civil state, Khalil thought it was important to introduce the concept to an Iraqi audience. He perceived the civil state as a democratic state, where individual freedom, gender equality, free markets, secularism, and civil liberties prevailed. One of its central components is the constitution, a form of voluntary contract between citizens who give up some of their natural rights and agree upon laws that apply to everyone. The constitution entails equality between all citizens, who all have the same rights and responsibilities and who elect the legislative and executive branches of the government. An important component of the civil state is democracy, which is not limited to the ballot, but consists of the respect for freedom and for the individual's rights to have a decent living; access to free education and health care; and the freedom to move, own property, practice religious beliefs, and express opinions without fear or constraint. Given its preservation of different forms of freedom and its functioning according to democratic rules, the civil state is the one state that can preserve civil peace in countries with diverse ethnic, religious, and national groups.

To Khalil, the United Kingdom—which consists of diverse ethnic, religious, and national groups—is an example of a civil, democratic state that protects civil peace. The different groups that constitute Britain enjoy the same rights and can practice religion without fear of persecution or violence and have their own places of worship. Since it is the people in the civil state who are the source of legislation, the religious establishment does not have the power to make political decisions or interfere in politics. In Khalil's opinion, what curtailed the emergence of the civil state in Iraq, in addition to the existence of the rentier state, was the nature of Iraqi society, which was dominated by the countryside. Rural relations are not conducive to the emergence of the civil state, since peasants' connection to the land is stronger than their connections to other people and deeper than their relations to the government; hence, peasants remains attached to their natural rights and to their family and tribe, and not to government institutions. By contrast, the accumulation of wealth in the city, which allows for diverse cultural and intellectual activities, creates the right environment for the emergence of a civil state. In the past, the rentier state did not allow for the emergence of civil society in Iraq, while the dominance of rural relations curtails the emergence of the civil state in the present. This state of affairs was further complicated by the institutionalization of a sectarian quota system after the fall of Hussein's regime. Khalil did not believe that the solution to sectarianism consisted in the elimination of sectarian affiliation. Rather, he believed sectarian identities and interests should be secondary, while the concepts of secularism and citizenship should take precedence.

To Khalil, secularism constituted an antidote to sectarianism. He believed that John Locke's call for a secular state, where the religious establishment does not interfere in the administration of the state and the writing of legislation, was not feasible. The United States is an example that shows the impossibility of the separation of the state from religion, such as when politicians vote against abortion bills based on their religious beliefs. What differentiates the democratic secular state from the unsecular state is the fact that it is a state where individual freedom and will are respected. The individual is free to adhere to different cultural and political views, including religious beliefs, and to act according to these beliefs without fear. The secular state, as such, refrains from interfering in the spiritual needs and beliefs of people and allows for the existence of diverse places of worship. To Khalil, the secular state does not indicate the erasure of religion; rather, it engenders a space of dialogue and compromise through respect for different beliefs. Khalil gives the United States and Britain as two examples of secular states where religious beliefs can inform the political sphere, where mosques, churches, temples, and synagogues exist, and where there are no incidents of sectarian or religious violence. For the secular state to function according to the ideals of tolerance and compromise, it needs to be a democratic state. Khalil recognized that secular states could flourish under totalitarian regimes, such as the Soviet Union, or Turkey under Mustafa Kemal Ataturk, when there were serious attempts to impose secularism and eliminate freedom of worship. To him, these are examples of failed secular states, since individual freedom is sacrificed. In Iraq, by contrast, secularism failed due to the institutionalization of a sectarian quota system and the alienation of the minorities—particularly the Sunnis—from the political sphere. In Khalil's view, the solution for the impasse of sectarianism in Iraq is the establishment of a democratic secular state that would guarantee individual freedom and the participation all of the citizens in the political sphere.

Khalil did not see his political views as aiming to develop a rigorous political ideology to fill the vacuum left by the disappearance of hegemonic ideologies. Rather, he saw these rudimentary ideas as a platform that would educate people about basic concepts related to democracy, citizenship, the civil state, and secularism that were necessary for building an inclusive and unified Iraq. He envisioned the Coalition of Democracy in Iraq as a forum that would disseminate these political ideas in diaspora and Iraq by bringing people from different backgrounds together to agree on a shared agenda that would keep Iraq unified. For almost twenty years, the Coalition of Democracy held annual conferences in London (and in Iraq after the fall of Hussein's regime) to debate these ideas and to envision an Iraqi future where a democratic, secular, civil state ensures the well-being of all the citizens.

Khalil's political views were linked to his belief in the possibility of an alternative future for Iraq, a future defined by inclusivity and stability. Unlike Hanan, for whom the failure of the postcolonial project engendered disenchantment and indicated a diminished future, Khalil aimed to shape the future through his political activism. The alternative future, however, was not defined by postcolonial dreams of national independence and social equality brought about through revolution. Rather, it was to be a future where a liberal democratic state would guarantee the welfare of all citizens, including women, through state institutions and civil organizations. Khalil no longer envisioned that sweeping revolutionary ideologies would engender radical reforms. Rather, political and social transformations could be achieved through deliberate work that revolved around the building of institutions and bringing people together. It was through the building of democratic institutions that a person's legal, political, social, and gender rights would be guaranteed.

Khalil's political thought aimed to forge an inclusive national sphere in Iraq, but it also shaped his own sense of selfhood. The Iraqi subject in his narrative was not constituted through revolutionary mobilization and reminiscences about the idealized past anymore. Rather, Khalil's new Iraqi was someone who took pains to engage in political activism throughout a life span, critically reflected on the practices of the past, and endeavored to build democratic and secular institutions. This self was no longer inspired by absolute conviction in the building of one's political project. Inspired by his experience in the British society, Khalil aimed to create a sense of selfhood based on notions of compromise, dialogue, and inclusion. While Khalil saw himself as a liberal in his belief in individual freedom and democracy, he described himself as a socialist democrat in that he was against the capitalist system and its exploitation of people. This self was still collective and nationalist in its outlook in that the welfare of the Iraqi people was the main point of concern and the incentive for political activism amid disenchantment and divisions. As such, the Iraqi subject was always becoming and evolving. No longer revolutionary, he was a compromising politician not tied to the romantic past and constantly looking forward to the future. Khalil fashioned himself as an Iraqi subject unbeholden to the rigidity of the past or to the sectarian discourse of the self, yet he still saw the ideal Iraqi as someone who was middle class and urban. This liberal self, with its sensitivity to the historical conditions that led to the rise of sectarianism and its reluctance to blame the turn of events in the present on notions of backwardness and religion, could not escape its middle-class and urban sensibilities. Peasants, in this framework, were incapable of breaking away from their inherent rootedness in land and family or of forming a sense of citizenship dedicated to the nation-state. The project of nation building and the construction of an Iraqi self remained the prerogatives of progressive, middle-classed Baghdadis.

## Optimistic Disenchantment

When I saw Khalil again in 2018 and 2019, it was hard to escape the sense of disenchantment he felt. After twenty years of political engagement, the Coalition of Democracy in Iraq stopped its activities in 2009. Most of its members were old men, who had either died or went to Iraq to hold positions. Part of the reason for dissolving the coalition was Khalil's conviction that change had to come from within Iraq. Following the failure of the exilic opposition to agree upon an agenda that would protect national cohesion, Khalil believed it was Iraqis inside Iraq who should take the lead in transforming the current situation. Despite his feelings of disenchantment, Khalil also held to the hope that a better future for Iraq was still possible. This hope was brought about by his visits to Iraq. While the deteriorating situation pained him, he admired the resilience and warmth of the Iraqi people. He no longer recognized Baghdad, yet he felt at home in the city because of what he saw as the generosity and honesty of the Iraqi people. It amazed Khalil that a taxi driver in Iraq returned money to him when he thought he had been overpaid, or that Iraqis received him warmly despite their negative experience with people who had returned from abroad. He read these little things as indications that Iraqis were genuinely open to someone who held Iraq's best interests at heart. He perceived his role as an Iraqi living abroad as limited to providing advice if asked by Iraqis inside Iraq. The protests against the Iraqi government that began and continued in Iraq following the Arab uprisings in 2011 gave him hope that the youth were fed up with the current situation and were taking to the streets to protest the corrupt government.

During my last interview with him, Khalil dwelled on the question of home. Though he could see that returning to Iraq was no longer possible, he still felt that Iraq, rather than Britain, was home. To him, he had a political role to play as an Iraqi. Political activism in the past and the present shaped his notion of subjectivity. He also felt a close affinity to Iraqis in Iraq for their resilience. When I interviewed him in 2018, I asked him if he thought that Iraq was over. He reminded me of the predicaments through which Iraq had suffered throughout history. He spoke of Hulagu Khan, the grandson of Genghis Khan, who laid siege to Baghdad in 1258. Hulagu figures prominently in Iraqis' historical memory as the Mongol ruler who ransacked the Grand Library of Baghdad and who turned the color of the Tigris blue because of the ink of the books thrown into the river. Khalil told me that Iraq lived through Hulagu and other foreign leaders, but it always survived invasion, destruction, and violence. Sooner or later, Iraq would survive the current crisis. He added that this might not happen during his or even my lifetime, but Iraq would "come back."

The metaphor of Hulagu Khan spoke to Khalil's sensibilities about foreign occupation of Iraq. In the past, Khalil perceived himself as a revolutionary subject who engaged in political struggle against the British presence in Iraq and dreamed of social equality brought about by a revolution. In the present, he saw his political engagement as a venue to build democratic institutions and, assisted by Iraqi politicians in exile, to resist an imperial project that aimed to fashion an Iraqi political sphere along sectarian policies. Not only did colonial and imperial realities shape Khalil's life prospects—in that they defined his political views and led to a lifelong exile—they also informed his visions of Iraqis and the future of Iraq. Though Iraqis in Iraq have lived through wars and violence for decades and encountered ongoing destruction of the social fabric, they still showed resilience and warmth. Read in the light of Hulagu Khan's siege of Baghdad and the departure of the British from Iraq in 1958, Khalil held on to the hope that Iraq would survive the impact of U.S. interventions in the country, including the occupation and the institutionalization of a sectarian quota system, and would eventually be able to build an inclusive country once people committed to the welfare of Iraq assumed power.

MEMORIES OF PERSECUTION

When I was growing up in the late 1970s and early 1980s, belonging to the Da'wa Party was a death sentence, at least in my mind. Whenever my parents and their friends whispered the party's name, they commented that so and so had been executed because of being a member. My parents did not know any members of the Da'wa Party personally; however, their friends and our neighbors told stories of relatives or acquaintances who had perished in jail due to their affiliation with the party. Rumors about families of prominent Da'wa members facing death or imprisonment were also rampant. Rumors about students who had relatives who were Da'wa sympathizers and were therefore disappeared also circulated. The Da'wa Party was surrounded by secrecy, fear, and death. I knew that my parents were communists, so they could never be accused of belonging to the Da'wa Party or be associated with the militant religious establishment in Iraq. To me, it appeared that my parents stood a chance of escaping the Hussein regime's tyranny as communists, but they would not have a chance of surviving if they were part of the Da'wa Party.

The escalating violence against the Da'wa Party and other critical religious scholars was another source of dismay and disbelief for my parents. To them, it was another instance of a brutal regime surviving despite unprecedented levels of violence against its people. I remember the execution of the prominent religious scholar Muhammad Baqir al-Sadr, who was the leader of the Da'wa Party, shocked my parents and raised their anxiety, since it showed the lengths to which the regime would go to suppress dissent. As the liquidation of the Iraqi Communist Party in the late 1970s was taking place, the regime turned its attention to clandestine religious parties, which had emerged as the main opposition in the country. However, no one knew anything about these parties because they operated in secret. Rumors related stories of attacks on state institutions coordinated by religious parties, assassination attempts of Iraqi officials, and quickly suppressed demonstrations. Along with the Kurdish insurgency in the north, the religious parties emerged as one of the only forces in the country challenging the regime. However, the brutality with which the regime treated religious opponents diminished any prospect that these parties could actually change the status quo.

The fear of the Da'wa Party intensified, as Hussein's regime was suspicious of religion when I was growing up in Iraq. It treated any public sign of religiosity—such as wearing a veil or growing a beard—as an act of defiance against its reign. While public signs of religiosity were few in Baghdad in the early 1980s, they became more frequent by the mid-1980s, especially as more and more women began to wear the veil. I vividly remember the reaction of my middle school teachers when one day a student, Noha, showed up veiled. She was one of the first students to wear the veil in school. While all the teachers expressed shock when they saw her, one teacher went after her. The teacher asked Noha to stand up in the middle of the class and began to interrogate her about why she wore the veil. The class went silent, which made me feel like Noha was on trial. She stood up in the middle of the class, not saying a word. When the teacher repeated the question, Noha replied that it was her father who had asked her to wear the veil and that she did not want to disobey him. I thought that Noha used her father as an excuse to deflect the persistent interrogation of the teacher. As all the students gazed at Noha, I just wished that the teacher would stop asking questions. After a while, the teacher told Noha to sit down, and she resumed the class.

This incident stuck in my mind for different reasons. It reflected the fact that newly emerging signs of religiosity in Iraqi society were seen as political acts of defiance by the regime. The teacher's interrogation of Noha, as such, laid bare the regime's anxiety over this new force that could undermine its control of the Iraqi society. The incident was a spectacle of the regime's power and, at the same time, its vulnerability; it also intensified my discomfort over the role of my teachers as agents of the regime. I always knew that my teachers had to join the Ba'th Party to keep their jobs and had to reproduce the state's glorification of Saddam Hussein. However, in this instance, I saw my teacher playing the role of a security agent in charge of safeguarding the regime. I feared that the teacher would accuse Noha and her family of being sympathizers of the Da'wa Party and would report them to the authorities. Luckily, this interrogation did not seem to have direct repercussions for Noha, who continued coming to school veiled.

( CHAPTER 3 )

# RELIGIOUS PATHS, SECULAR PASTS

I first met Ali at an Iraqi Shi'i organization in 2006. When we were introduced, I kept some distance between us and did not attempt to shake his hand. Because he worked at a religious institution, I assumed he was devout and would not shake hands with a woman. When I started fieldwork in 2006, there were uncomfortable incidents when I would put my hand forward to religious men only to have them put their hands on their chests, indicating that they did not shake hands with women. To avoid this embarrassment, I simply stopped trying to shake hands with people at religious institutions. Moreover, I expected that Ali might lecture me on the importance of wearing the veil, praying, and fasting. Some of the religious people I met did so, vocally disapproving of my appearance and lack of religiosity, yet they welcomed me as "one of them," since my father's family hailed from Najaf. On this occasion, I was visiting Abu Warda at the religious institution where he and Ali worked. When I walked into his office, Ali was there. Overturning my expectation, he stood up to greet me and held out his hand. We shook hands, and Ali and Abu Warda resumed their heated discussion about the turn of events in Iraq after 2003. Ali said that until recently he had considered himself to be an Iraqi, but not anymore, as "Iraq died when fellow Iraqis began to kill and take advantage of each other." He also criticized Shi'i Iraqis in power for their corruption and encouragement of sectarian divisions. Abu Warda disagreed with Ali and interrupted him many times. He defended

Shi'i politicians and claimed that Shi'is everywhere were under attack, citing the suicide bombings that targeted Shi'is in Iraq and the Israeli bombardment of Lebanon in the summer of 2006, which affected places where Shi'is lived. Listening to them, I wished Abu Warda would allow Ali to talk. I was surprised to come across a devout Shi'i Iraqi who was openly critical of the Shi'i religious establishment. Eventually, Ali appeared to realize the futility of the conversation and stood up to leave. But before he left, I asked him if I could interview him, and he welcomed the idea.

During our interviews, which took place at the religious organization, Ali talked at length about his family history and its impact on him throughout his life. Ali hails from a prominent upper-middle-class Shi'i family. His father is a well-respected religious scholar who, like his father and grandfather, studied Shi'i theology with renowned grand ayatollahs in the religious seminaries in Najaf. Ali's family background, which is tied to the history of Shi'ism in Iraq and revolves around the cultivation of a religious subjectivity, undermines the dominant discourse in London about Iraq as a secular place. It speaks to the experiences of devout Shi'i Iraqis who see Iraq as a country of holy shrine cities, namely, Najaf, Karbala, Samarra, and Khaddimiyya in Baghdad. To devout Shi'i Iraqis, Iraq is a holy land. Najaf is where Prophet Muhammad's cousin Ali, who was the fourth caliph and the first Shi'i imam, was assassinated and buried. Karbala is where the murder of Prophet Muhammad's grandsons at the hand of the Umayyad caliph took place. In this competing discourse, Iraq emerges not as a hub of secular politics but as a place rooted in a religiopolitical history that dates back to the seventh century. Unlike Hanan's perception of the religious establishment as a relic of the past, the Shi'i pious self has had a distinct political outlook in the twentieth and twenty-first centuries. Following the British invasion of Iraq during World War I, it was religious scholars who spearheaded the anticolonial opposition to the British, and they played an important role in mobilizing people during the 1920 Revolt. After decades of quietism, in the late 1950s, young religious scholars again began to mobilize the youth, this time against the popularity of the Iraqi Communist Party and the social reforms that undermined their authority. After Saddam Hussein took power, the religious parties posed a serious threat to his regime. Ali's father was exposed to this political mobilization through the latter part of the twentieth century and became involved in the opposition to Hussein's regime, even though his religious mentor, the grand ayatollah with whom he studied, adhered to quietism. In the late 1970s, as Hussein's regime increased its persecution of the Shi'i establishment and religious parties, Ali's father had to flee the country. He went to South Asia as the representative of his mentor to provide religious services for Shi'is there.

Ali was born in Baghdad, but he grew up in South Asia.[1] His family left Iraq when he was a few months old. The family hoped that their move to South Asia would be temporary and they would go back once Saddam Hussein was gone. After experiencing pressure from the government, which kept good relations with Hussein's regime, Ali's father relocated his family to London, as the British capital was emerging as a major center for Iraqis in Europe. Shi'i institutions and schools opened to serve the increasing needs of the community, and Ali grew up inhabiting a religious space that was dedicated to the cultivation of a pious self. This religious space was also rooted in transnational religious networks and institutions that were mobilized by the religious establishment at different moments in the recent history of Iraq to circumvent persecution and to provide support for a community of believers. Ali's family instilled in him a love for the twelve venerated Shi'i imams at an early age. He grew up yearning to pay pilgrimage to Iraq, to visit the holy shrine cities, and to experience the feeling of serenity and devotion in the presence of Imam Ali and Imam Hussein that his parents had told him about.

Ali's mother, especially, instilled in him a love for Iraq. Daily life was punctuated by her stories about the good times she had had in Baghdad with her family and friends and by her longing to go back home. She talked about picnics on the Tigris River with family members and trips to Hajji Zibala's shop to have the best sherbet in the country. She also talked about wonderful friendships and a bustling social life. In South Asia, there were not many Iraqis, and the family socialized with their neighbors there only in conjunction with his father's attending to the religious needs of the Shi'i community. As such, Ali was thrilled with the family's decision to move to London. Though he had a happy and carefree childhood in South Asia, he yearned to be around Iraqis. His parents' reflections on their lives in Iraq engendered a feeling of nostalgia for a place he did not remember and for people he had never met. He imagined that the move to London would introduce him to a pious Iraqi Shi'i community and to Iraqis from different backgrounds. However, the move resulted in disillusionment. Ali went to a Shi'i school in northwest London that was popular among Iraqis, but he found his Iraqi classmates were divided along sectarian and inter-sectarian lines, which left him feeling alienated. Over the years, the divisions only became more rigid, intensifying his disappointment. Mingling only with Shi'i Iraqis, Ali experienced the deep sectarian and ethnic divisions of the wider Iraqi community.

The exclusion of others in the Iraqi community by virtue of different religious practices led Ali to criticize those religious practices. He perceived religious people who endorsed a sectarian narrative to be misreading the true teachings of Islam, which are based on tolerance and respect for others. His differentiation between traditional Islam, which entailed following religious practices blindly and out of habit, and reformed Islam, which was based on the use of reason to reach the correct understanding of practices, had national implications as well. Living by the true teachings of Islam was conducive to tolerance, and hence national unity. At college, Ali met Iraqis from different backgrounds, including some who had lived through the 1950s or had parents who had experienced "the good old days." The contact with Iraqis who talked about the political and social vibrancy that dominated Iraqi society in the 1950s became crucial to Ali's sense of Iraqiness. While he was disillusioned with the sectarian sentiments among the Iraqi community in London, he lived with the hope that things in Iraq were different. He imagined Iraq to be a diverse, inclusive place where people coexisted with each other. However, the spiraling sectarian violence, which reached its peak between 2006 and 2008, and the rampant corruption in the country shattered this image of the ideal Iraq. Moreover, the turn of events in Iraq after 2003 confirmed Ali's misgivings about Shi'i politicians' and religious scholars' ability to carve out a national space to which all Iraqis could feel affiliated or to provide the much-needed social services the country had been lacking under Saddam Hussein. Not only did Ali become critical of religious practices among the Iraqi community, but he also came to believe in the necessity of separating religion from politics.

Whenever I met Ali, he reminded me of Hanan, even though they occupied two different worlds. They both shared a sense of heartbreak over the turn of events in Iraq and yearned for an idealized past. Ali was a sensitive person whose pain over Iraqis killing each other was conveyed by the sadness and anger in his voice. Like Hanan, he struggled to make sense of the political present that belied the romantic reminiscences of his mother and other Iraqis who lived through the 1950s. The political present shook his sense of what it meant to be an Iraqi and a Shi'i. Though he inhabited a religious space and embraced a secular past, his sense of belonging was marked by deferment. While Hanan yearned to visit the Iraq of the past and felt out of place when she went to Baghdad, Ali preferred to keep the picture of the idealized Iraq intact by refusing to visit the country. As he told me once, he was "an Iraqi of the 1950s." A return home was deferred until that past era of vibrancy and coexistence became possible again.

Ali's sense of belonging and selfhood, as such, was informed by U.S. imperial intervention in Iraq, his family's religious background and nationalist sentiments, middle-class sensibilities, and Iraqi communists' nostalgic reminiscences about the past. The confluence of these different players and political events in diaspora and Iraq constituted him as an exiled, nostalgic subject. Ali's life, since his childhood, has been defined by a feeling of rupture between the homeland he yearned for and his place of residence. The United States' support of Saddam Hussein in the 1980s and decision to keep him in power after the Gulf War of 1991 resulted in the displacement of Ali's family twice—once from Iraq and another time from South Asia—and rendered Ali unable to visit Iraq all his life. Moreover, his sense of exile was exacerbated by his mother's constant longing for the vibrant life she had once lived in Iraq. He grew up with an acute sense of missing out on an Iraqi experience due to exile. While his mother instilled the love of Iraq in him, his father's religious background shaped his efforts to cultivate a pious self. Eventually Ali began to advocate for the practice of reformed Islam as a way for a religious self to be accepting of difference and dedicated to the integrity of Iraq as a nation-state. However, Ali's modernist understanding of religion remained classed in its outlook in that he saw Iraqis in London who hailed from southern Iraq and who endorsed a sectarian discourse as the antithesis of "civilized Iraqis." Iraqis from the south were "the sheep," who followed religion blindly and jeopardized the integrity of Iraq through lack of understanding of the true message of Islam. Implicit in this narrative is the idea that middle-class Baghdadis were the ideal Iraqi citizens, dedicated to the notion of inclusion and the welfare of all Iraqi people.

Ali's sense of selfhood was both religious and nationalist in its aspiration. Unlike Hanan, who saw the religious political project as a sign of backwardness and ignorance, Ali developed an understanding of religion and Iraqi subjectivity based on his observation of religious practices in London. He believed that one could be a pious subject and a nationalist at the same time through the endorsement of what he considered secularism—that is, the separation of religion and politics. Following the failure of Iraqi religious politicians to promote a unifying national discourse and to provide basic services after 2003, Ali came to see that religion should be relegated to the private sphere and it should define the relationship between God and the individual only. Ali's encounter with Iraqi communists, with their emphasis on social justice and national unity, confirmed this conviction. He saw in the communist project an alternative vision of what Iraq could look like if principled subjects were in charge of nation building after the U.S. occupation. To him, the Iraqi subject was someone who endorsed a political project dedicated to Iraq first and foremost. This sense of the self was constituted through an intergenerational haunting, inasmuch as the communists' nostalgic reminiscences about the late 1940s until the early 1960s informed Ali's notion of an idealized Iraqi self that was a possibility at a specific historical moment.[2] Like Hanan, Ali was the nostalgic subject who found a utopia in the past, rather than the future.

## Religious Networks, Rebellious Sentiments

The modernist discourse of Iraqi communists—that religion was a marker of backwardness and ignorance, and religious scholars and their seminaries (the *hawza*) were relics of obsolete traditions—ignored an important aspect of the Iraqi political landscape: the role religious scholars had played in the political sphere since the establishment of the Iraqi state in 1921. This discourse was also silent on the experiences of devout Shi'i Iraqis, for whom Iraq was a sacred land and the burial site of venerated imams. In this framework, the political sphere was confined to the secular, and the modern Iraqi self was imagined to be anti-religious by nature. Any political action endorsed by religious people or scholars was seen as an infringement on the secular political sphere. Communists like Hanan in the past either ignored religious people, at best, or saw them as objects of ridicule. Interestingly, they singled out the Shiʻi religious establishment and people as particularly obscurantist. Reiterating the Orientalist discourse embraced by British officials, some communists perceived Shiʻi Islam as the cause of what was wrong with Iraq.[3] They failed to see that religious Iraqis had an alternative political project that was the product of political developments in the country and of a history of exclusion from the state. Ali's narrative undermines this discourse about the past. It speaks to the experiences of Iraqis who were dedicated to cultivating a pious self and establishing a space for their aspirations within the Iraqi state.

Ali's life trajectory was shaped by a shifting religious and political space that is rooted in transnational networks of patronage, religious institutions of learning, family lineage, and a history of political activism on the part of the religious scholars. Ali's father hailed from a prominent family of religious scholars from Najaf. Unlike Hanan and Khalil, who went to state schools with secular curricula, Ali's father followed his father and ancestors and joined the seminary in Najaf to study Shiʻi theology.[4] He studied with a renowned religious scholar, who later became his mentor, and quickly rose up the ranks in the *hawza*. At a young age, he became a close associate of his mentor and received the title of sheikh. This familial and scholarly lineage bestowed high prestige upon his father and his family. However, Ali's father was not only expected to attend to the religious needs of the community of believers in Najaf through his scholarly knowledge. As a representative of his mentor, he also had the responsibility of cultivating patronage through charity work, particularly the allocation of part of the religious taxes (*khums*) the believers donated to the mentor to assist the poor and to fund the seminary he supervised. Charity work was important not only because it conferred prestige, but also because it affirmed the centrality of religious scholars in society.[5]

Ali's father inhabited a religious space dedicated to the cultivation of a pious self, but he also inhabited a shifting political space that had repercussions for the religious establishment. He came of age in Najaf at a time when religious scholars began to be more politically active. Historically, the Shiʻi religious establishment—also known as the Marji'iyya, clerical class, or the ulama—led the opposition to British rule in Iraq as secular, anticolonial sentiments were starting to emerge. The ulama played a pivotal role in the 1920 Iraqi revolt, a national uprising against British occupation. The Shiʻi ulama led the revolt by the tribes against the British, but they could not overcome the British military, which put down the revolt by force. Following the revolt, the ulama spearheaded the opposition to the Anglo-Iraqi Treaty of 1922. Iraqi statesmen and nationalists from different political leanings opposed the treaty because it failed to grant Iraq complete independence. However, it was the ulama, led by Sheikh Mahdi al-Khalisi, who paralyzed the government by issuing a fatwa against the treaty and against the participation in the election of the assembly that would ratify it.[6] The British officials responded by deporting Khalisi and other prominent ulama to Iran on the pretext of being Persian subjects. This show of power on the part of the British put an end to the activism of the Shi'i establishment, which then adhered to apolitical quietism until the 1950s. Likewise, the Sunni religious establishment did not have a major role in the Iraqi political scene beyond their support of the 1920 revolt.

The fall of the monarchy in 1958 changed the religious establishments' apolitical stance. The revolution brought about social and political changes in Iraqi society, such as the decline of the old established classes, including the clerical class, the demolition of the Tribal Dispute Act, land reforms, a progressive family law, and unprecedented freedoms that allowed for the spread of the popularity of Marxist ideologies.[7] Young religious scholars responded to these political events by forming religious parties, such as the Muslim Brotherhood and the Da'wa Party. The emergence of these parties indicated a shift, especially among the Shi'i religious establishment, which was dominated by conservative scholars who shunned politics. Reforming junior Shi'i scholars and activists advocated for a universal Islamic agenda and thought the formation of a modern organization would help to fight the spread of Marxism.[8] In their early days, neither party sought regime change and were dedicated to leading an anticommunist campaign and mobilizing laypeople as well as conservative ulama, who were wary of political activism, to their cause.[9] Both parties were active under the Qasim regime, but their fates diverged under Ba'th rule. The Muslim Brotherhood remained dormant for decades under the Ba'th reign, and it was co-opted by the state after 1991.[10] But the Da'wa Party, along with other religious scholars, posed a threat to the Ba'th regime through its anti-government mobilization.[11] Ali's father joined the seminary in Najaf in the early 1970s as the Ba'th regime was attempting to co-opt the religious establishment and waging a campaign against Shi'i activists. Even though his mentor advocated quietism, Hussein's regime saw him as untrustworthy, and Ali's father came under pressure by virtue of his association with him.

Ali spent the first twelve years of his life in South Asia. As he told me, he was born and brought up in "an ultraorthodox Shi'i Muslim household." Ali was expected to pray, fast, refrain from lying, read the Quran, and commemorate the births and deaths of imams. His parents were particularly concerned that Ali and his siblings were growing up in a non-Muslim country and had to go to Catholic schools. They always used the terms *najis* (unclean) and *tahir* (clean) to comment on their surroundings and on their children's choices, such as visiting their non-Muslim friends' houses or buying food from non-Muslim shops. While Ali grew up with a strong sense of being a Shi'i, he also felt the burden of strict orthodoxy:

> Coming from a prominent religious family is a big burden. It still is, and I think it will be until the day I die. I think about every move a million times. Even from a very young age. I remember when I used to do something wrong and be punished for it, I used to remember hearing the words: "What are people going to say? You're the son of so and so, and you do something like that." I always thought if I've done something wrong, punish me, but don't punish me because of what people are going to say. It was always a problem, and it still is. I feel the situation took away a lot of my innocence because I couldn't do things on the spur of the moment because I'll be thinking: "Can I do this? Can I not do this?" And finally, when I do the thing, I thought about it so it wouldn't be a reaction. It would be a planned thing.

Though Ali felt at home in South Asia, he knew that he was still an Iraqi. While his father's name and family lineage situated him in a Shi'i religious sphere, his mother was concerned with keeping Iraq alive in her children's thoughts as well. Ali told me that the first words he ever learned from his mother were "May God curse Saddam." He said, "The one thing my mother was doing every day, every day, every day was waiting for Saddam to go so that she could go back to Iraq." His mother longed for her family and friends in Iraq and reminisced about trips to the Tigris and having a vibrant social life. Ali's only memories of Iraq were of a trip he had made to the country with his mother when he was only three years old. In the early 1980s, his mother went to Baghdad to give birth because she did not know anyone in

South Asia. Ali's parents thought that it was safe for her to make the trip, believing the regime would not go after a pregnant woman with young children. Despite his young age, Ali distinctly remembered how his maternal grandfather, whose house was on the banks of the Tigris, would take him to the river to buy a kebab sandwich and Pepsi from a man with a cart. They would sit on the banks eating and enjoying the serene sunset. Growing up, Ali cherished this memory, since it defined his "Iraqiness."

The United States' support for Saddam Hussein's regime during the 1980s meant that the family was not able to return or visit Iraq. Thus, after eleven years in South Asia, they hoped Saddam Hussein's regime would collapse following the Gulf War of 1991. The uprisings that broke out in the north and south only increased this hope. But the uprisings quickly failed, putting an end to their hopes of return and shaking Ali's family to the core. The family viewed the brutality of the regime in putting down the uprising as sacrilegious. According to witnesses who fled Iraq, the tanks were painted with the slogan "No Shi'is [will survive] after today," and the Republican Guard troops partially destroyed the holy Shi'i shrines in Najaf and Karbala and the famous cemetery Wadi Al-Salam (the Valley of Peace). In response to these unspeakable acts, Ali's father mobilized the Shi'is in the country where he lived to protest Saddam Hussein's brutality and attacks on the holy cities. In retaliation, Hussein's regime requested that Ali's father be turned over to the Iraqi authorities. Fearing for his life and the safety of his family, Ali's father fled South Asia and relocated the family to London.

The British capital at that time was emerging not only as a center of Iraqi opposition to Saddam Hussein's regime but also as a center for Shi'i Iraqis. The exodus of Shi'i activists and scholars from Iraq since the late 1970s had led to transnational networks of patronage in South Asia, East Asia, Iran, and Lebanon. Representatives of the renowned religious scholars who did not flee Iraq opened organizations and did charity work on behalf of their mentors. These projects included opening places of worship that provided religious, educational, and cultural services in Western cities—such as Paris, London, and New York—with the aim of widening the network of patronage. In London, eight Shi'i religious institutions—representing different religious scholars and Shi'i political parties—opened their doors in the 1990s to meet the increasing needs of the community of believers. These organizations benefited from

British charity laws, which allowed for the establishment of religious centers, and the British multicultural discourse, which encouraged groups to seek recognition on the basis of performing an ethnic or religious identity.[12] Unlike secular organizations—such as the Iraqi Forum, where Hanan volunteered—which struggled with funding, these religious organizations depended on their networks of patronage (in particular, religious taxes donated by devout Shi'is) to fund their organizations, as well as on investments in commercial businesses. Moreover, these organizations became the hubs of the opposition to Saddam Hussein's regime and opened channels of communication with the British and U.S. governments to advocate for regime change in Iraq.

## Shifting Terrains

At the age of eleven, Ali was thrilled by the family's move to London. London loomed large in his imagination, not because it was the British capital, but because it was a center for Iraqis. The family moved to a neighborhood popular with Shi'i Iraqis and was close to Shi'i organizations in northwest London. Ali went to a faith school run by an Iraqi Shi'i organization. The move to London, however, resulted in "a cultural shock," as Ali told me. The school catered to the Shi'i Iraqi community, and the students there did not engage with people from other ethnic or religious backgrounds, including Iraqis. Moreover, their religious practices seemed alien to Ali, who was brought up with strict values. He was surprised to see the kids his age at the school have lax religious values. One of the shocking things to him was that the kids in London had *turba* fights. To Ali, the *turba*—a disc or square made of the soil of Karbala, which is considered holy by Shi'is—was second only to the Quran in sacredness. His parents taught him that nothing went on the top of the Quran except the *turba*. When he pointed out to his fellow students that it was *haram* (religiously prohibited) to have *turba* fights, they laughed at him and called him an outsider. Ali thought that the move to London would provide him with an opportunity to inhabit a vibrant Iraqi space. Instead, he came to live in a closed community that still saw him as an alien. Despite his deep disappointment, Ali believed that he was a "true Iraqi," while the kids at the school "were the fake ones."

After spending a year at the faith school, Ali decided he wanted to go to a state school. Though his parents initially disagreed, they eventually relented.

However, things didn't improve; Ali went, as he put it, from "one hell to a bigger one." While the faith school was gender segregated and imposed strict social rules, the state school was not segregated and did not impose strict rules on smoking or dating, for instance. However, Iraqi kids attended the school, and they began to report to their parents what Ali did, who in turn reported the information to his father. Moreover, the Iraqi girls and boys at school did not approve of Ali's friendships with girls. In South Asia, Ali had had friends who were girls, and this was true at the state school as well. The other Iraqi students thought that "something wrong was happening," and they reported Ali to his father. While Ali felt socially alienated from the Iraqi kids, since they could not see eye to eye, he was also bewildered by the factionalization among them. At the faith school, the kids' families adhered to the religious scholar in Najaf associated with the charity that opened the school, but the Iraqi Shi'i kids at the state school were from families that followed different religious scholars and parties. There were two main camps at the school: the Hizb al-Da'wa kids (whose parents were affiliated with the Da'wa Party) and the Shirazi kids (whose parents follow the religious scholar Sayyid Sadiq Husseini al-Shirazi). Both camps saw Ali as an outsider because his father followed a different religious scholar. They ridiculed Ali because he had black and Asian friends and because he advocated for the respect of all religions.

As the years passed, Ali grew warier of the Iraqis he met at school and at the Shi'i organizations where he attended religious events. He was especially bewildered by an emerging Shi'i discourse that revolved around narratives of victimhood and of excluding others, particularly Sunni Iraqis. Ali's family had arrived in London during a pivotal moment for Shi'i Iraqis in the early 1990s. The arrival of thousands of Shi'i Iraqis following the failure of the uprising in the south changed the demographic constitution of the Iraqi community (in that Shi'i Iraqis emerged as the majority), but it was also accompanied by a shift in discourse among the newly arrived. This shift was marked by memories of the brutality with which Saddam Hussein put down the uprising in the south and by the perception that Saddam Hussein's regime had targeted the Shi'is as Shi'is, rather than as rebels who had risen against his regime. The events associated with the uprising are shrouded in uncertainty due to the lack of extensive media coverage and effective censorship by Hussein's regime.[13] However, they engendered communal myths that led to the rise of sectarian divisions among Iraqis. The anti-Shi'i slogans the Iraqi forces used and their destruction of the holy shrines in Najaf and Karbala as well as the Wadi al-Salam cemetery had engendered tropes of persecution and victimhood among Shi'i Iraqis. These events galvanized a distinct Shi'i identity that set it apart from the state and other Iraqis.[14]

This discourse of victimhood was intertwined with a distrust of Sunni Iraqis. Shi'i Iraqis perceived Sunnis not only as the beneficiaries of Saddam Hussein's regime, but also as complicit in his crimes because they had failed to support the uprising in the south. The assertion of a Shi'i identity by the rebels during the uprising led the rest of the Iraqi society to perceive them as Shi'i rebels who were backed by Iran.[15] The rebels displayed Shi'i symbols during the uprising, including images of Iraqi Shi'i religious scholars who opposed Hussein's regime, as well as pictures of Iran's Ayatollah Khomeini. In addition, they allegedly chanted slogans that demanded the establishment of a Shi'i state in Iraq, such as "There is no governor but Ali" (Prophet Muhammad's cousin who was the first Shi'i imam); "We want a Ja'afari [Shi'i] ruler"; and "We are your soldiers of liberation, oh Hakim march on" (Hakim was a Shi'i Iraqi scholar exiled in Iran).[16] The rebels in the heat of the moment had failed to appreciate the implications of using such slogans and images.[17] Fearing the establishment of a Shi'i government in Iraq that was beholden to Iran, Iraqis in the Sunni areas did not rise against Saddam Hussein. Shi'i Iraqis read the Sunni failure to support the rebellion in the south as an indication of their identification with the regime. As such, the uprising in the south reconfigured the political and religious landscape in Iraq by exacerbating the divisions between the Sunnis and the Shi'is.[18]

Iraqis who arrived as asylum seekers in London reiterated this narrative that Saddam Hussein had targeted the Shi'is while the Sunnis stood on the side of the regime. This view shifted the discourse of suffering from a narrative that Saddam Hussein targeted anyone who was against his regime to one that saw Shi'is as the main victims of persecution. During Ashura (the annual rituals commemorating the martyrdom of Prophet Muhammad's grandson Imam Hussein and his family), Ali listened to sermons that focused on Shi'i persecution (*mathloomiyyat al-Shi'a*) and the fate of the Shi'is who lived under, but also stood up to, unjust rule since the seventh century. Ashura, a key element in Shi'i self-construction, is an important cultural paradigm for

Shi'i Muslims, since it commemorates the battle of the righteous against tyranny and evil.[19] This battle took place after the residents of Kufa in Iraq invited Imam Hussein to Iraq to lead a revolt against the corrupt and unjust Umayyad caliph Yazid. Imam Hussein set out from Mecca with a small army, which clashed with Yazid's army in Karbala. Imam Hussein and all his men, including his brother Abbas, were killed on the tenth of Muharram. Throughout history, devout Shi'is have read the story of Imam Hussein through a contemporary lens, especially during moments of persecution. In London, Shi'i Iraqis saw themselves as victims of the unjust rule of Saddam Hussein, just as Imam Hussein and his family had stood up to the unjust Sunni rule of the Umayyad dynasty. In this narrative, Saddam Hussein plays the role the unjust Umayyad caliph who persecuted the Shi'is. Throughout history, this narrative of victimhood assumed sectarian tones whenever Shi'i Iraqis saw themselves as the victims of Sunni persecution. The sectarian discourse exacerbated divisions within the Iraqi community in London. Ali told me about an elaborate system of internal categorization—dominant among Shi'i Iraqis—that was based on religious and sectarian differences:

> People here have these pigeonholes, where they fit people in different categories. They can't bear a person who is not in a pigeonhole, so they see which [pigeonhole] is the nearest to put the person in, so that they know how to deal with you. They would like to have a few holes. The first one would be "he is one of us." The second one is "he is close to us." The third is "he is trustworthy." The fourth one is "he is religious." Then they have "he is from a such and such group." These are the close groups. Then come the people they don't like: "he isn't good," "he drinks," "he gets drunk," "his wife isn't veiled!" So what if a man's wife is unveiled. So what! "He doesn't pray." "He shaves his beard!" So what!

To Ali, not only did this thinking fail to read the true message of Islam, which is based on tolerance and equality, but it also exacerbated sectarian tensions within the Iraqi community. The first level of categorizing people was whether a person was Sunni or Shi'i. If the person was a Sunni, then he or she was the other and to be avoided. It pained Ali to hear Shi'i Iraqis in London "curse and abuse Aisha, Hafsa, Abu Bakr, and Omar" during religious events and daily conversations.[20] His argument was that "nobody is asking you to take them as your leaders. But what I'm asking you to do is to respect those who believe in them and who follow them." To Ali, just as Muslims expect respect and understanding and would be upset if Christians saw them "as crazy fools" who wrap themselves with a towel during Hajj, they should "give other people the same courtesy." The second level of classification was differentiating Shi'i Iraqis themselves on the basis of the religious scholar and political party they followed to figure out how "trustworthy" a person was.

This system of classification made Ali feel alienated from fellow Shi'i Iraqis. Not only did it undermine his vision of a unified Iraq, but it employed a religious narrative to exclude and reject those who did not belong. Ali believed in Imam Ali's saying that "a person is either your brother in faith, or your equal in humanity." He believed that Sunni Iraqis and Shi'i Iraqis who followed different religious scholars are his "brothers in religion."[21] He also felt a deep affinity to Iraqis who were not religious at all because they shared a common humanity with him. Ali believed that Allah said, "You have your own religion and I have my own religion." To him, this saying confirmed the Quranic verse that states, "There is no compulsion in religion." He thought that no human being could judge or reject another human being who adhered to a different religion or lifestyle; only God could judge a person. As such, Ali advocated an interpretation of Islam that saw religious rulings as carving out a space that accepted religious difference. By excluding others based on religious and sectarian differences, then, the devout Iraqi community was failing to live by the spirit of Islam. Ali attributed his view to his upbringing in South Asia; his experience at the state school, where he mingled with people from "all faiths and denominations," who sometimes did not believe in God; and his appreciation of the true message of Islam.

The religious and the political were deeply enmeshed in Ali's narrative. They were also situated in an Iraqi context. Whenever Ali criticized Shi'i Iraqis' religious practices, he was also making a political comment on the Shi'i Iraqi sphere in London. To him, their inability to see Sunni Iraqis as their "brothers in religion" and their exclusion of fellow Shi'is who followed different religious scholars spoke to a faulty understanding of religious practices and beliefs. Ali maintained that this rejection of other people stems from the fact that the majority of Shi'i Iraqis in London adhered to religious practices without truly understanding the meaning of these practices or having deep religious beliefs.

To him, a person who fasted, prayed, and commemorated the death of Imam Hussein but cursed the Sunnis was a person who followed traditional Islam. That person was performing religious practices without living by religious values that called for tolerance and respect of the other. Ali thought that religious practices were not enough in cultivating a pious self precisely because they were performative. They could be just part of a person's daily rituals, handed down to them from his or her family. The commemoration of the death of Imam Hussein in London, therefore, was an example of how religious practices failed to cultivate a pious self. Not only did these rituals become social occasions where people gossiped about friends and tried to fix up young women with eligible men, but they also became a space for the exclusion of other Iraqis by focusing solely on the plight of Shi'i Iraqis. In his view, the way the commemoration was performed failed to provide a space to experience true religious values, which were supposed to revolve around devotion and tolerance. A person could only cultivate a pious self through the use of reason to arrive at the most trustworthy and legitimate understanding of Islam.[22]

Though Ali identified strongly as a Shi'i, he saw himself as an Iraqi first and foremost. To him, religion was a relationship between him and God. From his experience with the Shi'i Iraqi community in London, Ali began to refashion his understanding of being an Iraqi: "I never doubted my Iraqiness. I'm most definitely Iraqi. I am a good Iraqi. I made friends with black people, Indians, and Somalis. Iraqi people in Iraq are like me, not like this [community here]. Everything was in Iraq itself. Although I did not remember Iraq, this is what I thought about. I ended up making friends with non-Iraqis and having them as my close friends."

Ali's notion of Iraqiness was defined by a sense of double exile. While he longed for Iraq as the place where things were different, he felt internally exiled from Iraqis in London, given the fragmentation of the community there. Exile, to him, not only entailed a physical separation from Iraq, but also posed a threat to the construction of a pious self. The rise of sectarianism and the diminishing of a sense of belonging to Iraq prompted Ali to critically reflect on religious beliefs and to cultivate a pious self based on acceptance and tolerance. Ali was "the good Iraqi" precisely because he accepted people from different backgrounds and nationalities. Moreover, this notion of the ideal Iraqi citizen was informed by the conviction that the real Iraqis were in Iraq, not the United Kingdom. Iraq emerged as not only a place of his mother's reminiscences about a vibrant social life, but also a venue for imagining an alternative political project, based on inclusion and providing a refuge from the contradictions of exile.

## Secular Longings

Going to college in the late 1990s gave Ali the opportunity to meet Iraqis from different backgrounds. Like other young Shiʻi Iraqis, Ali told me that he met Sunni Iraqis for the first time in college. Ali was happy to meet Iraqis from different backgrounds because he felt they shared many things in common. Moreover, he began to attend events on Iraq, where he met Iraqis who had lived there during the 1950s and early 1960s. Their reminiscences about the revolutionary past and the sense of camaraderie that existed made him idealize that time. Ali listened to their stories about a cultural renaissance in Baghdad, when Iraqi poets and artists were experimenting with different forms of expression. He heard about young men and women marching together in the street to protest Anglo-Iraqi treaties and going to modern cafés to discuss politics, art, and music. Ali especially yearned for this time because it seemed like sectarian divisions did not organize social and political relations. During those college years, Ali longed to see Saddam Hussein toppled so he could go back home and experience an inclusive Iraq. However, the arrival of the long-awaited moment of regime change shattered this image of Iraq:

> Iraq died after 2003. My mother passed away when I was seventeen. These whole seventeen years of my life, my mother waited for regime change so that she could go back to Iraq. To me, every day, it was the same story: we're children of Iraq, and we're waiting to be reunited with that country. But we waited and waited and waited. And finally the day came. On the night of April 9th, I went home early from work. . . . When I got home, I turned the TV on and saw the statue of Saddam brought down. It was unbelievable. I kept pinching myself. . . . This is the biggest nightmare that we have had since we were kids, and it is just going away so easily. And these people [Iraqi politicians and religious scholars who got involved in politics] came and killed it. Not the Americans, not the British. It is our people. May Allah never forgive them for that . . . because knowingly they came to efface our

country. . . . They killed it. They killed our hope. I don't think it will ever go back to the way it was before.

Unlike the majority of the Shi'i Iraqis I met in London who defended Shi'i politicians and politicized religious clerics, Ali often voiced this scathing critique of them for the role they played in inflaming sectarian divisions in the country and in failing to provide basic services for the Iraqi people. He believed that it was "a sad thing that these [religious clerics] got hold of Iraqi politics." Not only did they manipulate Iraqi politics, but they also paid lip service to democracy. Ali thought that most of these religious clerics probably believed that democracy was *haram* since it "was rule by the people, for the people." However, they participated in elections and spoke about democracy as a means to gain power. They also used the authority of—and people's love for—the grand ayatollah, Sayyid Ali al-Sistani, a spiritual leader in Iraq, for their personal gain. Ali believed that religious-clerics-turned-politicians took advantage of people's love of the *imama* (religious establishment) and of religion to enrich themselves at the expense of the Iraqi people. He recognized that there were many religious clerics who were honest and dedicated to people, but they were in the minority. For the majority of them, holding a religious position was just a job and a way to make money and gain influence. What saddened Ali further was Shi'i Iraqis' reaction to his criticism. When Ali expressed his opinion to other Shi'is, they dismissed his criticism and accused him of "becoming a communist."

In 2006, Ali was a rare voice in his critique of religious clerics. Most of the Shi'i Iraqis I met in London strongly defended Shi'i politicians in power. The suicide attacks that targeted Shi'i neighborhoods in Iraq—in particular, the destruction of a Shi'i holy shrine in Samarra—and the Israeli bombardment of south Beirut and south Lebanon in the summer of 2006 exacerbated the sense that Shi'is were under attack everywhere. After his experience with the Shi'i Iraqi community in London and updates about the turn of events in Iraq, Ali became convinced that the Shi'i political project, which advocated for the rights of Shi'is, was bankrupt and failed to unify the country. In the early days of the Iraqi state, the Shi'i political project was anticolonialist in its outlook and advocated for genuine independence; it became militant in its stand against Saddam Hussein's tyranny, but it failed to fashion a vision to tackle the challenge of building a unified nation-state after decades of war and oppression in Iraq. The failure of the political project advocated by Shi'i politicians confirmed to Ali that religion should be separated from politics and excluded from the public sphere. Ali began to develop the idea that the focus of religion should be the relationship between God and an individual person, with the aim of cultivating a pious life based on a modernist understanding of Islam rooted in the use of reason to reach the true interpretation of religious teachings. By 2018, I met many young Shi'i Iraqis who shared Ali's disappointment in Shi'i politicians and religious clerics.

Ali's experiences with different segments of the Iraqi community in London led him to categorize people into two groups: the sheep and the civilized. To Ali, the difference between these two groups was generational. Informed by Baghdad-based, middle-class sensibilities, civilized Iraqis included older people who had lived through the 1950s and arrived in Britain earlier, while the sheep consisted of the younger generation who arrived as refugees in the early 1990s and hailed mainly from southern Iraq. The sheep were the sectarian Iraqis who cursed Abu Bakr and Omar. Ali called them sheep because "they look at the shepherd, and whatever he says, they do. And the shepherds don't live in the UK. They live in Iraq or Iran or somewhere. Whatever tune they play, the sheep dance to that tune." By contrast, Ali felt affinity with the civilized Iraqis:

> They are the ones who planted the seeds of an ideal Iraq, because of their experience, because of what they used to see. My idea of Iraq isn't an imaginary or a made-up thing. It is a country; it is a system that existed. . . . I'm saying people are equal. Back in those days, people were equal. Now, if somebody said to you "I'm an Iraqi," he would say, "I'm Sunni or Shi'a or a Kurd." Religion is something between you and the Lord. It doesn't come into the public sphere. . . . I think these elder people planted the seeds of the ideal Iraq that did exist. I think some Iraqi communities try to live along these lines. I have friends in Sweden. Everybody hates them because they are secular and communist, and they drink. I've been to their gatherings, and it is nice. I would like to identify myself with them. These are my fellow Iraqis. They care for each other. They live as a community, not like here. . . . I say to these people: "Islam teaches you to do something, but you're not doing it, while these other people who you claim are bad, they're doing everything Islam says except

they don't pray and they drink *arak* [an alcoholic drink popular in Iraq]." You see, I don't think that my imagination of Iraq and my view of Iraq is a dream. It is reality. That [reality] was there one day, that might come back, hopefully.

While Hanan associated any sign of religiosity with ignorance and backwardness, for Ali, it was the blind following of religion that was the problem. The sheep in his narrative were backward not because religion was backward but because they and their leaders misused religion. His modernist approach to religion revolved around the idea that it was an individual's responsibility to interpret the true message of Islam and to use reason to practice religion correctly. To follow religious clerics without questioning, even when some of the teachings of these clerics were problematic, was to be a sheep.

Ali's thoughts reflected classed understandings of religion; people from southern Iraq were the sheep, whom he saw as failing to endorse a modernist understanding of religion. The civilized people, by contrast, had been politically involved in the past and had tried to bring about social and political reforms that would benefit all Iraqi people, regardless of their ethnic, gender, and sectarian background. Though they did not practice religion, the civilized people lived by what Islam preached by caring about the well-being of the marginalized; they showed that it was possible to create an Iraq based on inclusion and equality. The communist political project, to Ali, did not constitute a radical rupture with efforts to cultivate a pious self, because the essence of Islam and the aspiration of the communists were not mutually exclusive. They both advocated for the rights and acceptance of others. In Ali's narrative, the secular and the religious are entangled and situated in a modernist understanding of the self informed by notions of equality and inclusion, which were dominant in the 1950s. While Ali believed that Islam called for equality among all people, he saw this notion implemented in practice in the communist political project. The religious and the secular did not occupy opposite poles, as in Hanan's narrative, but were constitutive of each other in that they both aspired to reach the same goal, namely, the building of an equal and prosperous Iraq.

## Deferred Returns

Before the fall of Saddam Hussein in 2003, Ali yearned for Iraq. For him, Iraq represented the antithesis of the status quo in exile. While the Iraqi community in London was divided along sectarian and ethnic lines, Ali believed that the situation in Iraq would be different. When the spiraling sectarian violence and the rampant corruption after 2003 destroyed this image, Ali began to identify as an Iraqi of the 1950s and 1960s:

> I was born in Iraq. I lived the whole of my life as an Iraqi. I will die as an Iraqi. But the Iraq I affiliate with isn't the Iraq that exists today. Also, I don't affiliate with the Iraqi people or the Iraqi community. . . . I'm an Iraqi, but I think the Iraq that I would want to go back to is the Iraq of the 1950s or 1960s. That is the Iraq when my grandfather lived. . . . All the good things we hear about Iraq, they all happened in that age. I'm an Iraqi of that age, which is why I don't want to go to Iraq right now. I want to go for *ziyyara* [pilgrimage to holy shrines in Iraq], but I don't want to go and see the people or see the society because I'd like to have fond memories of Iraq. Although I've never seen it, these are my fond memories. So I'm an Iraqi of that age, not this age. I think the Iraqi people now unfortunately have done themselves more harm than good by embracing sectarianism. . . . I'm an Iraqi of my idea of Iraq, not of the existing Iraq.

To a great extent, Iraqi communists' narrative about the idealized past shaped Ali's sense of belonging. It produced an idea of the ideal Iraq that stood in contrast to the bleak present. It was an Iraq defined by aspirations for social equality, justice, and tolerance. It was this image that captivated Ali's imagination and shaped his exilic yearnings. To Ali, Iraq was not a physical space that existed in the present, but rather a misty memory of the past. Thus, Ali longed for a home that no longer existed, and his nostalgia was a romance with his idea of what Iraq was like in the past.[23] This identification with the Iraq of the past produced a desire to inhabit Iraq temporally, not spatially; he was not interested in visiting Iraq as an existing physical space. He would wait until the sentiments of the past became a possibility again. Ali did not visit Iraq after the fall of Saddam Hussein, though some of his family members did. Like some other Iraqis I met in London who decided not to visit the country in its present condition, Ali wanted to keep the image of the idealized Iraq intact and alive. Stories he heard about the destruction of the country and the disrepair of Baghdad raised fears that the reality on the ground would dispel forever his ideal of Iraq. That ideal was the only thing he had left. He thus deferred return until the ideal Iraq at least became a possibility again. Ali enjoyed the company of Iraqi communists because through them he could get a glimpse of that Iraq in their stories of the past. These reminiscences and his vague memory of having a sandwich by the Tigris with his grandfather were all he had to hang on to.

Ali's refusal to go to Iraq was closely intertwined with the U.S. imperial intervention in the country. The United States' support of Saddam Hussein's regime in the 1980s and its prolonging of the Iran-Iraq War had caused Ali's family to not return to Iraq in the 1980s. Moreover, the U.S. decision to keep Saddam Hussein in power after the Gulf War of 1991 led to the second phase of displacement for Ali's family when they had to flee to London. Finally, it was the U.S. institutionalization of a sectarian quota system in post-Hussein Iraq, which reorganized the political landscape along sectarian and ethnic lines and brought to power Iraqi politicians who were concerned with personal gains, that intensified sectarian violence and dimmed the possibility of his return or visits to Iraq. Nevertheless, despite U.S. imperial formations in Iraq, as well as his admiration for the communist political project of the past, Ali did not endorse an anti-imperialist position. Rather, he blamed the turn of events in Iraq after 2003—including sectarian violence, corruption, and lack on basic services—on Iraqi politicians who employed religion as a means to wield power and acquire wealth. His disillusionment was the product not of imperial powers, but of the religious establishment he had grown up venerating. Religious Iraqi politicians, in his view, enabled the success of the imperial project in Iraq.

Although Ali was the nostalgic subject, aspiring after the communist political project of the past, he did not attempt to get involved in politics. While Hanan and Khalil had thrust themselves into the revolutionary tide in the past and were politically active, Ali, like most people of his generation, had an aversion to politics. He saw political work as dominated by corrupt politicians who would not allow for the emergence of a democratic political system in the country. Ali's ideal Iraq, where national unity and the welfare of all Iraqi people were paramount, remained oriented toward the past, rather than the future. Despite his young age at the time I interviewed him, Ali could not look forward to the future. The utopia he dreamed of had existed in the past.

And the bleak present forestalled any course of action that might change the status quo and engender a possibility for an alternative future. The Iraqi subject was no longer someone who was a revolutionary or a political activist who believed that activism would change the course of history. Rather, the nostalgic self was paralyzed by the loss of an era it had never experienced and by the inability to envision that its agency could transform its world.

# IN THE MIDST OF WAR

My sister and I were close to Nour, who was my sister's age, and Abeer, who was two years older than my sister. We would wait together for the school bus to take us to and from school. After school, we played together in the streets. One day in the early 1980s, we went to the bus stop, and Nour and Abeer were not there. Their house looked quiet. After school, my mother explained to us that Nour and Abeer, whose father had left Iraq to avoid military enlistment during the Iran-Iraq War, had been deported to Iran with their mother. Growing up under Hussein's reign, I often heard stories about the disappeared. Some of my father's friends disappeared after they were arrested, and our neighbor always talked about her disappeared brother. Rumors about people being arrested and never released circulated widely. However, I had not realized that my friends could also disappear.

What happened to Nour, Abeer, and their mother was part of a deportation campaign initiated by the Hussein regime in the early 1980s. It targeted the so-called Iraqis of Iranian origin. The regime sent thousands of families to the border with Iran after it confiscated their property, documents, and belongings. I still remember my mother's disbelief that Iraqi citizens who had been living in Iraq for generations and identified as Iraqis were suddenly designated as Iranians by the regime and deported. Unlike the majority of deportees who were sent to Iran, Nour, Abeer, and their mother reappeared after a few weeks. My mother warned us that we should not ask the girls any questions and that we should behave as if nothing had happened. Moreover, we were made to understand that their mother was being forced to collaborate with the regime and had to write reports on neighbors in order for her and her daughters not to be deported. While we went on playing with Nour and Abeer and pretended that everything was normal, we exercised caution and self-censorship.

The deportation campaign, the increasing brutality of the regime, and the Iran-Iraq War intensified the sense of foreboding in the country in the 1980s, which compounded my personal anxiety about my mother. By the time I began primary school, at the age of six, self-censorship and apprehension were already deeply ingrained in me. Being at school only intensified my worry. Not only did I have to watch what I said constantly, but I also had to resist the pressure to join the Ba'th Party. Ba'th members often came to schools and forced students to join the party by making them sign a membership application and pay a fee. The possibility of these random visits made me fret. My mother warned my sister and me against giving in to pressure. She told us that we should say that we could not sign anything without her permission, but I always doubted my ability to stand my ground if I were put in this situation, especially if a Ba'th official screamed at or threatened me. Luckily, teachers sometimes told us ahead of time when Ba'th members were coming to the school. During these days, my mother would keep us home.

The Iran-Iraq War also entered the school in a direct way. Every Thursday morning, which was the last day of the school week, there was a flag-raising ceremony. After singing the national anthem, three students unfolded the flag and raised it on a pole. Teachers and students then delivered speeches in which they praised the regime and the performance of the Iraqi army. The last part of the ceremony featured a soldier firing a rifle. Everyone dreaded this moment. We tried to put our hands over our ears to dampen the sound, but our teachers yelled at us and demanded that we show courage, which was necessary to defeat the enemy. Sometimes, this chiding was short, immediately followed by the firing of bullets in the air. At other times, the headmistress rebuked us at length, reminding us of Iraqi soldiers who were dying for our sake while we could not even bear the sound of a few bullets. She ordered us to stand straight and still and look ahead. This long berating made things worse for us, since it delayed the firing of the gun. The anticipation was almost unbearable.

My mother and her siblings talked fondly of the teachers they had had when they were young, who encouraged them to read and introduced them to prominent Arab and other writers. I knew that all my teachers, however, had to be Ba'th members. They could not be trusted or confided in. After all, they had to make sure that we sang the pro-regime national anthem, as well as songs glorifying Saddam Hussein and the Iraqi army's "victories" on the battlefield. They also had to ensure that we memorized Ba'th literature and Saddam Hussein's speeches. For our composition assignments, teachers asked us to write about "the president's wisdom and genius" in leading the Iraqi army to victories during the Iran-Iraq War. While I never liked my teachers, I understood that they were bad-tempered because they themselves felt trapped and had been forced to join the Ba'th Party to keep their jobs.

Predictably, the regime also used schools to indoctrinate students with its ideology. The humanities curriculum—in particular, Arabic literature, language, history, and national education—was designed to extol Hussein. My education was based on rote memorization. We were not allowed to ask questions or disagree with the content. This stood in stark contrast to my mother's education, which had emphasized inquiry and close engagement with readings. My mother was worried that my sister and I were not getting a solid education. To compensate, she made sure we read and studied during our summers. She focused on Arabic and English and encouraged us to read both Arabic and translated literary works. She also made sure that my sister and I understood that the regime's version of modern Iraqi history—which teleologically cast the Ba'th Party and Hussein as saviors of Iraq who managed to prevail despite imperial and internal conspiracies—was inaccurate and nonsensical. We knew, however, that we had to reproduce the official version in school in order to pass.

During the 1980s, the Iran-Iraq War dominated the social scene. Black banners with information about martyrs who had died in the war filled Iraq's public spaces. While television and radio stations spouted songs and military communiqués about the Iraqi army's victories and the Iranian army's poor performance, the banners betrayed a different story: that the Iraqi army sustained considerable losses on the battlefields. Khaki became an unpopular color, since it was associated with war and with state officials—including Saddam Hussein, who wore it all the time. Rumors about summary executions of deserters circulated widely. The regime, some said, decided to hang deserters in front of their houses at the start of the war to deter soldiers from fleeing. Relatives of soldiers talked about harsh military training and horrific war scenes. In addition, the regime made sure that the reality of the war reached every Iraqi house. Saddam Hussein's honoring of Iraqi soldiers was broadcast on television during the news hour. The broadcast of these ceremonies entailed the interruption of regular programs and the prolongation of the news program until the ceremony was over, which sometimes lasted three to four hours. In addition, a program entitled "Pictures from the Battlefield" showed horrific pictures of dead Iranian soldiers. As soon as we heard the foreboding music accompanying the program, we turned the television off. Hundreds of war songs, which often celebrated Saddam Hussein as heroically leading Iraq to victory, were written and broadcast on television and the radio.

Amid this atmosphere of fear and persecution, rumors flourished. In its efforts to keep people in the dark, the regime controlled television and radio stations as well as local newspapers, and it censored all newspapers and magazines published abroad. Rumors became the major source of information about developments within the country. There were always rumors about failed coup d'états and the regime's swift and ruthless retaliation, heavy military defeats in the war, staggering national debt, brutality against opponents of the regime, summary executions, and people who had succumbed to pressure and joined the Ba'th Party or the intelligence agency. But rumors were tricky. A trusted friend or neighbor repeating what she had heard did not raise a red flag. A person outside the trusted circle freely volunteering information and openly criticizing the regime raised suspicions. Such behavior indicated that the person was doing the regime's bidding by spying on and baiting people, whether willingly or by coercion and co-option. We always had to be cautious about whether a person was, or had become, a regime loyalist or was still a trustworthy friend. Stories of friends informing on friends were rampant. In fact, I did not have an Iraqi friend with whom I did not have to censor myself until I began my fieldwork in London in 2006.

We thought that the 1980s was a liminal decade. We never lost hope that regime change was imminent and that the nightmare we were living would soon come to an end. My dream was to live a life that was carefree and spontaneous and not defined by anxiety. Instead, I lived in a state of relentless vigilance and worry. But I also could not complain. After all, our situation was not that bad. There were people who were forced to cooperate with the regime or who languished in jails or were tortured. Some did not know if missing family members were dead or alive, and others lost loved ones to the war. The harassment we experienced paled in comparison to what other Iraqis went through.

This distorted sense of privilege intensified in the first half of 1988. The atrocities that the regime committed reached an unprecedented level in the months preceding the end of the Iran-Iraq War. The regime pounded major Iranian cities with hundreds of Scud missiles provided by some European governments and the United States. Television programs were constantly interrupted to broadcast war communiqués about the number of missiles falling on Iranian cities. Unlike Iraq, Iran did not have many Scud missiles and retaliated by launching what few it did possess on Basra and Baghdad, with some landing in areas close to our neighborhood. During these months, fierce fighting on the front lines took place as well. There were even rumors that the regime sent death squads to the front lines, whose task was to shoot at Iraqi soldiers who tried to flee. Finally, rumors about the regime's use of chemical weapons against the Kurds spread widely. There being no mention of it on the news, we heard through friends about thousands of Kurds who had instantly perished from mustard gas. Today, we know of this incident as the Halabja massacre and al-Anfal campaign.

( CHAPTER 4 )

# ITINERARIES OF HOMECOMINGS

One hot summer day in 2006, I was walking toward a café near Paddington in the center of London to meet with Hadjar. I did not know what to expect because my meeting with her was arranged by a common acquaintance, and I had not had the chance to communicate with her directly. The only information I had was that I was meeting her near the law firm where she worked and that her family had been deported from Iraq to Iran in 1980. As I approached the café, I saw a tall, slim, veiled woman sitting outside eating Middle Eastern food. When I introduced myself, Hadjar, who like me was in her early thirties at the time, welcomed me warmly, and our conversation flowed smoothly. We soon realized that we shared common experiences as children who had grown up in Iraq during the rise of Saddam Hussein. We exchanged stories about the fears and anxiety we had felt as children, as well as stories about loss and death, and aspirations and hopes. Hadjar, who is an immigration lawyer, was as curious about my life story as I was about hers. I felt I owed her a candid account of my life, as she was remarkably open and forthright about the hard life she had had until she came to Britain at the age of sixteen. During our conversation we developed a close bond that has persisted throughout the years, even though we are not in touch that often. We are very different in some respects. Hadjar is a devout Shi'i Muslim whose religiosity is an integral part of her identity and daily life, while I am irreligious. But our stories of endurance and displacement under Saddam Hussein's regime provide a common ground.

During our conversation, Hadjar told me how Saddam Hussein's tyranny shattered her world when she was young. At the age of seven, she was snatched from the comfort of her middle-class home and taken to the Iran-Iraq border by security agents because her father was *taba'iyya*: an Iraqi of "Iranian origin." Her family's deportation was part of the regime's massive expulsion campaign in the early 1980s that targeted Shi'i Arabs and Shi'i Kurds—like Hadjar's family—who had held Persian nationality under the Ottomans and who came to be seen as a threat to the Iraqi nation under Hussein's regime. The expulsion campaign was accompanied by the confiscation of the deportees' documents, property, and belongings. Stateless and penniless, Hadjar's family found themselves in a new country where they did not speak the language or have the means to start anew. While Hadjar's father was a successful merchant in Baghdad who had provided his family with a comfortable life, he could not establish a business in Iran to provide the same standard of living, and the family suffered financially. Also, Hadjar's family was confronted with Persian nationalism, which perceived them as outsiders—specifically, Arabs, though they are Kurds—who did not belong in Iran even though they are Shi'i Muslims and even though the father had relatives in the country. This furthered her family's inability to start anew in Iran. After nine years of economic hardship and marginalization, Hadjar's family relocated to London, where one of her brothers lived, worked, and supported his family. The family decided that they had no future in Iran and that a return to Iraq was no longer feasible with the consolidation of Hussein's power. Britain offered the prospect of a secure and comfortable life, albeit culturally different from the Middle East. It was to be a new home, where they felt that the children could have a better future.

Hadjar also dwelled at length on how questions of selfhood and home became a pressing issue for her from a young age. In Iran, familial expectations complicated her desire to blend with Iranian society and to escape the label "Arab." Her family—particularly her eldest sisters, who came of age in Iraq—grew anxious that Hadjar was taking on Iranian, rather than Iraqi, norms and manners. In Britain, her veil, life experiences, and accent set her apart as the "other," and she missed Iran terribly. Her identity crisis reached a peak when she was in her mid-twenties. At the time, Hadjar felt lost, confused, and alienated from her family and religion. Her social life revolved around her British friends. But at the age of twenty-seven, she experienced a turning point in her life when she read a book by a renowned Lebanese Shi'i scholar about the struggle of young people with religious faith. The book renewed her faith and gave her an anchor, starting her on a journey to reconnect with her roots and religion. Hadjar went on a trip to Damascus to visit a Shi'i holy shrine, followed by a pilgrimage to Mecca for the first time.

After the fall of Saddam Hussein, Hadjar went to Iraq, which she hadn't been able to do for almost two decades. The visit provided her with an Iraqi experience she had always missed when she listened to her sisters reminisce about their life there. It also cemented her Shi'i faith through her visits to the holy shrine cities of Najaf and Karbala. Hadjar's search for roots took her to different cities. At the same time, she began to develop a strong British identity built on the notion of hybridity. Britishness became a marker of inclusive identity that encompassed different aspects of belonging, whereby Hadjar could claim that she was Muslim-British or Iraqi-British. London became the place from which she embarked upon recurring journeys that shaped her multiple identities as Iraqi, Kurdish, Shi'i, Muslim, and British.

Unlike Hanan, Khalil, and Ali, who thought of Iraq as their homeland, home was not a stable, fixed, or taken-for-granted thing for Hadjar. Instead, home was a shifting and contested concept that constantly needed to be reaffirmed through journeys to other places. It was a place rooted in—and routed through—multiple locations, but with an ongoing expectation of homecoming. Hadjar was constantly embarking on journeys to Baghdad, Najaf, Karbala, and Mecca, only to come back to London. And then a new journey would begin whenever she had the opportunity. While in London, she yearned for these distant cities, but as soon as she was away, she yearned for London. It is through these processes of travel and homecoming that Hadjar carved out an Iraqi-British and Muslim-British subjectivity that marked a shift from the discourse of an Iraqi subjectivity centered on national struggle and political activism. Each journey affirmed some aspect of her identity because they enabled her to establish roots in different places and enjoy everyday happenings that she could not experience while she was in London. Hadjar felt at home whenever she arrived in Iraq, heard Iraqis shout at each other in the Iraqi dialect, sat on an Iraqi sofa (*karawita*), visited and touched the shrines of Imam Ali and Imam Hussein, went on pilgrimage and felt proximity to God and the Prophet, and returned to the gloomy skies and queues of London. She inhabited a subjectivity that was reproduced in processes of homecoming. The search for a home and a sense of selfhood was constantly reenacted through journeying.

As I listened to Hadjar reflect on her trajectory, I could discern how her construction of subjectivity and home has been historically entangled in forms of nationalism, colonialism, and imperialism, as well as transnational connections. For example, the British colonial legacy manifested in the first Iraqi Nationality Law, which relegated Iraqis who held Persian nationality under the Ottomans to second-class citizenship, or *taba'iyya*, putting these Iraqis in a precarious position. Decades later, Saddam Hussein's regime relied on this law to denaturalize and expel Hadjar's family and thousands of other families. Also destabilizing her notion of home were the centuries-old regional networks between Shi'i communities in Iraq and Iran, which connected families across national borders. Hadjar's paternal grandfather hailed from Iran and was engaged in trade and familial networks that spanned Iran and Iraq. In addition, the exclusionary discourse of both Persian and Arab nationalism, predicated on mutual fear and suspicion, eventually rendered Hadjar's family stateless and in search of a home. Britain, the old colonial motherland, thus became a place for Hadjar's family to find refuge. Then the U.S. invasion of Iraq and the fall of Saddam Hussein opened up the possibility for Hadjar to return to Iraq. For her, homecomings—and the very feeling of home—was articulated, rearticulated, and disarticulated in these nexuses of power, mobility, transnationalism, and family networks.

Hadjar's narrative indicated generational shifts in the understanding of home and subjectivity. To Khalil and Hanan, Iraqi subjectivity was constituted in political struggle and activism with the hope of building a democratic and unified country. This perception of Iraq informed Ali's vision of the idealized past while he searched for an alternative to the divided present. To Hadjar, the construction of home and subjectivity was an ongoing process that was informed by familial memories of Iraq, religious faith, experiences of marginalization and exclusion in exile, and British multiculturalism. Hadjar's life story provides an alternative to the dominant middle-classed discourse endorsed by Hanan about Iraq as a hub of progressive politics, anticolonial struggle, and cultural renaissance. It speaks to the experiences of Iraqis who were not politically inclined but who still suffered persecution under Saddam Hussein's regime. The fashioning of an Iraqi self in this instance was rooted in everyday practices—such as walking in Baghdad or eating Iraqi dishes, sharing tales of direct persecution, and having religious experiences. No longer a revolutionary who dreamed of changing the status quo, the young Iraqi in Hadjar's narrative was an individual who was entangled in the contradictions of exile and familial expectations and sought an Iraqi experience through daily practices. Though Hadjar grew up listening to her sisters' reminiscences about their middle-class life in Baghdad, she did not perceive middle-class Baghdadis as having a quintessential Iraqi experience. To be an Iraqi in her narrative was to be able to enjoy the common, quotidian experiences that the majority of Iraqis took part in.

Moreover, Hadjar's narrative indicates the multiple ways in which a religious subjectivity is constituted. For Ali, Shi'ism was rooted in transnational religious networks, family lineage, and established religious institutions (such as the faith school or Shi'i organizations he attended in London). Hadjar, however, aimed to carve out an Iraqi religious subjectivity through travel and through her personal pursuit of religious understanding in order to find answers to challenges she faced as an exiled individual who inhabited different places. Religion was not just a relationship between God and the person, but also a platform to craft a subjectivity situated in different localities. In addition, to Hadjar, religion and gender were deeply intertwined in that she found her role models in strong religious women who lived in the past, rather than in the modern Iraqi women who took part in anticolonial struggle. She attributed her strength, resilience, and faith to her readings on Prophet Muhammad's daughter and granddaughter, who led pious lives, wielded tremendous religious knowledge, and dedicated themselves to the well-being of the community. In her daily life, she aimed to emulate these women in order to create a gendered subjectivity that revolved around individual independence and piety.

## Displacement from Home

Hadjar's childhood was neither carefree nor spontaneous. From an early age, she sensed her parents' and relatives' fear and anxiety at the increasing authoritarianism of Saddam Hussein. But her parents were afraid to say anything about Hussein's regime in front of their children for fear that they would repeat what they had heard at school. Stories circulated frequently among Iraqis of people ending up in prisons because their children, when asked by teachers at school, mentioned that their parents cursed Hussein or spat on pictures of him printed in newspapers. Early on, Hadjar realized that all was not right. She heard her parents and relatives whisper behind closed doors and saw them stop in the middle of sentences when they realized that the children were nearby:

> I remember my folks didn't talk about politics in front of us [the children]. Yet at times, you feel there is something not right. The minute we walk in, they stop talking. When we go out, [we overhear them] say they can't speak in front of children. Then they go on to speak about and curse Saddam. . . . So I noticed this, and I remember I used to say to Mom, "Why are you treating me like a kid! I'm not a kid! I know I shouldn't say things outside." She used to get mad at me and say, "Who told you this? There is nothing wrong. We love the president. His picture is hanging on the wall."

One day, the family's caution in front of Hadjar dissipated unexpectedly. Saddam Hussein paid a visit to her school and he talked to her. He asked her if she recognized him:

> I remember I had to be quiet in order to say the right thing. I remember I was thinking, "I must say the right thing." So I went on saying, "Of course I know you. We have your picture on the wall in the house." When I said that, I had a flashback of my brother-in-law spitting on his picture one day but pretending to be cleaning it when he saw me. I remember I also said, "My brother has your picture in his wallet." He said, "Well done. Good girl." I remember the teachers were looking at me anxiously.

Though Hadjar was only around seven years old when she met Hussein, she already understood that her answers would determine the fate of her family. After school, Hadjar ran home to tell her mother that Saddam Hussein visited her school. She found her mother and maternal uncle full of anxiety. The headmistress had already called them and told them that Hadjar had talked to Hussein, and they were worried that Hadjar had said something that would jeopardize the safety of the family. Her uncle held her, kissed her head, and said, "For love's sake, I hope you didn't say anything wrong." This event had caught the family off-guard, and Hadjar experienced her family's fear directly. Later that day, Hadjar received an invitation from Hussein to attend his birthday party. Her mother bought her a new dress for the occasion and warned her not to say much during the party. Hadjar went to the birthday party along with some other children who had been chosen to attend. Hussein put her on his lap and gave her presents. Hadjar found Hussein to be "such a nice guy." She could not believe that this same person was the cause of her and her family's misfortune when her life turned upside down shortly afterward.

One day in 1980, Hadjar's father went missing. He had gone to a meeting at the Chamber of Commerce and did not come back. No one knew his whereabouts. Hadjar's mother and sisters were extremely distressed and cried all the time. Visits and calls from relatives only exacerbated their distress, and her mother began to pack suitcases. Hadjar, only seven at the time, did not understand what was going on but clearly felt the sense of foreboding in the house. She then realized that her family was preparing for deportation and that the visits and calls they received were relaying news of the denaturalization and deportation of friends and relatives. A few days after going missing, her father called to let them know that he was in Iran.

What happened to Hadjar's father is known among Iraqis as the deportation of the merchants, which signaled the start of the expulsion campaign against the *taba'iyya*. On April 7, 1980, the Chamber of Commerce summoned around eight hundred influential and wealthy Shi'i merchants in Baghdad to a meeting, supposedly to provide them with new licenses. The merchants were told to bring all the documents they had—including identity cards, certificates of nationality, property deeds, and licenses. After the merchants arrived at the Chamber of Commerce, state agents ordered them to hand over all their documents and get on buses parked outside the building. The buses drove them to the border with Iran, and there they were told to get out and walk across. The families of these merchants, like Hadjar's, were left to wait anxiously for them to return from the meeting, not knowing what had happened. Bit by bit, rumors of the deportation began to circulate. And before long the merchants' families all faced the same fate.

The expulsion campaign that followed targeted Shi'i Iraqis who were seen as a threat by the regime, especially after the Islamic Revolution in Iran in

1979 and the rise of the Shi'i ulama-led opposition against Saddam Hussein's regime at the end of the 1970s. The regime came to perceive Shi'i Iraqis who hailed from Iran or whose grandparents and great-grandparents held Persian nationality under the Ottomans as a threat to the Iraqi nation.¹ An attempt on the life of Tariq Aziz, a close associate of Hussein, was used as a pretext to expel "the Iranians" from Iraq. At the time, Saddam Hussein said, "Take your belongings and leave. You have come to us bare-foot, and now that the country has educated you into a civilized human being, you are seeking [to rejoin] your paternal uncles [the Iranians]. Go back to them then. This is what we have done in Iraq. . . . There are some Iraqis who have come 50 years ago or their seventh grandfather was non-Iraqi. But once they misbehave, they will remind us of their past affiliation. Then we tell them: You have remembered your background. Leave in a hurry."²

Hussein's statement reflects a long-standing anxiety over the presence of "Iranians" in Iraq, which dates back to the establishment of the Iraqi state in 1921. During the early days of the modern state of Iraq, the presence of "Persians" preoccupied British officials and Iraqi statesmen. For the British and Iraqi ruling elites, the "Persians" (often Shi'i individuals of Arab descent who acquired Persian nationality under the Ottomans) challenged their rule and demanded the genuine independence of Iraq.³ In addition, the Iraqi ruling elites' anxiety over the "Persians" in Iraq was couched in their Arab nationalist ideology, which perceived Sunni Arabs as the quintessential Iraqis and viewed the presence of others—Jews, Kurds, Christians, and Shi'is—as a threat to the nation. Iraqis who held Persian nationality under the Ottomans, or who hailed from Iran generations ago, became suspect in their loyalty to Iraq, especially when they were critical of the government. Decades later, Saddam Hussein employed a similar nationalistic discourse to discredit political opponents, who were characterized as foreign elements within the nation intent on destroying the country. However, Hussein went further than just the use of nationalistic rhetoric to exclude some Iraqis. The British colonial legacy in Iraq, represented by the first Iraqi Nationality Law of 1924, provided the legal apparatus to deport these citizens. The legislation allowing the *taba'iyya* denaturalization, Resolution No. 666 of 1980, was in fact an adaptation of the first Iraqi Nationality Law of 1924, which British officials had drafted and Iraqi statesmen approved in the 1920s. Though the law of 1924 appears on the surface to consider all inhabitants of Iraq as citizens, it relegated the inhabitants who held Persian nationality to a second-class status.[4] The Iraqi Nationality Certificate, an identification document that was attached to the Iraqi Nationality Law, institutionalized differential inclusion in the country by categorizing people on the basis of the nationality they held prior to the establishment of the Iraqi state. Iraqis who held Ottoman nationality were considered first-class citizens, while those with Persian nationality were deemed second-class citizens. These categories were passed from a father to his offspring. It was through this categorization that the label "Iraqis of Iranian origin" became attached to Iraqis who held Persian nationality under the Ottomans.

Hussein's remarks also gesture toward the historic trade and religious networks between Iran and Iraq. These networks spanned Shi'i holy cities in the two countries—in particular, Qum, Najaf, and Karbala—as well as cities on the Iran-Iraq border.[5] Inhabitants of these cities often moved between Iran and Iraq and had family members who were settled in different cities. Religious pilgrimages to holy cities and trade networks were consolidated by family connections that spanned the border. Hadjar's family history was imbricated in these historical transnational connections. Her paternal grandfather came from a city on the Iraq-Iran border whose inhabitants historically had close contacts with Iraq. He settled in Baghdad in the late nineteenth century and established trade networks that spanned the two countries for decades. Under the Ottomans, the father's family opted to keep their Persian nationality to avoid military service in the Ottoman army and taxes, a practice that was common among the Shi'i inhabitants of Ottoman Iraq, whether Arabs or Iranians. After the establishment of the Iraqi state in 1921, the family renounced their Persian nationality and acquired Iraqi citizenship, since they had developed a strong attachment to Iraq.

While the family lived in Iraq for decades with no problems, these transnational connections and networks became suspect under the Ba'th regime, which came to power following the 1968 coup. In 1971, following a dispute between Iran and Iraq over water borders in Shatt al-Arab and the failure of the Ba'th regime to co-opt the support of the Shi'i establishment in this dispute, the Ba'th regime deported around twenty thousand Iraqis of "Iranian origin" to Iran.[6] With the rising tensions between Iran and Iraq following the Islamic

Revolution in Iran and the increasing opposition to the regime from the Shi'i religious establishment in Iraq, Hussein's regime embarked on a massive expulsion campaign in the early 1980s.[7] This time, the expulsion of thousands of families was accompanied by widespread brutality. The regime held families in prisons and prison camps for months before abandoning them on the border with Iran. It confiscated their property and documents and, in some cases, subjected them to rape and torture. The state also ordered the detention of young men between eighteen and twenty-eight. The regime killed many of them and buried them in mass graves. Those who were not deported were forced to collaborate with the regime when the expulsion campaign subsided.

Shortly after the phone call from her father, Hadjar's family was deported. One day, early in the morning, state agents came to the house. Hadjar remembers shouts and screams when the state agents entered the house. The neighbors were out on the street, watching what was going on. Hadjar began to cry because her best friend was crying, knowing that Hadjar was leaving. Her eldest sister, who lived nearby, came when she heard that state agents had come for Hadjar's family. She was not allowed to go with the family because she was married to a cousin whose family held Ottoman nationality. As the family was led to a van, her sister sat on the ground, crying, screaming, beating herself, and throwing dirt on her head. As the van moved away, Hadjar could see her sister and the house disappear in the distance. Hadjar remembers waking up in the middle of the night to her mother's voice. She was asking the driver to continue driving and to forget about a suitcase that had fallen from the roof of the car. Hadjar's mother feared for her daughters because stories of deported women being raped were rampant. Shortly after that, the family arrived in a prison camp, which consisted of a huge room covered in square rugs. Each family was assigned to a square. Hadjar's mother began to talk to other families and learned that some of them had been in the camp for months. The family had to live in deplorable conditions. Taken away from the comfort of their middle-class home, they had to sleep on dirty floors, eat mediocre food, and share utterly filthy bathrooms with other families.

Luckily for Hadjar's family, their stay in the prison camp did not last more than a week. A few days after their arrival, a state agent drove them to the Iran-Iraq border. Hadjar sat in the front with her mother while her five sisters sat in the back. As they approached the border, Hadjar could see her father from a distance. Seeing him for the first time in weeks came as a shock to her. Hadjar was used to seeing her father dressed in traditional Arab clothes. She always thought of him as a strong, confident, and handsome man. However, at the border, Hadjar saw a broken, disheveled man. He was wearing only a *dishdasha* (a plain gown worn by men), and his headgear was untidy. He had a beard, and Hadjar thought he looked dirty. The family reunion was emotional, and everyone, including an Iranian border guard, began to cry. Hadjar's mother tried to reassure her husband, reminding him that he was a merchant and that he could make it all over again. After weeks of anxiety and uncertainty, the family thought the worst had passed. They felt that the family connections and the property Hadjar's father had bought in Iran would enable him to start a new business in Iran and provide the family with a comfortable life for the duration of their stay in Iran.

## Years of Marginalization and Alienation

Unlike many Iraqi deportees who ended up in camps in Iran, Hadjar's family stayed with relatives in the city from which her paternal grandfather hailed. Her father's relatives entertained the family, and they felt welcomed and safe. The family was also relieved that Hadjar's eldest sister and her husband managed to flee Iraq and join the family in Iran. Despite this generosity and support, the family yearned for their own space, so a few weeks after their arrival, the family managed to rent a small house. The gold Hadjar's mother had smuggled from Iraq covered the rent and daily expenses. Hadjar's father thought he would be able to provide his big family with a decent life in Iran because he owned land, but as it turned out, the relative who had the land registered in his name refused to acknowledge the sale. The news left her father in such a shock that he had a stroke and was bedridden for a few months. Her parents had to rely on their eldest son, Ibrahim, who was studying in London, for financial support. He had to cut his studies short to join the family in Iran. During these months, the family was hopeful that their exile in Iran was temporary and that they would go back to Iraq after the regime changed. They believed that Hussein could not stay in power with all the atrocities he was committing. This hope of return was crushed with the outbreak of the Iran-Iraq War in September 1980. At that point, Hadjar's father had recovered from his stroke, and he decided to find a job to support his family.

The outbreak of the Iran-Iraq War not only signaled the loss of the hope of returning to Iraq, but also made life in Iran harder. Because the city where the family lived was on the border with Iraq, Hadjar and her family experienced intense bombing by Iraqi airplanes and later Katyusha rockets. Following the bombing of Hadjar's school during a school day, the family decided to relocate to Mashhad in northeastern Iran. There, her father started a poultry business, and Ibrahim, thinking that the family would be safe and prosperous there, decided to go back to London to finish his studies. The years in Mashhad proved to be difficult, however. The poultry business began to fail when the chickens became infected, and her father was taken ill again. Ibrahim did his best to help the family, but it was not enough:

> The conditions in Mashhad were really bad. The economy was bad. We lived in poverty, poverty, poverty. The poultry died because of an infection, so there was a big loss. My brother had to work in the UK and send us money. So I would say: two years of hell. My shoes had holes in them. Mashhad was cold in the winter. . . . Because the shoes had holes in them, water got into them. I wore plastic bags and then a pair of socks and then another plastic bag and then another pair of socks and then the shoes. The shoes belonged to my sisters. When things did not fit them, I took them.

These economic hardships were exacerbated by political exclusion in Iran. The life of Iraqi deportees, who arrived in Iran with no resources, was made more difficult by the measures taken by the Iranian state. In Iran, the deportees were called "unwelcomed guests" and were seen as Arabs who were competing with the Iranians.[8] They found themselves caught up in a Persian nationalistic discourse that perceived Iran as a Persian nation threatened by others—particularly Arabs following the outbreak of the Iran-Iraq War.[9] This discourse rendered the deportees stateless and without legal rights. They were not allowed to go to universities after finishing high school, buy property, be employed in state positions, or acquire Iranian nationality. Even families like Hadjar's that had ancestors that came from Iran had no rights. The family had the so-called green card, but Hadjar described it as "a humiliation card." The green card represented something negative: that she and her family did not have a nationality or a passport. When she went to register for school, the school administration did not accept her green card and informed her that she had to pay because she was a foreigner. Her father tried to get Iranian nationality, but he was not successful. The family felt lost between two nations. In Iraq, they were told that they were Iranians who did not belong there, while in Iran, they were considered Arabs who could not make claims on the state. Not only did these nationalistic discourses render them stateless, they also left them with no resources to sustain themselves or pursue their goals.

Legal exclusion was accompanied by social prejudice. Hadjar felt that neighbors looked down upon them because they were "Arabs." As a kid, she got into fights with other kids in the street because they called her an Arab. She recollects that "in Iran we're told, 'You're Arabs.' Iranians say Arabs brought us problems and war. People were thinking your airplanes are bombing us." Though Hadjar's family were Shi'i Muslims, like the majority of Iranians, they were still shunned socially due to national differences. The social exclusion Hadjar suffered made her anxious; she just wanted to blend in and "to get lost among the Iranians." She dressed like other Iranian girls her age and spoke perfect Persian. Unfortunately, her mother wore the traditional *abaya*, which showed that she was an Iraqi, thus broadcasting the fact that they were foreigners. When the school administration requested the presence of her mother for Hadjar to register, Hadjar feared they would say she was an Arab. To further complicate matters for Hadjar, her family rejected "the culture of the Ajam [Iranians]" and worried that she was turning into an Iranian girl:

> When I was growing up, my mother would tell me, "I don't want to see you with Iranian girls. You're friends at school only. Outside school, I don't want to see you with them." One of my sisters used to say, "Your behavior is not nice, and you're unrestrained." This is just because I laughed in the street. In Iraq, it is unacceptable for a girl to laugh aloud in public. I remember once my sister saw me walking home from school. I looked back twice. She went mad. She asked me why I was looking back. As soon as I got home, she slapped me, "What is this? Are you looking for boys?" In Iraq, if a girl turns her head, it means she is looking for boys. For Iranians, this wasn't a big deal. Around the age of fourteen, all Iranian girls start looking for a boyfriend. . . .

The Iranian girls noticed I was different and used to ask, "How come you don't have a boyfriend?" I would reply, "This is unacceptable to us. And I prefer to focus on my studies." Blah blah blah. . . . It was these simple things. I remember I used to be stuck in these simple things. It was a different culture.

Moreover, Hadjar grew up feeling that she had missed out on Iraqi experiences. She listened to her sisters reminisce about a culture of Ramadan in Iraq that they thought did not exist in Iran, about trips to holy Shi'i shrines, about night visits to Abboussi Ice Cream, about Iraqi foods like *qaimar* and *pacha*,[10] and about strolls on Abu Nawas Street in the evening. In Iran, Hadjar grew up feeling that she "belonged nowhere." She had no memories of Iraq, and her family and Iranian neighbors did not allow her to be an Iranian. This sense of alienation was aggravated by another, more symbolic, loss. "Hadjar" was not her actual name. She was born Hazar, which is a Kurdish name. However, at the Iranian border, the Iranian official wrote "Hadjar" instead, an Iranian name. For years, Hadjar complained about this name change and always maintained that her name was Hazar. At school, she encountered some problems with her documents due to this name difference. Eventually, the teachers summoned her mother to discuss the discrepancy. At the end of the meeting, her mother asked her to forget about "Hazar" and to accept the fact that she was "Hadjar" now. Hadjar was very upset and cried for a long time. But finally she decided, "I can always call my daughter Hazar when I grow up and have a daughter. The thing is, somehow I let go of 'Hazar,' but I always knew I was 'Hazar.' It was not lost. I decided to give it to someone when I grew up."

Despite these layers of alienation, Hadjar was surrounded by Iraqi culture through her family. Her sisters all married Iraqi men. They rejected well-to-do Iranian suitors and chose Arab Iraqis who had fled persecution in Iraq and made it to Iran. At home, she was not allowed to speak Persian; she spoke Kurdish with her mother and the Iraqi dialect with her sisters. A vague sense of Iraqiness was instilled in her through her sisters in particular:

> I can always say that my family didn't want me to lose their memory, and I think they kept it alive in me by trying always to teach me about it. . . . Everything was Iraq. And I think somehow I saw that. I saw the struggles. I saw that when my sisters said, "Shame on such and such. How could he do such

things! In Iraq, we wouldn't do such things. . . ." I so loved my eldest sisters because they were the most beautiful, the most amazing, the best looking. When they put on lipstick, I used to love it. This is why I had that connection with my sisters. So when they say something like "you behave like Iranian girls," I would say, "No! I'm not Iranian."

Hadjar's eldest sisters, through their reminiscences about Iraq and criticism of Iranian lifestyle, managed to keep the notion of Iraq alive in her. They employed a sisterly bond to make sure that Hadjar did not lose connection with their home country.

## The Search for Roots through Routes

After the end of the Iran-Iraq War, Hadjar's family decided to join Ibrahim in London. The fact that Saddam Hussein remained in power after the war further dimmed the hope of return. They thought that they had no future in Iran and that relocating to London would provide the family with legal protection, citizenship, and a stable life. Her family applied for asylum to the United Kingdom through the United Nations. Since her brother was living in Britain at the time, her family got asylum easily and was granted indefinite leave to remain status upon arrival in the airport in London. The British government provided the family with council housing and social benefits.

Hadjar was sixteen when her family arrived in London. The move was a cultural shock to Hadjar. Everything was a source of surprise: a woman in a miniskirt at Heathrow Airport, a Coke bottle in a vending machine falling at the press of a button, and Indian, Chinese, and Black students in her classroom. Hadjar felt lonely in the United Kingdom, and she yearned for Iran and her Iranian friends. Unlike Ali, who went to a faith school and lived in a neighborhood in London popular among Iraqis, Hadjar lived in a neighborhood where few Iraqis lived and went to a state school not frequented by Iraqis. The fact that she could not speak English well made it difficult for her to make friends at school or in the neighborhood. These difficulties were exacerbated by her family's inability to understand why she was always tearfully asking to go back to Iran. While she had the support of her sisters, she felt that she struggled more because of her veil (her sisters were not veiled at the time). Things only began to change a year later when she came to terms with being different and learned to speak English without a Persian accent. Nevertheless, her anxiety about her sense of belonging persisted. She was in a country she could not relate to, but she could no longer see herself as an Iranian, Iraqi, or Kurd either. In London, she met Kurds, but she felt she had nothing in common with them. At this point, faith began to play a central part in her life. It became a means to construct a Shi'i subjectivity that connected her to Iranian, Iraqi, and Shi'i Kurdish roots. Shi'i Islam was the one thing that she shared with these three groups. Religious beliefs, in addition to giving Hadjar comfort that she was special to God, became a way for her to affirm a sense of national belonging.

In her mid-twenties, Hadjar's feeling of loss and confusion again became aggravated. She felt alienated from the Iraqi and Muslim communities in London, and her connection to her faith waned. She kept wearing the veil, but only out of habit, rather than religious conviction. This period of turmoil was compounded after the engagement of her sister Shaima, who was four years older. During their stay in Iran, the family had charged Shaima with watching over Hadjar, and the two sisters had formed a special bond. Now Shaima's engagement reordered her world. Hadjar felt that she was losing Shaima, who had always held her hand. At the same time, she began to see a therapist to deal "with wounds" she had left untended to for decades. During this time, she said, her family became her "worst enemy." She was hardly ever at home, and she looked for an apartment to move to. All she wanted was to have fun, relax, and fill the vacuum left by Shaima's marriage. She then met an English man, John, who made her feel even further removed from her family. Although she felt happy with John, she became anxious about the relationship—especially with regard to premarital sex. It was not so much that it was immoral, but that "it was not possible because it is not part of my life." Though Hadjar was rebelling against her family, she could not escape the Iraqi social norms instilled in her by her family, which dictated that a woman should wait until marriage to have sex. In this instance, sexuality connected Hadjar to Iraq through her gendered embodiment of "the good Iraqi girl."[11] Thus, Iraqi social norms doomed the relationship, and after a while the couple broke up.

A year after Shaima's marriage, Hadjar went through a religious transformation. On a visit to one of her sisters, she was looking at the books on the shelves and found a volume by the prominent Lebanese Shi'i scholar

Mohammed Hussein Fadhallah. The book was titled *Dunyia ash-Shabab* (The world of the youth), and it consisted of questions and answers concerning issues facing young Muslims. Intrigued by Fadhallah's openness, Hadjar spent hours reading through the book, despite her weak Arabic. Fadhallah argued that belief in God and his Prophet is enough for a person to go to Paradise. After reading this comment, Hadjar felt that she had a chance to be accepted by God again, even though she was no longer praying or fasting. A day later, she went to another sister's house to spend the night and came across some pamphlets for Hajj left on a table. Hadjar picked up a pamphlet and thought that, after all, she could go on a pilgrimage because God had not forsaken her. At night, Hadjar dreamed that she was stuck in a train in London and could not breathe because of the heat. English people around her were asking her to take off her veil. Then a breeze came from one end of the train. Hadjar looked up and saw a man chanting a prayer that Muslims recite during a pilgrimage: "Ever at Your service, O Allah, ever at Your service. Ever at Your Service, You have no partner, ever at Your service." Hadjar began chanting as well, and the breeze came her way. Hadjar woke up from the dream screaming the chant and decided to go on Hajj.

Going to Mecca for the first time became part of the journey Hadjar embarked on in 2002 to "know herself." On her way, she visited the shrine of Sayyida Zainab in Damascus to connect with her Shi'i faith. In the story of Ashura, Sayyida Zainab was a model of strong Muslim womanhood. Ashura commemorates the martyrdom of the Prophet's grandson Imam Hussein in the seventh century in Karbala. After the martyrdom, the women and children were taken as captives to Yazid in Damascus. Sayyida Zainab, who was Hussein's sister and a granddaughter of the Prophet, showed tremendous courage and leadership at the time and challenged Yazid's authority. She also became important in narrating the events in Karbala for posterity. While the trip to Damascus affirmed Hadjar's Shi'i faith by connecting her to the martyrdom of Hussein, it also served to link her to a female role model in Zainab, a powerful Shi'i Muslim woman that Hadjar could look up to. Hadjar believes that her own strength, independence, coping skills, and leadership are inspired by Zainab's qualities. To Hadjar, Sayyida Zainab was "an independent, strong-minded, outspoken Muslim woman, who challenged the concept of a repressed Muslim woman." Hadjar's perception of Zainab as a female role model reflected a shift in the discourse on gender among devout Iraqis. Rather than look to the modern Iraqi women who were politically active in the 1950s, Hadjar looked for role models in the history of Shi'ism.[12]

After spending a few days in Damascus, Hadjar went on a pilgrimage to Mecca and Medina to connect with God after years of lack of practice. Rather than trying to prove the existence of God, Hadjar wanted God to prove to her that He had not forsaken her:

> When I was on pilgrimage, every time I talked to Him, in seconds something happened, and He gave me the answers. That was the reason for my Hajj. I am not trying to prove You exist, but I want You to prove to me that You are looking at me, that You notice me, that You feel me. Glory to God, He never failed to prove that to me. During Hajj, I would make a request, and He would grant it to me. Once, I got lost in Hajj, and I would pray: "God, how am I going to find my way?" All of a sudden, I saw someone from my group in front of me. . . . There were many incidents like that. . . . At the time, I felt, "I'm chosen. I'm the special one. You chose me for Hajj."

Visiting the house of God in Mecca and Sayyida Zainab in Damascus affirmed Hadjar's sense of belonging as well as her faith as a Shi'i and as a Muslim. Rather than familial memories about Iraq or forbidden attachments to Iran, Hadjar could have her own experiences and memories of places. These journeys enabled her to cultivate a religious subjectivity anchored in sacred localities. Her connection to the sacred, whether the feeling of proximity to God through Hajj or the story of Karbala, entailed journeys to holy places. These sacred localities, moreover, enabled Hadjar to fashion an identity connected to physical places.[13] While Iran and Iraq were elusive places, Mecca, Medina, and Damascus emerged as concrete locations where Hadjar could feel at home. Hadjar went on the pilgrimage to connect with God and Sayyida Zainab, but her journeys were characterized by unexpected encounters that connected her to specific geographies. Inhabiting a religious self was rooted in, and routed through, holy places.

These journeys also made Hadjar yearn to visit Iraq—in particular, Najaf and Karbala. The trip to Sayyida Zainab filled her with veneration for Imam Hussein and the tragedy of Karbala. It was not Iraq per se that she wanted to visit, since it represented a place that "destroyed my father, destroyed me, and destroyed us." Rather, Hadjar wanted to visit the holy shrine of Imam Hussein. Going on *ziyara* (religious visit to a holy place) to Imam Hussein would complement her pilgrimage to Mecca. After returning from Mecca in 2002, she went to the Iraq embassy in London to apply for a visa. Hadjar took a copy of her father's nationality certificate, which her mother had smuggled out of Iraq. Upon looking at the document, the Iraqi employee at the embassy informed her that she was not allowed to go to Iraq because her father was *taba'iyya*. Hadjar's began to cry when she heard the word *taba'iyya*. At that moment, she felt that she was an Iraqi because she had been born in the country and that a representative of Saddam Hussein's regime had no right to tell her that she was not. When Hadjar left the embassy, she prayed to Imam Hussein that Saddam Hussein's regime would be toppled soon so that she could go and visit the imam. Less than a year later, the U.S. invasion brought down Saddam Hussein's regime. Hadjar, who believed that the invasion was Imam Hussein's response to her prayer, had mixed feelings about it:

> I couldn't believe the fall of the regime. It was like, "Wow. I'll go to Iraq. I'll go and visit Imam Hussein." But the feeling was very mixed. I so wanted Saddam to be gone so that I could go back. At the same time, I was angry with the Americans and the Brits, that they waited too long, and the only reason they took action was because Saddam was turning against them. I was quite angry with them that they allowed this guy to do all these things, and now they wanted to get rid of him in the name of freedom of Iraq. I didn't buy the story. They did it for their best interests. I thought we could do something about America. We can get rid of them one day, but at least we got rid of Saddam. It is like choosing between the lesser of two evils. The war meant I could go back.

Hadjar's position on the U.S. invasion echoed the views of most Iraqis I met in London, who had grown desperate for regime change to come from within the country. Hadjar imagined external military intervention was the only possible way to remove Hussein from power. Despite her ambivalence toward the invasion, she welcomed it. As she told me, she did not care about the worldwide antiwar protests. What she cared about was "a free Iraq" that she could visit. As such, the invasion signaled the end of exile and the possibility of visiting Iraq after more than twenty years. Iraq was no longer a forbidden place to her. Within months after George W. Bush announced the end of the military campaign in Iraq, Hadjar bought an airplane ticket to Amman to go to Baghdad.[14] After buying the ticket, she informed her family of her decision to go to Iraq. The decision caused an uproar. Though Hadjar had traveled abroad alone before, her family did not approve of a single woman going to Iraq on her own. They feared that Iraqis in Iraq would frown upon such a visit and would consider her family unconcerned about the reputation of their daughter. However, Hadjar stood her ground. She refused to cancel her trip and argued that Imam Hussein would protect her in Iraq. In the end, the family came around, and Hadjar went to Iraq.

As soon as Hadjar landed in Amman, her family got in touch with friends in Amman to find a trustworthy taxi driver to take her to Iraq. Though Hadjar arrived in Amman at night, she decided not to wait until morning to leave for Baghdad. She arrived at the Iraqi border at dawn. As she walked into the immigration building, she saw Iraqi men shouting and screaming and wearing *dishdasha*:

> I thought, "This sounds like home." I can't tell you how fantastic it felt to be somewhere where everybody spoke the same language. . . . Then I got to the immigration officer. He looked at my passport and asked why I was visiting Iraq. Honestly, I had no answer. I just said I wanted to come home. It came out naturally. It just came from the bottom of my heart. He asked me to go back to the taxi. After five minutes, he came back and said in English, "Welcome home, ma'am." Oh, my tears. It was so emotional. Then we were on the highway. I could see American soldiers and burned tanks. . . . I saw Iraqi cars with signs: "Iraq/Baghdad," "Iraq/Karbala," etcetera. I was looking in disbelief. Then I saw palm trees. I screamed, "Oh my god! This is a palm tree." . . . These little things were Iraq. Then I saw a sign: "Baghdad Welcomes You." And I began to cry. I could not believe it. . . . It hit me when we got to Tahrir Square.[15] That was it. Tahrir Square represented Baghdad to me. Every time we saw the Iraqi TV station, it was Tahrir Square on the news.

Arriving at her cousin's house, Hadjar relished the little details that constituted Iraq to her, such as sitting on an Iraqi sofa (*karawita*), sleeping on the roof, walking in Adhamiyya, going to Abboussi Ice Cream, sitting in the garden, seeing the Tigris, and eating famous Iraqi dishes, such as *pacha*.

To her, these little things represented home and constituted her as an Iraqi. Hadjar had yearned for these experiences all her life as she grew up listening to stories her sisters told about Iraq. The trip presented her with the opportunity to have her own experiences of Baghdad. However, her arrival in Baghdad was accompanied by disenchantment as well. As Hadjar passed through neighborhoods with her cousin, she could not believe that these areas were the same ones her sisters remembered fondly. The sisters reminisced about beautiful, well-kept neighborhoods, but Hadjar saw neglected and dusty streets. She was particularly shocked when she could not recognize the house where she had grown up. The house had been turned into a police station after her family was deported. After the fall of Hussein's regime, the house was abandoned and left in poor condition. As Hadjar walked in, she saw a once-beautiful house that was now "bare and horrible." The balconies were no longer there. The windows in the bedrooms were bricked up. The kitchen, which her mother had refurbished with wood cupboards and marble floors before their deportation, consisted only of a sink and a faucet. Hadjar began to cry. She cried for her mother, father, and sisters. She had flashbacks of her mother screaming from the kitchen and her father walking in after work. The current condition of the house left her shaken and shocked.

Hadjar's next destination was the holy Shi'i shrine cities of Najaf and Karbala. She was eager to visit the tomb of Imam Hussein in Karbala, but her cousin told her that people visit Imam Ali's tomb in Najaf first, and then they visit his sons in Karbala. The visit to Imam Ali was very emotional for Hadjar, who was "awe-stricken." Najaf had been a forbidden place to her, since she could not visit Iraq until the regime change, and now to stand in the presence of Imam Ali's tomb felt like "entering paradise." Hadjar grabbed the bars of the tomb and sat on the floor, crying and trembling. After Najaf, Hadjar went to Karbala. She felt that Karbala was more welcoming and calming, despite the injustice associated with it because of the martyrdom of the grandson of the Prophet. She recalled, "I felt Imam Hussein embrace me. I could not believe that I'm saying the prayer of Imam Hussein in his presence. For years, I said the prayer from afar. For once, I could sit and say, 'As-salamu 'alayka, ya aba Abdullah.'"[16] He was in front of me. It was really fantastic." Like the trips to Damascus and Mecca, the trips to Najaf and Karbala enabled Hadjar to embody a religious subjectivity that is performed in the acts of visitation and prayer. This subjectivity, moreover, had a distinctive Iraqi and Shi'i element in that it is a story of a Shi'i tragedy that unfolded in Iraq. Becoming a Shi'i Muslim was rooted in a religious trajectory that was produced and reproduced in the act of homecoming.

Hadjar stayed in Iraq for two weeks. She visited different parts of the country and Baghdad. The trip allowed her to begin to have her own memories of Iraq. And having a firsthand experience of Iraq, she was truly able to identify as an Iraqi:

> I'm glad I went to Iraq in 2003. That was it. When I came back, I knew where I came from. I was so proud of myself, so proud of being an Iraqi. I got in touch with Iraqi culture, Iraqi music, Iraqi this, Iraq that. . . . Now I knew what my family talked about. I heard a lot about Iraq from my sisters. Now, I can say I was there. All of a sudden, it is a reality. It was no longer a vision from my sisters. . . . At first, I wanted to go to Iraq in order to visit Najaf and Karbala. I think by going there, everything came to one place, and I was Kurdish, Shi'i, and Iraqi. They all represented one country for me. My identities started to intermix. As a Kurd, I'm an Iraqi. As a Shi'i, I'm an Iraqi. That was it. I'm Iraqi, which means I'm Kurdish-Iraqi, Shi'i Iraqi. That was my identity now. . . . I'm also British-Iraqi. I know I'm not English, but I'm British. This is important, because you can still be an Iraqi as well as British. Being British means I can be an Iraqi, and I can be a Muslim. You can be anything because it is a nationality. I studied here. I grew up here. It was my Britishness that allowed me to go to Iraq.

Hadjar, like most young Iraqis I met in London, was concerned about the question of home and selfhood, and she had a complex understanding of what constituted them. Unlike Hanan and Khalil, whose notion of home was straightforward and rooted within the parameters of a secular, Iraqi nation and a disavowal of sectarian and ethnic markers, the younger generation's notion of home was not fixed or clear. Hadjar was attuned to the discourse of hybrid identities and multiple homes dominant in the United Kingdom, and she perceived of her identity as consisting of multiple religious, ethnic, and national components. Iraqiness became a prism that included other identities. Unlike Iraqi nationalists, who perceived the religious and the ethnic as a threat to the nation-state, Hadjar saw national, ethnic, and religious identities as intertwined in ways that affirm each other. This multifaceted subjectivity was coupled with a distinctive British identity as well. Hadjar expanded the notion of Britishness to include Iraqi and Muslim components. Britishness is no longer limited to categories like British-Irish or British-Welsh, but accommodates categories like British-Iraqi and British-Muslim. Hadjar, moreover, thought that it was her Britishness that enabled her to discover her Kurdish, Shi'i, Iraqi roots. Home itself became an elastic notion that included multiple locations and affirmed multiple subjectivities. It was rooted in, and routed through, journeys to Mecca, Baghdad, Najaf, Karbala, and back to London.

## Shifting Identities and Homes

Since I met Hadjar in 2006, she has been to Mecca, Baghdad, Karbala, and Najaf many times. She has constantly felt the need to make these journeys to affirm her Shi'i faith and her sense of belonging to her Iraqi and Kurdish roots. It was through the performance of religious rituals and mundane Iraqi acts—such as eating certain dishes or taking walks in certain neighborhoods in Baghdad—that Hadjar cultivated a religious and national subjectivity rooted in these places. These constant journeys, however, were defined by unexpected encounters that shifted Hadjar's notion of home and subjectivity. When I interviewed Hadjar again in 2017, she emphasized the importance of a British identity to her, though she still identified as Iraqi-British. She thought her previous identity as a Shi'i-Iraqi and Kurdish-Iraqi were extenuated due to her frequent visits to Iraq and Saudi Arabia. During her trip to Iraq in 2014, Hadjar decided to get her family's national documents so that they could claim the properties that had been confiscated under Hussein's regime. But encountering the Iraqi bureaucracy, a corrupt system defined by long delays and expectations of bribes, her sense of Iraqiness was shaken. She also complained when people cut in line. This attitude—refusing to give bribes and insisting that people wait their turn—made her an object of ridicule. People laughed at her and told her that she was "an outsider" coming from London. Moreover, during that trip, Hadjar saw more cruelty in Baghdad, such as a woman hiring a child to carry her heavy groceries or a man kicking a child for making a mistake. She thought this kind of treatment would not be tolerated in the United Kingdom, where child protection laws penalized such acts.

Hadjar thus began to feel that she did not "fit in," that she had found something during that trip that she did not want to be part of. In addition, daily life in Iraq seemed to get more difficult with each visit. She remarked, "During that trip, I could see everything. I could see the traffic, the meaninglessness. It was so ridiculous why people had to live like that. The fear of bombing. The fear of whether you'll come back or not come back." She still wanted to belong to Iraq, but she was happy that she could leave the country.

In addition, during her frequent trips to Mecca and Medina to perform Hajj, or 'Umrah,[17] Hadjar met more Sunni Muslims who had views similar to hers, except that they believed that Omar and Abu-Bakr, rather than Imam Ali, were "the chosen ones."[18] Though Hadjar saw herself as a practicing Shi'i Muslim who followed Imam Ali and commemorated Ashura, simply being a Muslim became more important to her. For instance, back in 2006, Hadjar thought that she would never marry a non-Shi'i man. But a decade later, sectarian differences were no longer an important issue to her. Hadjar's frequent trips to Saudi Arabia caused a shift in her understanding of faith. The performance of Hajj and 'Umrah with millions of Muslims at the same time enabled her to carve out a Muslim subjectivity open to the broader Muslim world beyond Shi'i doctrine.

Hadjar also began to have more difficulty connecting with her Kurdishness. She still could not connect to Iraqi Kurds in northern Iraq due to linguistic differences (Hadjar spoke Fayli Kurdish, dominant among Shi'i Kurds, while the majority of Iraqi Kurds spoke Sorani Kurdish) and different ideas about the future of the Kurds within the Iraqi state. Hadjar also felt alienated from the idea of Kurdish racial superiority embraced by the two main Iraqi Kurdish parties in Kurdistan, since it prioritized the notion of race over Iraq, whereas she prioritized the integrity of the Iraqi nation-state over an independent Kurdistan. What defined her relationship to Shi'i Kurdishness was a familial connection—in particular, the connection to her father and his family from Iran—rather than a nationalistic affiliation with Kurdistan. Nevertheless, she went to the city on the Iran-Iraq border from which her grandfather hailed to become acquainted with her Kurdish roots. Moreover, Hadjar's understanding of her Kurdishness had a gendered element. Hadjar ascribed her independence and strong character to the fact that she is a Kurd. Kurdish women, she believed, "are not controlled like in some other cultures," and a Kurdish woman is "her own boss." Thus, being an independent woman became closely intertwined with Kurdishness in Hadjar's narrative. While faith and national belonging became loosely associated with Iraq over the years, family roots and female independence were linked to Kurdishness.

These shifting identities—whether Iraqi, Shi'i, Muslim, or Kurdish—made Hadjar feel more British:

> When we last spoke [2006], it was much more about being Iraqi, and that meant a lot to me. It is now that, but it is no longer a strong part. I'm Iraqi. I'm Kurdish. I'm Muslim. I'm Shi'i. These are all my identities, but I think my Britishness comes up a lot more. . . . I think being British allowed me to be different. While if you're Iraqi, it is either this or that. Being British means you can be Asian, Chinese, Black African, Middle Eastern. In that way, I always say being British is a combination, and I'm British-Iraqi. Previously, I was Iraqi, Shi'i, Muslim. I'm not sure if that is a major identity for me at this stage. It was at that point in my life. Maybe my Britishness is very much about my ideology in life and the way I see other people.

Over the years, Hadjar grew wary of naming her Shi'ism, Kurdishness, and Iraqiness as the main markers of her selfhood. She thought these identities marginalized and excluded people different from her: "If I say I am a Shi'i, it means I reject the Sunnis or I'm prioritizing my faith over somebody's else. If I were to say I'm Muslim, it means somebody else is a Christian, not necessarily equal to me. I'm Iraqi, but what about the Iranian side of me? And then I'm Kurdish, but what about the Shi'i in me, because the Kurds are Sunnis and they are rejecting Arabs? When I say I'm British, I'm allowed to be everything." Britishness came to indicate a marker of inclusion, not only of Hadjar's multiple identities but also of groups who are religiously and ethnically different. It is associated with hybridity, rather than the racial superiority of whiteness. Being British enabled Hadjar to write each of her multiple identities into the social fabric of British society. For her, British subjectivity is defined by heterogeneity and diversity. This vision marks a disavowal of provincial identities and celebrates the nation-state as a space of inclusion. However, it is Britain, rather than Iraq, that emerges as the cosmopolitan place capable of inclusion.

Though Hadjar attempted to subvert the dominant association of Britishness with Englishness, she still subscribed to a Western multicultural discourse. In her narrative, Britain emerges as a "multicultural society" defined by tolerance of others. Hadjar believed that if she were to say that she was Kurdish or Iraqi, she would not be "as tolerant of other people's differences and religions." Interestingly, like many young Iraqis I met in London, Hadjar reproduced the discourse dominant in Western societies that perceives the West as a place of tolerance while associating non-Western societies with intolerance. During my interviews with her, I asked her many times about her experience in Britain—in particular, if she had faced discrimination or marginalization due to her otherness. She always asserted that British society was open and accepting and that she had never experienced discrimination at work or in the street.[19] To her, Britain was the country that granted her and her family legal papers and a future, unlike Iraq or Iran. This idealistic view of Britain silenced the colonial and imperial legacy of Britain, as well as the history of discrimination and exclusion of others within British society. Indeed, when I asked Hadjar how she felt about the fact that Britain occupied part of Iraq in 2003, she was taken aback by the question and was silent for a long time. She said that she never thought about this issue, maybe because it was a difficult one to come to terms with. She remarked, "I don't have an answer for it. I think I have two separate selves. They don't meet halfway. You know, the split personality. I don't see myself as either Iraqi or British. I see myself both. If I was just Iraqi, then I would have issues with them invading Iraq. If I was just British, or the other way around, how do I feel? I'm more angry at the Americans. Maybe because I'm able to do that. . . . To me, the Brits didn't do a dirty job as the Americans did in Abu Ghraib. The Brits just went to Basra and played football with Iraqis."

## A Graveyard

As I was wrapping up my last interview with Hadjar, I asked her what she identified as her home. Hadjar was silent for a long time. She finally said that it was odd to say, but there was not just one place. After a few seconds, she told me that London was home, since she always returned there after her journeys and since this is where she had lived the longest time. After a short pause, she talked about her trip to Wadi al-Salam cemetery in Najaf, where her parents were buried.[20] There were six spots left in the family lot. Hadjar chose one of them to be her grave. "I want to be buried there. When you said where is home, I straightaway had a flashback to that place. You'll be surprised. I slept in it for a second. I went inside it to know what it is like. I said I'll come here when I'm dead." She elaborated on the experience:

> When I slept in the grave, I felt comfortable. It was nice and chilled and comfortable. I had no fear. I just lied there in it, and my cousin pretended he was reading to me the final verses they read to a dead body before they shut the grave. He started reading that to me. I felt so good in there. I touched the ground and I said I'll come back to you. I didn't plan it. I was there. I wanted this for me. I talked to the grave and said, "Don't take anyone except me." I said to the grave, "Don't allow anyone. You're mine." My mom always said if you give something to the earth, it'll never betray you, but if you give something to a human being, they will always betray you. I took her word for it. I never thought about [where home is] until you said it. You said "Where is home?" and I had a flashback of the grave.

Death would entail yet another journey for Hadjar: to be buried in a place where she felt home. The sacredness of the soil of Najaf offered permanence to her identity in death, unlike the fluidity of her identity in life.[21] However, death would not only entail a permanence of identity, but would also negate the colonial and imperial legacies that shaped Hadjar's life. The British colonial rule, through the legislation of the first Iraqi Nationality Law, rendered Hadjar's family second-class citizens and led to their deportation to Iran under Saddam Hussein's reign. The United States' support of Hussein in the 1980s and the decision to keep him in power in the 1990s prolonged Hadjar's exile for more than two decades. The U.S. occupation of Iraq in 2003 both opened up and foreclosed possibilities for Hadjar. On the one hand, the invasion led to regime change and enabled Hadjar to go and visit Iraq. On the other hand, it revealed to her the harsh realities under which Iraqis lived. As such, colonial and imperial realities led to displacement from Iraq and disillusionment with the status quo there.[22] However, upon her death, Hadjar wanted to make one last journey to be reunited with the soil of Najaf and to negate the imperial conditions that she would constantly struggle with during her life in her efforts to define home and to shape a coherent subjectivity.

# IN THE AFTERMATH OF DESTRUCTION

The Iran-Iraq War came to a sudden end in August 1988. The cessation of hostilities brought relief and, with it, the tragic realization that regime change was not in view. While the fighting had stopped, the apparatus of the security state remained unchanged and the targeting of dissident voices continued. In early 1990, when the regime unexpectedly lifted the ban on travel, we decided to go to London to visit my mother's two sisters. It meant that I would have two months' peace of mind, without the need for self-censorship or the feeling of being on heightened alert. The first month provided a great respite, but before long everything was turned upside down. On August 2, we woke up to the news that Iraqi troops had invaded Kuwait. The following month was filled with anxiety and uncertainty. Should we stay in London, or should we return to Iraq? Is a war going to take place, or not? Is the Iraqi army going to withdraw at the last minute, or is Saddam Hussein going to drag Iraq into yet another war? My mother thought that it was best to return. She also firmly believed that the regime would not survive this fatal mistake. With or without a war, the regime would collapse. My sister and I were worried about staying in the United Kingdom because switching schools was intimidating. Staying also meant that my mother would lose her job in Iraq, as well as everything she had built over the last twenty years. We finally agreed to go back.

The Iraq we returned to was different. The markets were filled with looted merchandise from Kuwait. We had heard about the looting on the news when we were in London, but to see its magnitude firsthand was sobering. Like many Iraqis we knew, we boycotted the looted goods. In addition, the price of food suddenly increased due to the trade and financial embargoes that were part of the UN-imposed sanctions on Iraq following its invasion of Kuwait. The prices of basic commodities like rice, flour, sugar, and oil more than quadrupled. Iraq was allowed to import certain medications and food items, but with restrictions. The regime started a monthly ration to make sure that everyone had enough food. There was also an acute sense of uncertainty among people, which only intensified on the eve of January 15, 1991, the UN-designated deadline for Iraq's withdrawal from Kuwait. In the meantime, military bravado pervaded daily life. The regime named the imminent war that the U.S.-led coalition forces were about to wage as the "Mother of All Battles" and bragged that all Iraqis would defend their country against all invaders.

On January 17, our neighborhood, like most of Baghdad, became eerily quiet. Most people had fled Baghdad in anticipation of the war. We went to bed that night not knowing what the next day would hold. Around 2:30 a.m., we woke to the sound of bombs. The bombing was relentless for the first three days, particularly at night. On the third day, we decided to leave Baghdad after Iraq launched missiles into Israel. We made plans to go to Najaf to stay with one of my father's distant relatives. My mother grew increasingly uncomfortable having two girls in the house when young men who were not from the neighborhood began to roam the streets. We were also afraid that Baghdad would be the target of a chemical attack by the coalition forces led by the United States. The bombing was much less intense in Najaf. After about three weeks, we heard that people were returning to Baghdad. Some people said the coalition forces were targeting bridges. We did not want to get stuck in Najaf in case all the bridges in Baghdad were bombed, so we decided to go back home.

Baghdad was surreal. The city was engulfed in black smoke. The streets were empty. As we approached Al-Sarrafiyya Bridge, my sister drove extremely slowly for fear of falling into the Tigris if the bridge was bombed while we were on it. When we got home, we discovered that someone had broken into the house. We entered cautiously in case someone was still there. Thieves had emptied all the drawers of their contents and thrown them all over the house. Many precious things were gone. That night, the sounds of bombing invaded the house just like the strangers who had robbed us, and we sensed the profound insecurity that would come to define life in the 1990s.

The end of the Gulf War left us in disbelief. The regime had managed to survive yet another devastating war and brutally put down uprisings in the south and north of the country. Immediately following the war, we began to remember the 1980s with nostalgia as a time of comfort and plenty. The heavy bombardment of Iraq, coupled with the sanctions, had taken its toll on Iraqi society. The war had destroyed most of the country's infrastructure. Although a reconstruction campaign began immediately after the war, basic services—especially electricity and telephone lines—were never restored to prewar levels. Power cuts became common and lasted for hours at a time. During the academic year, we relied on candles and lanterns to study at night. These outages hit the hardest during the summers, when temperatures got as high as 120°F (50°C). Perhaps even worse, the regime failed to inform people when it stopped purifying the drinking water due to the lack of necessary chemicals. As a result, there was an outbreak of gastroenteritis in 1992, which caused me to be hospitalized for three days. Water often tasted metallic and was undrinkable on some days. Everyone started boiling water before drinking it. The impact of the heavy bombardment on the environment was felt immediately and daily. During the war, the ground was always covered with a layer of soot after it rained. When the war was over, trees suddenly dried up and died. People were diagnosed with cancer and babies were born deformed or sick.

Things continued to get worse. Prices of basic food items kept going up because the food ration was not enough. Medicine became even harder to find. In 1993, the regime took a step that literally changed life overnight. It severed the Iraqi dinar from gold and began to print massive amounts of currency. The value of the dinar plummeted, and inflation, which had begun with the imposition of the sanctions, reached staggering levels. In 1980, one Iraqi dinar equaled three US dollars; around 1992, twenty-two dinars equaled one US dollar; and only a year later, around two thousand Iraqi dinars equaled one US dollar. If you had fifteen thousand Iraqi dinars in 1980, you could buy a small house. In the 1990s, fifteen thousand dinars would only buy five kilograms of tomatoes. People's savings and salaries became worthless. This exacerbated the postwar state of insecurity in Baghdad. Gone were the days when we went to bed without locking the main door or the car. Robberies were common, and we had to install an alarm system in the car and put a chain with a heavy lock on our gate at night. Either my sister or I had to go with my mother to the market to stay in the car because if left unattended someone might try to steal it. And almost always one of us stayed in the house to make sure no one broke in.

Corruption and bribes became commonplace and publicly visible. Government employees demanded bribes for processing any paperwork. Prostitution was rampant, as were young children begging in the streets. My mother's students openly boasted of getting high grades on certain courses because they got their professor's car a set of tires—an especially popular item among university professors—and would ask my mother if she needed anything. Some of my mother's colleagues urged her "to ease up" and accept student "assistance," but she refused to compromise her integrity. We managed to make ends meet by relying on my mother's salary, exchanging dollars we had saved, and using food we had stored before prices went up. In Iraq, most people had a pantry and big freezers in the house. Under Hussein's regime, shortages of one kind or another were part of everyday life. Sometimes there was a rice shortage. At other times, soap was not available. Meat, chicken, and eggs were always scarce. We always stocked up on whatever was available in the market, anticipating future shortages. We managed to accumulate hand soap, detergent, facial tissues, salt, rice, tea, oil, and sugar, all of which could last us for years. My bedroom became a storage space. During the 1980s we froze meat, chicken, and eggs for years. Expiration dates on medication or food items were ignored. The dry-stored items especially came in handy during the blockade. My mother's salary mainly went to fill the car with gas and to buy basic items, such as fresh vegetables and fruits, gas cylinders, and heating oil.

The rhythm of daily life changed as well. We began to spend more time preparing food. For instance, we had to bake our own bread. The quality of the flour used in bread sold in the market was very bad, as was the flour distributed in the ration. We had to sieve the flour many times before using it to make our own pita bread, a tiresome and time-consuming task, especially in the summer heat. Also, the dried food distributed in the ration or sold in the market—such as dried broad beans and pasta—was often rotten. Pasta bags had dead worms in them, and we had to wash the pasta many times before boiling it. Broad beans often had worms in them, too, and we had to soak them for hours before cutting each one open sidewise to remove the spoiled part. Nobody would even consider the idea of throwing away food in the 1990s.

Even though we managed to make ends meet, we were always worried about the future. We could take nothing for granted anymore. What if prices kept increasing? What if we could no longer sell the US dollars we had from the trip to London, especially because they were technically illegal to sell? What if we ran out of food? The specter of hunger and destitution was real and manifested itself all around us. People's clothes became shabby, and during the winter, everyone shivered in the cold, not having enough money to buy warm things. Many began to look malnourished. To make ends meet, people began to sell household and personal items, such as rugs, jewelry, cars, china sets, and even the doors of their houses. But thanks to my mother's thrift, which she had learned from her mother, we managed to maintain a decent standard of living.

( CHAPTER 5 )

# DISPOSSESSION AND AUTHENTICITY

I met Rasha for the first time in 2006 during a dinner get-together organized by a group of young British-Iraqis in London called We Are Iraqis. Rasha had only left Iraq in 2004 following the death of a close friend in a car explosion near the Green Zone in Baghdad and the bombing of the international humanitarian organization where she worked. During our conversation, I learned that Rasha's family had fled Iraq that summer and arrived as refugees in Damascus due to the spiraling sectarian violence in the country. The family had received death threats from extremist groups because they belonged to a minority group in Iraq. Rasha, who had to support her family in Syria, hoped that her family would get settled in a European country through the United Nations High Commissioner for Refugees. She was concerned about the welfare of her family, in particular about the future of her nieces and nephews. She thought that her family had no prospects in Syria and that a European country would provide a decent life for them. Rasha also shared with me her own legal struggle in the United Kingdom. Though the British government was part of the occupying forces in Iraq, it rarely granted asylum or visas to Iraqis after 2003 for fear of an influx of Iraqi refugees. In 2004, Rasha managed to get a tourist visa—through a miracle, as she described it—and came to London for a short visit. After experiencing life without wars, bombs, or power cuts, she decided to stay in Britain. Through contacts with the international organization where she worked, she found a job with the same organization in London. Though Rasha managed to get a work permit and to live and work legally in Britain, securing a more permanent legal status, such as the indefinite leave to remain (ILR), proved elusive. British immigration laws kept changing, and Rasha lived in constant fear of losing her legal status.

Rasha took an avid interest in my story and research. We soon realized that we had gone to adjacent universities at the same time, that we both had degrees in English literature, and that she was a friend of some of the students I went to college with, but our paths had never crossed in Baghdad. After I told her that my parents were communists, Rasha shared with me that her father was also a communist and that he had been imprisoned for four years following the Ba'th coup of 1963. Despite these intersections in our lives, I kept my distance from her. I could not tell if Rasha was a loyalist of Saddam Hussein's regime, especially because she worked at an international organization. Under Hussein's regime, people who worked in embassies or international organizations were under tremendous pressure to cooperate with the regime. During the following weeks and months, Rasha kept sending me emails about events organized by Iraqis in London and suggested people for me to get in touch with for my research. After a few months, we agreed to meet for coffee. During that meeting, Rasha talked about the challenges she had faced in Iraq and the persecution her family had endured under Hussein's regime due to the father's communist past. She also opened up about the difficulties she faced with the Iraqi community in London. On the one hand, Rasha enjoyed being around Iraqis in London. On the other hand, she felt that Iraqi men thought that they could hit on her because she was a single young woman with no family to protect her. That meeting was a turning point. After that, we became close friends. In fact, Rasha was my first close Iraqi friend; I had never had close friends in Iraq because I never felt like I could fully trust other people.

Rasha is a vivacious, cheerful young woman. She always dispelled the gloomy mood over bad news from Iraq with Iraqi jokes and funny anecdotes about her early days in London. She often had a joke ready, depending on the conversation and company, and she never failed to lighten a serious situation or create rapport with new acquaintances by making them laugh. She built a wide network of Iraqi friends and acquaintances, both in Iraq and London.

Rasha grew up navigating different class, ethnic, and religious spheres in Iraq. She hails from a lower-middle-class family that lived in southern Iraq and relocated to Baghdad when she was only four. Her father was a schoolteacher, while her mother stayed at home to raise Rasha and her four siblings. In Baghdad, Rasha lived in a modest mixed neighborhood and went to school with students from different ethnic and religious backgrounds. In college, she met people who belonged to different classes as well, and she had to adapt her behavior and use of slang to meet the dominant middle-class Baghdadi norms and avoid being an object of ridicule. Her work at an international humanitarian organization further widened her circle of Iraqi contacts. This life experience made her well versed in different belief systems and dialects. Within two years of her arrival in London, Rasha had managed to establish a wide network of Iraqi contacts there. On different occasions, I watched her navigate various Iraqi scenes in London. With Shi'i woman at religious events, she spoke in Shi'i religious terms, while with young Iraqi women who defied Iraqi social customs and had relationships with men, she cracked jokes about sex and hymen reconstruction (which a woman may need to have done to prove to a husband that she is a virgin). With young Iraqis who grew up in London, she talked about her experiences of growing up in Iraq under a dictatorship and through several wars. With Iraqi men, she was a serious, proper Iraqi girl who politely engaged in political discussions about the current situation in Iraq. With middle-class Iraqis, she employed the Baghdadi dialect, while with people from the south, she used a heavy southern slang. Given her wide range of contacts, Rasha became a pivotal link between the Iraqi community in London and Iraqis in Iraq and the surrounding region. She mobilized these networks to help Iraqis in Iraq, Syria, and Britain. If a British journalist needed to be in touch with Iraqis in Jordan or Syria to do research about the life of Iraqi refugees, they would reach out to Rasha. And if an Iraqi family in Britain was trying to secure a British visa for a relative, they would get in touch with Rasha because of her knowledge of the British immigration system.

Rasha was popular with Iraqis in London not only because of her pleasant demeanor, openness, and connections. She was also seen as an "authentic" Iraqi. This was partly because her family hailed from the south and had lived in destitution under the monarchy. Iraqis in London thought Rasha's roots in southern Iraq signified her closeness to the downtrodden, who represented the "true Iraq" because of the decades of marginalization and injustice they had endured, unlike middle-class Baghdadis. In addition, Rasha was perceived as an authentic Iraqi because she had experienced the full reign of Saddam Hussein and had lived through the Iran-Iraq War, the Gulf War of 1991, the sanctions years, and the U.S. occupation of Iraq. She represented a link to the years that Iraqis in London had not experienced. This notion of authenticity indicates an emerging shift among the community in London: from a glorification of Iraqis who had lived through the 1950s as the ones who had experienced the "real" Iraq to a concept of selfhood associated with a discourse of the endurance of hardships experienced under the monarchy, Saddam Hussein's reign, wartime, and the U.S. occupation. This discourse of endurance was also marked by a classist shift from Baghdadi middle-class sensibilities to those attuned to the experiences of the marginalized majority. In this framework, the more one suffered under different regimes, the more one was an Iraqi. Moreover, this notion of authentic citizenship was gendered in that the community idealized the strong Iraqi women who had lived through hardships but remained unwavering in the face of uncertainty and difficulties. Over the years, I watched Rasha perform an Iraqi subjectivity attuned to the expectations of the Iraqi community. She performed this through "proper" behavior, humor, updates about Iraq, and tales of hardships and ongoing struggle to find a secure future for her and her family.

Rasha's life trajectory—in particular her socioeconomic background, life in Iraq throughout Hussein's reign and the early years of the U.S. occupation, and experience with legal precarity in Britain—stood in stark contrast to that of Hanan, Khalil, Ali, and Hadjar. However, like them, her life has been shaped by U.S. intervention in Iraq from the 1960s until the present. Her father was imprisoned for four years after the CIA-backed Ba'th coup in 1963, cutting short his dreams to be the first one in his family to attain a college degree, and he and his family lived in fear of him being recruited in the Iran-Iraq War, which was prolonged by the United States. Moreover, the United States' and Britain's role in undermining all efforts to lift the harsh economic sanctions imposed on Iraq exposed the family to destitution and downward mobility. The U.S. invasion of Iraq led to the displacement of Rasha and her family and furthered their economic and legal precarity until 2010. These imperial events in Iraq had engendered chronic conditions of dispossession for Rasha and her family since the early 1960s. Living under these persistent conditions of hardship made Rasha an enduring subject, as far as the Iraqi community was concerned. They saw Rasha, who had supported her family and laughed in the face of adversities, as the model resilient Iraqi woman. Endurance here was not only about staying in Iraq and persevering in conditions of inequality and marginalization; it also opened a space to redefine political belonging by displacing the prevailing discourse about the self and producing alternative imaginations about Iraqiness.[1]

## Alternative Narratives

Unlike some young Iraqis I met in London who were influenced by communists' nostalgic reminiscences about the period from the late 1940s to the early 1960s in Iraq, Rasha did not yearn for that time as the golden age. Growing up, she had listened to her parents' stories about deprivation, disease, and poverty under the monarchy. Whereas Hanan saw the monarchical rule as a time when Iraq lacked national independence and opponents of the regime were persecuted, Rasha's parents spoke of it as a time when people were "barefoot" and "hungry." Her parents, who were born in the 1930s, like Hanan, lived in a small town in southern Iraq that had little access to health care, education, or sanitation. Rasha's maternal grandfather was a blacksmith who repaired guns, while her paternal grandfather was a carpenter who specialized in making boats. Her grandparents' modest professions meant that their families had to live in houses made of reeds and mud, since they could not afford bricks. Rasha's paternal grandfather died of tuberculosis when her father was only nine, and her paternal grandmother had to work to support the family. With no education or pension, she made and sold reed baskets and rugs and used traditional medicine to cure an eye disease associated with planting rice. Unlike Hanan's parents, who took it for granted that both their sons and daughters would go to school and later on to universities, Rasha's grandparents did not have the means to grant all their children an education. While Rasha's father went to school, since he was the only boy in the family, his sisters stayed at home and helped with the housework. Likewise, Rasha's mother did not get an education. Instead, she contributed to the housework, baking bread in a mud oven outside the house, washing clothes by hand, making fuel for the winter from cow feces, and milking the family's cows. Throughout her life, Rasha was reminded of economic and gender disparity through her paternal aunt. Her aunt and father got an eye disease when they were young. Their family had to go to Kuwait to seek medical help, as there were no hospitals nearby. In Kuwait, the family and the doctors paid more attention to Rasha's father because he was a boy and neglected her aunt, who, as a result, lost her eyesight.

Her parents' standard of living changed tremendously following the fall of the monarchy. Abdul Karim Qasim's reforms—including the opening of hospitals throughout the country, the allocation of affordable loans to build houses, and the expansion of free education—opened up a different future, especially for Rasha's father. As a result of these reforms, her father went to Baghdad to study for his BA in Russian literature and got involved in the Iraqi communist scene in the city. After the CIA-backed Ba'th coup of 1963, he was sentenced to four years in the notorious Nugrat al-Salman Prison in the south due to his communist activities. After his release, he could not resume his college education. Instead, he took a preparatory course to become a schoolteacher in his hometown. A few years after marrying Rasha's mother, the family decided to move to Baghdad. Rasha's parents were keen to ensure that all their children would have access to a good education, and they thought the move to Baghdad would open different horizons for the family. By the time the family relocated to Baghdad, in the late 1970s, Iraq had witnessed further social and economic changes. As a result of the increase in oil revenues and the nationalization of oil in the early 1970s, the Iraqi government made expansive investments in health, education, housing, and infrastructure.[2] Some of the revenues also went into establishing industries, implementing agrarian reforms, and expanding the state bureaucracy. This increase in expenditure resulted in momentous social transformations, such as a decrease in infant mortality, increases in literacy and life expectancy, a boost in migration from the countryside to the cities, and a rise in people's salaries.[3] These developments created unprecedented prosperity that especially raised the standard of living for those in the middle and lower classes. For some Iraqis, the 1970s came to be seen as a golden age, despite the increasing persecution of opponents of the regime by the end of the decade.

When she was young, Rasha envisioned the 1970s and 1980s as a better time than the 1940s and the 1950s. As she grew up listening to her parents' stories of hardship and destitution, she understood that people who came from her socioeconomic background did not have an easy life under the monarchy. Rasha felt especially fortunate that, unlike her mother and aunts, she had access to a good and free education and lived in a household defined by plenty. Despite the economic prosperity the family enjoyed in Baghdad, life under Hussein's reign returned them to a life defined by fear and uncertainty. The increasing oppression of communists under the reign of Ahmed Hasan Al-Bakr and later under Saddam Hussein exposed the father to the possibility of arrest and disappearance, a fate many of his comrades faced in the late 1970s. Fearing for his life and succumbing to his wife's imploring, the father's ended his political activity. But despite the increasing oppression, Rasha still remembered the late 1970s fondly:

> I remember the good days as well. For instance, we used to sleep on the roof. We were spoiled. We read a lot. My parents focused on our study because education was free. Also, the Iraqi society was going through a renaissance. It was moving from a backward and old society to a modern one. There was some openness. We wore clothes different from the clothes people wear now. We wore sleeveless shirts and short skirts. We used to go to parks. We used to go out a lot. Life was more beautiful, as people say. It was a prosperous life.

Unlike Hanan, who was silent on the reforms that engendered widespread economic prosperity under the Ba'th regime and who thought of the 1970s and 1980s as a time defined by oppression and disappointment, Rasha's memories were refracted through her parents' narratives of economic hardships under the monarchy. She remembered the radical economic progress that began under Abdul Karim Qasim and continued in the 1970s and early 1980s due to the oil boom. Thus, Rasha's reminiscences about the past oscillated between anxiety about persecution and nostalgia about their comfortable life and the promise of upward mobility. This oscillation between negative and positive memories was constantly reconfigured vis-à-vis the present. As Rasha spoke about the past, she recognized how hindsight made it seem like a better period. Though her parents talked about poverty under the monarchy, they also remembered those days as "a simpler time" when people had "a peace of mind" and when oppression of political dissidents was not as widespread or brutal as under Saddam Hussein's regime. They also perceived the early 1970s as a time of prosperity that was marred by the rise of Saddam

Hussein to power and the beginning of the Iran-Iraq War. In these ongoing reminiscences over the past vis-à-vis the present, the past was not necessarily an idealized time that promised an alternative future. Rather, it kept shifting along lived political and economic realities that were constantly evolving.

Even Rasha herself began to remember the past differently. She vividly remembered the outbreak of the Iran-Iraq War as a time that transformed Iraqi society overnight and furthered the family's anxiety. The school year was delayed and war songs celebrating the prowess of the Iraqi army and the wisdom of Saddam Hussein dominated popular culture. More importantly, the establishment of the Popular Army by the government to replenish the regular national army during the war meant that Rasha's father could be sent to the front at any time, even though as a teacher and sole breadwinner in the family he should have been exempt from military service. To have some peace of mind, her father spent his summers in Poland, until travel was banned in 1983, and then spent them in Mosul. Rasha's cousin was killed in the war, and her aunt's fiancée went missing four days before their wedding and was never found. These personal tragedies were a source of anguish for the family. The atmosphere of fear brought about by the war and the increasing oppression of political opponents permeated their house. Rasha, like Hadjar, remembers how her parents were afraid to criticize the regime in front of the children for fear that they would repeat these comments at school. She recalled how their neighbor's son, a classmate, said to the Ba'thist teacher that his father usually spat on the television whenever Saddam Hussein appeared. The neighbor's family lived in tremendous fear until they realized that the teacher had decided not to report the incident to the authorities. Moreover, even as a child, Rasha came under pressure when the regime tried to recruit children to the Ba'th-backed organization. Rasha's father had a discussion with his children about why they should not join, and the children understood that it was their responsibility to avoid the Ba'th members who came to school to recruit students.

## Precarious Existence

Despite increasing oppression and the Iran-Iraq War, Rasha began to yearn for the 1980s as a time of plenty and a time when people were "stronger and more optimistic." To Rasha, the 1990s were defined by the hardships that resulted from UN-imposed sanctions, which pushed the family to the verge of destitution. The sanctions, which were imposed to pressure Iraq to withdraw from Kuwait, were comprehensive and bound all members of the United Nations Security Council to observe them. Iraq couldn't export oil or import goods, including everyday items that could be used for military purposes, or food. Though the sanctions debilitated the Iraqi economy, they failed to pressure Iraq into withdrawing from Kuwait. When Iraq failed to meet the deadline imposed by the United States to withdraw from Kuwait, a coalition of allies, under the auspices of the United Nations, began Operation Desert Storm in early 1991. The campaign targeted both military facilities and civilian infrastructure—such as milk factories, roads and bridges, power plants, communication lines, water treatment plants, storage facilities, and civilian buildings—and left the country destroyed.[4] During a six-week period, the coalition forces dropped 130,000 tons of ordnance on Iraq, and the damage to Iraqi infrastructure was estimated at $232 billion.[5]

The Gulf War quickly resulted in the withdrawal of Iraq from Kuwait. However, the sanctions were not removed until the fall of Saddam Hussein's regime in 2003. The United States and Britain played a major role in keeping the sanctions in place and linking the lifting of them with regime change in Iraq. Given that the unprecedented economic and social affluence that Iraq witnessed in the 1970s and 1980s had been dependent on state salaries and expenditures, the majority of Iraqis experienced economic hardship when the state ceased to provide social services and the currency collapsed due to exponential inflation. The war also compounded the impact of the sanctions on Iraqi society. The heavy bombardment relegated Iraq to the preindustrial age and led to a massive breakdown of the infrastructure, including water and sewage treatment, agricultural production and food distribution, health care, communication, and electricity.[6]

When I first met Rasha in 2006, the financial and economic hardships her family had endured during the 1990s still preoccupied her. While she talked extensively about the sanctions, she seldom mentioned the Iran-Iraq War, the invasion of Kuwait, the Gulf War, or the failed uprisings in the north and the south. This silence in her daily conversations was especially poignant in light of her family's experiences during the Iran-Iraq War and the Gulf War. As I mentioned earlier, her family feared that her father would be conscripted into the Popular Army, and they lost two relatives in the 1980s. Furthermore, they lived near the Amiriyya Shelter, whose bombing by the U.S.-led coalition in 1991 made news headlines in Iraq and abroad when four hundred trapped people burned to death inside. It was only when I interviewed her and asked her about her experiences during these events that she talked about them, and even then, her comments were brief. Instead, she spent more time reflecting on the hardships her family experienced under the sanctions. After her father retired, he opened a gold shop to supplement his pension. However, he could not cope with the fluctuating market and the inflation of the 1990s. He lost most of his money in the unstable economy:

> My father lost everything: the building he owned, his gold shop, our house, and the two cars he had. We sold our house and had to rent a house in a cheaper area. We also sold the chinaware in order to make ends meet. The economic insecurity took its toll on the family relationships. We began to have a lot of fights because we didn't know how to organize a budget. The pension wasn't enough. I was in tears many times because I wanted the bus fare and my father didn't have money to give me. I was in college at the time, and I had to tutor children in our neighborhood to make some money. The education system collapsed at this point, and teachers were no longer teaching, so students who can afford it relied on tutors. It became very hard to buy a new shirt, for instance. It took tremendous efforts of me to get a new shirt.

These economic hardships led to social changes that made Iraqi society unrecognizable to Rasha. As a result of the inflation, the middle class began to lose ground, and traditionally lower-class jobs gained new value. Handymen, mechanics, and drivers began to make more money than state employees, teachers, and doctors. Blue-collar workers would take a doctor as a second wife, since a doctor earned 3,000 dinars (two dollars) a month, according to Rasha, while a driver or mechanic would give her 10,000 dinars a month if she quit her job. In addition, more people began to embrace religion when a state-sponsored Faith Campaign began in 1991. Islam became a major course in school, and religious programming increased on television. Rasha thought more and more people flocked to religion to cope with their economic hardships and the increasing oppression of the regime as they lost hope in regime change or the end of sanctions. Though travel was no longer banned in the 1990s, most people could not afford the exit fees and the cost of a hotel in

Amman, given the collapse of the Iraqi currency. Rasha felt like a prisoner who did not know what was going on in the world. Her family no longer went out to socialize with friends or visit stores to buy luxury items and could not afford to travel abroad. The sanctions engendered cultural and scientific blockades. According to Rasha, women dreamed of finding an Iraqi groom who lived abroad even if he was below her in education and social status.

After Rasha finished her undergraduate degree in English literature, she decided to do a master's degree in the English language and continue her work as a tutor to pay for her expenses. Unlike Hanan, who took it for granted that she would find a good job after finishing college, Rasha could not find a full-time job after getting her degree. She was so desperate that she agreed to work in a lawyer's office where she had to clean the bathroom and serve water and tea to clients. She had to quit when one of her sisters got mad that Rasha had taken a job that was beneath her. After a short while, she took two jobs: a morning job in a translation and photocopying office and an evening job teaching English as a second language at a university. At the former, Rasha spent all of her time in the office photocopying and had to do the translating at home, even though she had applied for the job of translator. She had to accept her boss's unfair demands because she needed the money. Rasha's second job at the university was short-lived. Soon after the start of the academic year, a student approached her and told her that he was "Uday Saddam Hussein's man" and that he wanted to have an affair with her. Rasha could not tell if the man was truly part of Uday's clique or if he was lying. She replied politely that the best relationship they could have was that of a professor and student. As Rasha walked away, she decided she would not set foot on that campus again. She was too afraid, however, to even call the chair of the department to inform him of her resignation. Moreover, she did not tell her family about the incident because she feared they would not allow her to leave the house again.

This economic precarity further kindled Rasha's nostalgia for the late 1970s and the 1980s. However, it was not nostalgia for a romantic past of grand ideas, but for a time in which she had been able to survive comfortably. Rasha was anxious about her and her family's capacity to find food to eat, study when the power was on, have drinkable water, and take a bus to go to college or work. It was nostalgia for a time when daily life was taken for granted and when quotidian things did not appear to be tremendous obstacles to surmount. What Rasha appreciated about the 1980s was the fact that, despite the fear and uncertainty that characterized that time of war and authoritarianism, life did not teeter on the verge of destitution. It was nostalgia for a time when daily life for her and her family was relatively easy, rather than a persistent round of hardships. Rasha looked to the past for comfort because the present and the future were defined by the impossibility of a simple existence.

In 2000, Rasha found a job as a translator in an international humanitarian organization. The job not only enabled Rasha to work in her specialty, but also brought about a reprieve from economic hardship, as the salary matched the inflation rate. Rasha became the main breadwinner in her family, and the income allowed her to have the kind of social life that she had missed terribly. She began to go out with her friends again and take her sisters on shopping sprees at secondhand stores. However, the job came with its challenges. Rasha's colleagues were suspicious that she got the job because she worked for the intelligence agency (*mukhabarat*). They could not believe that she got the job because of merit. Moreover, since Rasha worked at an international organization, she came under tremendous pressure to cooperate with the regime. One day, an official in the intelligence agency requested a meeting with her. After delivering a talk about national security and the need to protect Iraq, he asked her to work as an informer. Rasha was obliged by the international organization to keep her neutrality and to refrain from conveying information to the government. Shaken by the request, and expecting direct threats, Rasha replied with a cliché about her love for Iraq and left. This encounter made Rasha suspicious of her colleagues, who might face the same pressure, and might succumb to it.

## Being an Iraqi under Occupation

By the end of 2002, Rasha began thinking that there was finally hope that Iraq would become a prosperous and democratic country again. Like the majority of Iraqis she knew, Rasha supported the U.S. invasion of Iraq. To her, the invasion represented the only way to topple Saddam Hussein and end the sanctions. She was particularly upset to see the worldwide demonstrations against the war. In retrospect, she realized that she was naive to think that an imperial war could promise a different future:

I, as all Iraqis who were oppressed and lived in darkness, supported the war. We didn't know what was going on around us. We couldn't travel. We couldn't have a comfortable life. The regime was totalitarian and ruthless. To us, the war would get us out of this situation. Everyone I talked to, with few exceptions, supported the war. The picture wasn't clear. We thought we would live in a rosy dream after the fall of the regime. We thought the United States, the most advanced country in the world, would take care of us. We thought they would bring us democracy. We thought we would surpass the Gulf countries because we have a secular tradition and a diverse society. We saw the big demonstrations in the United Kingdom and Europe and everywhere on the news. No one wanted the war. We used to say, "For heaven's sake, can't they shut up and leave us to live. Isn't what we have been through enough?"

Rasha's family did not leave Baghdad during the war in 2003. They thought they would be trapped if they went to the south, where the family had relatives, since the land invasion was starting there. As the war broke out, they tried to listen to international news on the radio (Hussein's regime had banned the acquisition of satellites) to know how the invasion was progressing. Iraqi radio and television broadcast propaganda news about the victories of the Iraqi army, like it had done during the Iran-Iraq and the Gulf War. For the first few weeks of the invasion, Rasha's family was mostly in the dark about what was really going on. When people toppled Hussein's statue in Firdous Square, Rasha and her family were not aware of the event. Rasha's sister who lived nearby, like a small number of Iraqis who defied the ban on acquiring satellites, watched the event live on television. Afterward, she went to her family's house to relay the news:

> My sister who lived nearby came to see us with her husband. They had a satellite and a generator so they were watching the news. She came before anyone knew about the fall of the statue. She was still at the entrance of our home when she began saying, "Congratulations, Saddam is gone. The regime fell." We opened the door and told her to shut up in case someone hears her and we'd all be in trouble. We tried to use the few Mandaean words we knew to ask her to shut up. She said, "I'm telling you Saddam is gone. Can't you understand!" She got inside the house and she told us about what she saw on TV. We had different reactions. I was surprised that this had become a reality.

> Saddam to me was like God, an unchanging fact in life. He is there all the time whether you like it or not. Imagine you wake up one day and you're told there is no God. I was dazed.

As Rasha heard the news of the fall of the regime, she thought about how the hardships she had lived through—whether economic deprivation or political persecution of the family—had come to an end. However, news of looting and the destruction of state institutions that began after the U.S. military entered Baghdad soon followed. She did not know whom to blame for the chaos: Saddam Hussein's loyalists, who did not want to see a stable Iraq; the criminals that Hussein had released from prisons shortly before the war; or the U.S. military, which was behind the chaos and looting, as claimed by conspiracy theorists. The following weeks and months intensified Rasha's disappointment, especially after the establishment of the Iraqi Governing Council and the institutionalization of a sectarian quota system. Rasha had hoped that the "technocrats"—people who would be selected based on merit and experience—would take over and govern the country. She had never heard of the term *technocrat*, but the word became popular on the eve of the invasion. This political disappointment with the institutionalization of a sectarian quota system and the increasing violence in the country brought about by the U.S. army and insurgent groups was accompanied by further everyday hardships. Power cuts became more frequent than they had been under Hussein's regime. Water was no longer consistently available. Fuel became scarce, and long queues at the gas stations became a common scene. Ordinary people's purchasing power plummeted. The dismantling of the Iraqi army and the Ba'th Party left thousands of people without jobs. Manifestations of religiosity by Shi'i Iraqis, who could not perform most of their rituals under Hussein's regime, became more apparent. Shortly after the invasion, a massive march took place on the anniversary of the murder of Imam Kadhim, one of the twelve imams venerated by Shi'is. According to Rasha, Baghdad was cloaked in black banners for the occasion. The reconfiguration of the Iraqi political scene through sectarian rhetoric permeated social life as well. Rasha all of a sudden found herself referred to as a minority, rather than an Iraqi. She felt that everything around her was "collapsing."

Not only did Rasha have to grapple with these radical transformations, but she became surrounded by death as the violence accompanying the occupation increased. Shortly after the fall of the regime, Rasha lost a Canadian colleague who was shot in the crossfire between U.S. troops and Hussein's loyalists. A few months later, another incident occurred where she herself escaped death only because her driver was an hour late due to traffic. It happened as they were approaching the office. Rasha and her driver heard a loud explosion. Within minutes, they heard on the radio that the organization where Rasha worked had been targeted. Rasha got out of the taxi and walked to the building. Sneaking in through a back door, she went to her office and saw that all the windows were broken. She imagined herself sitting behind those windows and cut into pieces. She moved through the office and went to the front door, where the explosion had occurred, and there she stepped into a pool of blood. Her colleagues were screaming that it was Hani's blood, that he had been killed. At that point, she began to scream. Just a few days earlier, Rasha had had a conversation with Hani, who was trying to raise her spirits. Rasha and her colleagues had decided to get a small plant for the office to remind them of their Canadian colleague who was killed. As the death toll around the country increased, Rasha had asked Hani how many plants they were going to need to get, saying that one day, "there would be nobody left to plant anything." Ten days after that conversation, he was gone. It was a tremendous loss for Rasha. She and Hani had been close friends, and it was Hani who had accepted her application when she applied for the job.

In early 2004, Rasha lost another friend, Sulaf. Rasha, Mary, and Sulaf worked in the same building between 1998 and 2000 and became close friends. Following the U.S. occupation of Iraq, Sulaf and Mary applied for a job to work as interpreters for the Coalition Provisional Authority in the Green Zone.[7] One day, Rasha was in her office when she heard an explosion. It took place at the entrance of the Green Zone. She worried that Mary and Sulaf were hurt. She tried to get in touch with them, but with no success. A few hours later, she got a phone call from Sulaf's mother letting her know that Sulaf was missing and asking her if she knew anyone who could help the family find Sulaf. Her mother knew that Rasha had a wide network of contacts through her work at the humanitarian organization. Rasha also learned that Mary was badly injured in the explosion, though her wounds were not life threatening. Rasha mobilized her contacts to see if she could get some information on the whereabouts of Sulaf, to no avail. Three days after the explosion, she went to visit Sulaf's family. She found Sulaf's brother crying at the entrance of the house. When he saw Rasha, he asked her to wish Sulaf peace. Rasha could not believe that Sulaf was dead. Just three days before the explosion, Sulaf and Mary had paid Rasha's family a visit to check on her father, who had been in a car accident. The young women and the family were laughing and had a good time that evening. Sulaf's brother also told Rasha that he had been able to identify Sulaf's body from the ring that Rasha and Mary had given her on her birthday a month earlier. Sulaf had been engaged to an Iraqi man who lived in Europe, and she was supposed to have joined him in a few months. The friends had wanted to give Sulaf a special present before she left Iraq

Losing three friends in the span of nine months was tremendously depressing for Rasha. She began to fear for her own life since more and more people who worked for international organizations were being targeted. A French colleague advised her to go to Jordan for a training course and then try to go to London for a few days for a change of scenery. She was thirty years old by then, and it was the first time that she had left Iraq. Arriving in Amman, she realized that life could be different. There was a stable and safe environment in Amman, where electricity and water were available all the time and where the markets had high-quality food. Rasha recalled that she "felt amazing" and enjoyed going out with friends without fear of violence. Shortly after arriving in Amman, Rasha applied for a British visa and could not believe that she got it so easily, since the British government wasn't issuing many visas for Iraqis for fear of an influx of refugees. When Rasha landed in London, she was overwhelmed with emotions and impressions:

> I felt I was dreaming. At last, I'm in a strange new world. I am so excited about the experience. I'm not with my family. I am a grown-up. It is London, the long-heard-of London. I'm going to see lots of English people. I'm going to test my English. I don't know what I'm going to see but it looked quite green from the outside as we were landing. The smell of air felt very different. I was just smiling. So cheerful. My cousin and his English wife came to pick

me up, and they wanted to talk. I didn't want to talk. I was looking at things. I wanted to see the greenness.

A few days after her arrival in London, Rasha decided that she would not return to Iraq. She got in touch with the French colleague she worked with in Iraq to see if she could find a job with the British branch of the international organization where she worked. The colleague used his contacts and was successful in securing a secretary job for Rasha. Though the position entailed a demotion, she felt happy that she could sort out her legal status through a job. Rasha did not want to apply for asylum in Britain. Even though she had been in London for less than a week, she had heard many stories about the near impossibility of getting asylum and about the limbo in which asylum seekers lived. Despite regulations that required applicants to leave Britain and reenter the country with the new visa, Rasha managed to change her status without leaving the country. She was concerned that if she applied for a different type of visa at a British embassy, she would not be able to get it. Getting a work permit and having the ability to stay in Britain legally did not confer security or stability, however, as Rasha's visa was to be renewed annually, and the laws for acquiring the indefinite leave to remain kept changing. When I met Rasha, she was living in constant fear of losing her legal status due to changes in the law. Unlike Hanan, Khalil, Ali, and Hadjar, who had encountered no difficulties in getting the indefinite leave to remain through work, investment, or asylum in the late 1970s and 1980s, Rasha left Iraq at a time when to be an Iraqi meant to be seen as an unwanted asylum seeker and a burden by authorities. Rasha joined thousands of Iraqis who found themselves unable to leave Iraq or stranded in different countries—in particular, Jordan and Syria—unable to get a visa or a legal status in a host country.

Rasha's anxiety about the future was compounded when her family—including her married sisters, who no longer lived with the family—had to flee Iraq for Syria in 2006. In Iraq, her family had received anonymous death threats because of their minority status and because a family member—Rasha—worked for an international organization while she lived in Iraq. The family decided to move to Syria, since, unlike Jordan, the Syrian government still allowed Iraqi refugees into the country. The family joined almost one million Iraqi refugees in Syria. The influx of refugees put a strain on social services and the infrastructure in the country. While Iraqis were allowed to settle and young children could go to school, they were prohibited from working legally. Rasha's youngest sister, Rana, who had finished high school in Iraq, could not go to college in Syria. Rasha's brother and a brother-in-law had to work off the books to make money to support their families. Another well-off brother-in-law paid smugglers and managed to go to Sweden with his wife. Rasha had to support her parents and Rana. Meanwhile, the family applied for refugee status with the United Nations High Commissioner for Refugees and hoped to be settled in a European country. The family lived in limbo and did not know when their asylum application would be processed—or even if they would be granted asylum at all.

## Enduring Subjectivity

The emerging discourse among Iraqis who did not belong to the upper-middle and middle classes revolved around the notion of endurance—of persistence and perseverance in conditions of chronic uncertainty, precarity, and destitution, which disproportionately affected the lower-middle and lower classes in Iraq. Iraqis in London who could not relate to the prevailing discourse of the older Iraqis saw Rasha, who left Iraq only in 2004, as representing the "real Iraq" through her and her family's experiences of hardship and resilience. They invoked the Arabic concept of *tahamul* to describe Rasha's abilities to put up with hard conditions and support her family. *Tahamul* comes from the verb *hamal*, which means to carry. And while *tahamul* suggests an existence defined by carrying a weight, it also indicates the capacity to carry on in the face of difficulties. In addition, this alternative narrative revolved around everyday practices. Rasha was not just someone whose family had suffered through the various troubles that had afflicted Iraq over the years. She also brought an Iraqi touch to daily life through humor and her cooking of Iraqi dishes. Over the years, I saw Rasha perform a subjectivity attuned to the narrative of precarity while also creating excitement through meals and laughter.

Moreover, the trope of "the strong Iraqi woman"—who constituted the essence of the nation through endurance during times of wars, persecution, and loss—was dominant among Iraqis in London. Iraqi women increasingly became the heads of households as single mothers during the Iran-Iraq War and the Gulf War, when the men were sent off to fight, were killed, or perished in the regime's prisons. While women ensured the continued operation of the state through their professional jobs, they also took care of their families after work. The sanctions years affirmed this trope of the resilient Iraqi woman when women had to make ends meet during a time of scarcity. Iraqis in London heard stories about female relatives and friends in Iraq who had to be practical and resort to different socially acceptable means to complement their valueless salaries—such as sewing clothes, selling food and bread, and tutoring students in the neighborhood. The true Iraqi woman was no longer the revolutionary who fought for social justice and women's liberation, but the enduring woman who held the nation and the family together during decades of crises. When Iraqis in London met Rasha, they saw a woman who had risen to the occasion and taken care of her family both in Iraq and in exile.

I often heard Iraqis tell Rasha, "You lived through it all," "You suffered a lot," "You've seen a lot," and "You are the real Iraqi" (*Iraqiyya asliyya*). After spending decades in exile, Iraqis in London perceived their experience of Iraqiness as defined by a lack, an absence. The majority of them had arrived in London in the late 1970s and early 1990s. Rasha had lived through an Iraq they had only heard about: decades of persecutions, the Iran-Iraq War, the Gulf War, the sanctions, the U.S. invasion, and the increasing instability in post-Saddam Iraq. Though Iraqis in London were preoccupied with the ongoing violence in the country and were worried about relatives and friends still in the country, they themselves had lived lives of relative security and plenty in London. They realized that their pain could not match the suffering of Iraqis living in Iraq who daily struggled with immediate violence and hardships. The intertwinement of having "lived through it all" and being "a real Iraqi" ties endurance and authenticity together. The more a person endured hardships, fear, and persecution throughout her life in Iraq, the more she was an Iraqi. As a new arrival in London in 2006, Rasha represented the ultimate Iraqi experience to the community.

Furthermore, this Iraqi authenticity was tied to a notion of economic and legal precarity. Rasha's Iraqi friends and acquaintances in London saw her connected to the downtrodden, whose experience represented the majority of Iraqis, rather than to Baghdadi middle-class elites. The fact that Rasha hailed from a modest background rooted in southern Iraq, where people struggled to make ends meet under the monarchy, resonated deeply with Iraqis who could not relate to the discourse endorsed by Hanan and her friends. To them, Rasha represented an Iraq not defined by a romantic past but by daily hardship and struggle. Her experience with precarity was not limited to family experience under the monarchy but extended to the period of sanctions, which most Iraqis in London only heard about through relatives in Iraq. This economic precarity was compounded by the precarity of trying to secure legal status in a foreign country. Rasha lived in legal limbo in Britain for years, while her family became refugees and hoped for resettlement in a European country. In the post-Saddam era, the figure of the true Iraqi is no longer the optimistic revolutionary who had worked toward a promising future, but a person who had lived a simple life rooted in the land and who had endured persecution, wars, sectarian violence, deprivation, and legal uncertainty following displacement.

Thus, Iraqis in London admired Rasha as someone who had suffered, but they also enjoyed her company for her sense of humor and the Iraqi dishes she made. Despite the legal uncertainties that engulfed her and her family, Rasha was always cheerful and had a joke ready to tell. During social gatherings, she would become the center of attention through the jokes she narrated. Most of the jokes she told provided a moral critique of the present through parodying the daily hardships of the U.S. invasion, discrimination, power cuts, and so on. One night in the winter of 2007, she and I were invited to a dinner at a common friend's house. As we got to the house, we found the guests talking about the stories relayed to them by their relatives in Iraq about the lack of basic services there. The conversation went for at least fifteen minutes. I glanced at Rasha, who was growing uneasy. I knew that Rasha sometimes got fed up with the excessive dwelling on Iraq among Iraqis in London. She often found that the conversations depressed her and raised her anxiety about the future. Thus, at a lull in the conversation, she offered a joke: "An Iraqi and Chinese were challenging each other with the achievements of their civilizations. The Chinese man said, 'We have the Great Wall of China.' The Iraqi replied, 'Well, we have the Great Queue of Gas.'" Everyone in the room burst out laughing. "And once a boy drank some oil," Rasha said, "so his father took him to the hospital. The doctors brought gallon containers and queued at his bed." Through her jokes, Rasha lightened up the mood in the room while at the same time acknowledging and criticizing the present political conditions.

On another occasion, Rasha and I went to a dinner, and as we arrived, we found two guests engaged in a heated discussion about the deterioration of the situation in Iraq. Ziad, who was a Sunni, was blaming the Shi'i politicians for the lack of services and the spiraling sectarian violence in the country, while Ghassan, who was Shi'i, was defending Shi'i politicians and pointing fingers at the Sunni insurgents as the source of insecurity and instability. Other guests joined the discussion, taking sides with Ziad or Ghassan. The discussion got more heated, and tension was rising along sectarian lines. Rasha interrupted the conversation and gave her take about sectarianism in Iraq, the reality of displacement, and discrimination Iraqis encounter abroad: "Once, a Jordanian man found a magic lantern and said to the genie, 'I would like you to remove all Iraqis from Jordan.' The genie replied, 'Mate, may your father's soul rest in peace, what have we done to deserve such a treatment?'" The joke ended the heated discussion and eased the tension in the room. Through such humor, Rasha not only brought Iraqis together, but she also enabled them to better deal with times of difficulty and uncertainty.[8]

Rasha's sense of humor both conveyed her resilient spirit and created a sense of unity in the Iraqi community in London despite the sectarian tensions. She had been surprised, upon her arrival in London, by the level of fragmentation in the Iraqi community and by the efforts of Iraqis she met to situate her in a sectarian pigeonhole that did not allow for inclusion or elasticity. In Iraq, Rasha saw herself as mainly an Iraqi and thought her minority identity was a marginal issue as far as how people perceived her. What preoccupied people in Iraq was the experience of hardship and persecution, rather than sectarian divisions. As she once told me, "Iraqis living under Saddam's rule did not have the luxury to be sectarian." In London, Iraqis perceived Rasha as mainly a minority. While some Iraqis welcomed her unconditionally, others reminded her constantly of her minority status. To fight against these divisions, Rasha got involved in a campaign called "I'm an Iraqi" organized by a group of Iraqis in London, which aimed to emphasize a unified Iraqi identity over sectarian affiliations among the community. However, her efforts failed; Iraqis in London could not agree who constituted an Iraqi—whether it was a communist, an Islamist, a Shi'i or a Sunni, someone from the middle or lower class, or someone who suffered under Hussein's reign. Rasha envisioned that anyone who identified as an Iraqi should be considered one, regardless of religious, class, and political background. Thus, she sought to bring Iraqis together and ease sectarian tensions through humor.

In addition to Rasha's sense of humor, she also brought an Iraqi touch through cooking, especially the breakfast dish *qaimar*. Though Iraqis in London made Iraqi dishes themselves or went to Iraqi restaurants, they missed *qaimar*, which is a layer of thick cream made from boiling water buffalo milk. It reminded them especially of weekends in Iraq when families gathered and ate *qaimar* for breakfast. People in Iraq usually bought *qaimar* and did not make it at home. Rasha had learned to make it for her mother. In 2002, her mother had back surgery, and the doctor recommended eating products high in calcium. Water buffalo milk was high in calcium, so Rasha began to make it at home. When she came to London and saw how Iraqis missed that dish, she decided to find buffalo milk and make the dish, even though she did not really like it. With Rasha's first attempt, London's Iraqi community agreed that her *qaimar* tasted exactly like *qaimar* in Iraq. It created a sensation among her wide circle of friends, and she often brought along some *qaimar* when friends invited her to lunch or dinner. Rasha told me that she enjoyed making *qaimar* because she saw how it made London's Iraqis happy and enabled them to relive memories of home. They would share stories about childhood, family gatherings, and funny anecdotes about their lives in Iraq. During these personal reminiscences, they would forget about the bleak realities of the U.S. occupation and sectarian violence and dwell instead on fond memories associated with *qaimar*.

## Living in Diaspora

When I first met Rasha in 2006, she was haunted by the death of her friends in Baghdad and troubled by the displacement of her family to Syria, news of the deteriorating situation in Iraq, and her legal status in the United Kingdom. In 2006, her parents, her unmarried sister, her brother and his family, her separated sister and her child, and her other sister and her family all had to flee to Syria. The family went to Damascus, where they lived in a poor neighborhood inhabited mainly by Iraqi refugees. The entire family shared a small, cold apartment that lacked basic functioning amenities. Their rations from a charitable organization and the United Nations did not last very long, and the low-skilled jobs that Rasha's brother and brother-in-law took could not support the family for a whole month. Rasha's brother, who had a degree in administration, had to work as a porter, while her brother-in-law, who was an electrician, sold fruits and vegetables to make ends meet. Rasha had to send them money, and she learned to be financially prudent in order to continue her own life in London.

During the years I have known Rasha, she has always been preoccupied with Iraq, enjoying the company of Iraqis, savoring Iraqi food, and attending lectures and film screenings about Iraq. She will often grow emotional and cry when she hears a song about Iraq or sees pictures of destruction in Baghdad on the television or in newspapers. She has also helped Iraqis by putting them in touch with lawyers, charities, or journalists, and she follows the news of her Iraqi friends in Iraq and diaspora. However, though Iraq looms large in her daily life, she has not expressed any yearning to return to the country. She told me that when she first arrived in London, she was so nostalgic about Iraq that she insisted on going back to visit on the first anniversary of leaving the country, despite strong opposition from her family. They feared that Rasha would be killed or kidnapped as soon as she landed. Following the fall of Saddam Hussein, gangs began to kidnap Iraqis coming from abroad for ransom and sometimes even killed them after the ransom was paid. When Rasha got to her parents' house, her mother would not allow her to leave and did not even tell her neighbors that Rasha was visiting. Rasha could only see her sisters and brother, who came and visited her. During that trip, Rasha was shocked to see the terror in which her family lived. The family distrusted everyone—including their best friends and neighbors. They spoke in riddles, laughed nervously, and made jokes when they were leaving the house that they may not come back (due to the possibility of dying in a car explosion or suicide bombing). One day, Rasha managed to convince her brother to take her to her favorite neighborhood, Karradah. She yearned to walk on the Muʻlaq Bridge and watch the Tigris flow by. Her brother agreed but told Rasha that she had to cover her hair so that nobody would suspect that she had come from abroad. They parked near the bridge, Rasha got out of the car, let her cover slip, and stood on the bridge, watching the Tigris.

Shortly after that sole excursion in Baghdad, Rasha went back to London and no longer felt nostalgic for Iraq. Her thought was that "Iraq was gone." The image she had of Iraq as a bustling place, where she had once had a busy social life, was erased; that Iraq was now only a deeply cherished memory. As she once told me, "Iraq is the past, my roots, family, and friends. Britain is the present, the future, security, and the guarantee in life." She compared her relationships to Iraq and Britain to a married person who had moved from her parents' house to a new house after marriage. That person would not be disconnected from her family, but she would no longer live with them. Despite her lack of nostalgia, Rasha still saw herself as an Iraqi first and foremost. She thought of Iraq as "the cast that molded her." Her memories and roots were deeply ingrained in the country. What aggravated her ache and the sense of loss "was the knowledge that the place you left is bleeding, in pain, and being devoured by fire." Rasha felt sad that the feelings she had for Iraq were those of compassion, not nostalgia. Iraq was an open wound that could not heal because the situation in the country kept deteriorating.[9]

In 2009, both Rasha and her family had a break from their legal uncertainty. Rasha's family was resettled in Finland early in the year, and she managed to get indefinite leave to remain shortly afterward. The resettlement of her family in Finland was an emotional and financial relief. Her parents and single sister, her brother and his family, her separated sister and her child, and her married sister and her family each got a nice furnished apartment with a stipend that ensured a middle-class standard of living. I vividly remember the two phone calls Rasha made to convey the good news. Her voice was beaming with happiness and a sense of relief. In both calls, she expressed joy that she and her family would no longer lose their legal status and be forced to return to Iraq. She voiced fears that she had held for years but was afraid to articulate because just uttering the thoughts disturbed her. She had lived with the fear that she would have to leave the United Kingdom if the laws kept changing, that she would have to join her family as a refugee in Syria. She was also concerned that her family would have to live in limbo in Syria for years, like the majority of Iraqi refugees living there. After she heard the news that she had received indefinite leave to remain, Rasha told me she "could start living now." After decades of wars, sanctions, persecution, and legal uncertainty, she felt she could finally have "a normal life" defined by security and plenty. For the first time, she could "make plans for the future," such as planning a vacation, saving to buy property, or looking for a different job. In the meantime, Rasha met an English man, and they got married in 2010. A year after her marriage, Rasha acquired British citizenship, which changed her life significantly. She could now go anywhere in the world without needing a visa. While an Iraqi passport marked Rasha as an outcast, incapable of securing a visa to go anywhere except Syria, a British passport opened the world for her. Like Hadjar, who took advantage of British citizenship to become more mobile, Rasha began to travel and have experiences she had long yearned for.

Moreover, Rasha's sense of selfhood began to shift over time. While she enjoyed the fact that Iraqis in London were interested in her life story and saw her as an enduring Iraqi subject, she began to grow anxious about this perception. She thought that Iraqis inside Iraq were suffering more because the sectarian violence in the country was reaching its peak between 2006 and 2008. Rasha came to see her life in London and the assurance that her family was safe in Europe as signs of privilege. She once told me that she was afraid she would become like Iraqis in London—namely, a diasporic Iraqi who did not suffer as much as Iraqis in Iraq. But after 2010, Rasha was elated that the relentless precarity was lifted and that she could now plan for the future for the first time in her life. Over time, I saw how Rasha came to see Iraqis who left Iraq after her as Iraqis who had endured and suffered more than her.

## The Taste of Home

In 2011 and 2012, Rasha became a mother to a boy and girl. Since then, she has been haunted by the prospect that her children might grow up not knowing Iraq. It broke her heart that she could not take them to Iraq to show them the town where she had been born, or the school she had gone to, or the house where her grandmother had lived. She thought that her children's friends had continuity with the roots of their mothers. They could go to Scotland or northern England to see their grandparents, while her children would not have this experience. The fact that her children might grow up disconnected from Iraq became a source of anxiety for her, especially because they were not keen on speaking Arabic. The integrity of Iraq became more important to her as her children began to grow up and ask her about the country. The prospect of the disintegration of the country presented her with a further dilemma. If

Iraq were divided into Sunni, Shi'i, and Kurdish provinces, she would have to tell them that she was born in a province called Basra, rather than a country called Iraq; this was painful. To her, the possibility of the division of the country meant that Iraq would cease to exist and that her life experience and history there would be erased and reconfigured along sectarian entities rather than a unified Iraqi entity. Since then, Rasha has begun to instill a notion of her homeland for her children through food. Rasha told me that she purposefully cooked Iraqi food for her children because she wanted them to learn to love Iraqi dishes, particularly rice and stews, which the children preferred over British food at the time. If they could not see Iraq, then at least they could get a sense of its culture through the taste of its food.

# WITH NO RAY OF HOPE

Following the failed 1991 uprising in the south, the virtual secession of the Kurdish region, and Iraq's regional and international isolation, the regime became relentless in its oppression. Its policy was "you are either with us or against us." My mother became more concerned about the increasing pressure that the regime put on her. Phone calls from newspaper editors insisting that she write articles praising Saddam Hussein became more frequent. Students of "special admission" increasingly criticized the regime and related stories of oppression in front of her with the hope that she would slip and also condemn the regime. And some of her colleagues' open criticism of the regime made her unhappy because she did not know if she could still trust them. At school, and later in college, I pretended not to hear what other students said about the regime. I was so scared that any gesture or move would be counted against me—and my mother. Yet we both worried most about my sister because she was more rash and hot-headed, and she sometimes said things that she later regretted. Once, she told someone who was openly criticizing the regime that Iraq had lost the 1991 war. For two days, we worried that she would be arrested. Luckily, the person did not report her.

Things took a turn for the worse in 1993. My sister finished her bachelor's degree in computer science that year, and she applied for jobs. After a successful interview, a high-ranking government employee told her that she would be hired but just had to wait for official approval. Two weeks later, my sister went to see him; he told her that she had failed to secure the regime's permission to work. We were all in shock when she told us the news, and we realized that it meant pressure was mounting on my mother. It was then that we decided that it was time to leave Iraq. This was not an easy decision for my mother, given her attachment to the country. But she thought that it was best for my sister to go to Lebanon, where my maternal grandparents were originally from; she and I would follow after I finished college in two years.

But the decision to leave Iraq had come too late. My sister was prevented from traveling. During the blockade, the regime could no longer enforce a travel ban. Instead, it put in place legal and monetary obstacles to stop people from leaving. One of these was the introduction of the *mahram*, or a male legal guardian, which required women under the age of sixty to travel in the company of a husband or non-marriageable relative—a brother, uncle, or father—to protect their honor abroad. Legally, my sister and I should have been exempted from this law since we did not have a male legal guardian. However, the regime refused to grant an exemption to my sister. My mother asked an influential acquaintance to intervene on my sister's behalf in the Ministry of Interior. This acquaintance promised us that she would get her exemption and that we should hear good news from the ministry very soon. I still remember my mother leaving the ministry two weeks later looking anguished and defeated. The woman in charge told her that all the exemption cases had been approved except for my sister's case. The door for leaving the country had closed for us.

Having failed to find a job or leave the country, my sister stayed at home and spent her time reading. After I finished college, I did not even apply for an exemption or a job, knowing that rejection awaited me. I joined my sister and spent time reading and sewing. My dream of starting a PhD in English literature abroad was put on hold. I decided to make the best of a bad situation by reading books I had never had the chance to read before. In the meantime, my mother was getting increasingly uncomfortable at work. She thought that it was time to retire to have some peace of mind. She submitted her retirement paperwork, but the university did not approve it. The rejection of her retirement application was another blow, since she was legally eligible to retire. When the new academic year started, my mother decided not to go to work. A few weeks later, she received a letter stating that she had resigned and, hence, lost her right to her pension. Now, we were left with no steady source of income. We began to sell jewelry to survive. Since the price of gold was high, we managed to subsist on the money we received for a small piece of jewelry for at least three months, but we did not know how long our jewelry would carry us. We knew that we had to be careful with money and only spend it on food.

In late July 1997, we decided to commit suicide. We chose to end our lives because we believed that there was no other way of escaping the tyranny we had long endured under Saddam Hussein. The regime seemed strong, and there was no hope that the sanctions would be lifted. The future looked bleak. Death seemed like the only way out of the situation. My mother and sister died, but I lived.

( CONCLUSION )

# ENDURING LEGACIES

My story is a typical Iraqi tale, in that death had become a part of everyday life in Iraq. In fact, to many Iraqis I encountered in Iraq and London, I am considered lucky—and I agree with them. I know how my parents and sister died. I know where they are buried. I had the luxury to mourn their deaths and eventually find some sort of closure. That means I am unlike many Iraqis who had family members disappear in the regime's prisons or wars, leaving their relatives questioning how and when they died and where they were buried.

When I lived in Iraq and in London during my fieldwork, Iraqis I met felt that we were pawns in an international game of politics and that our lives did not matter. Iraqis in Iraq and in diaspora saw the Iran-Iraq War as a war of attrition supported by the United States and European countries to bog down two powerful countries in the Middle East. They also saw the sanctions as a way of punishing the Iraqi people while enriching those affiliated with the regime. Moreover, they were acutely aware of the role of the United States in supporting Saddam Hussein in the 1980s and in keeping him in power in the 1990s for fear of the establishment of an Islamist government. Iraqis reckoned that the United States decided to invade Iraq and bring about regime change to better serve U.S. interests in the region. Over the decades, U.S. imperial intervention in Iraq consolidated the power of an authoritarian regime, which resulted in the deaths of millions of Iraqis, destroyed the Iraqi social and environmental fabric, and led to a massive exodus of Iraqis from the country and the formation of Iraqi diasporic communities abroad.

This history of U.S. imperial entanglement means that Iraqis have constantly lived in the shadow of wars, authoritarian brutalities, and imperial violence. For decades, violence has constituted the rhythm of everyday life in Iraq, rather than being an interruption of it. U.S. violence in Iraq has rendered Iraqis disposable human beings whose suffering and death warranted little attention.[1] Through military interventions, the prolonging of wars, and the support of Saddam Hussein, the United States has created conditions of dispossession and death for Iraqis inside Iraq and in diaspora. As an empire, the United States has resorted to practices and policies that unequally distribute life and death, has exercised the power to kill populations outside its national territories. Within an imperial logic of managing populations in the expanse of empire, "those whose rights and protection are presented as the *raison d'être* of war are sanctioned to death and therefore live a pending death precisely because of those rights."[2] While the United States sometimes killed Iraqis directly through bombardment of Iraq and the imposition of sanctions, it also was responsible for the death of Iraqis at the hands of Saddam Hussein through the support of his regime and prolonging of wars. In these instances, it was not only an illiberal state that was killing its own citizens, but also a liberal state eliminating the lives of imperial subjects in the name of national security, democracy and freedom, and the protection of global peace.[3]

The imperial encounter between Iraq and the United States has produced conditions of precarity for Iraqis. Through wars and violence, the United States inscribed itself onto Iraq, "sustaining populations on the edge of death, sometimes killing its members, and sometimes not; either way, it produces precarity as the norm of everyday life."[4] The United States' support of the first Ba'th coup in 1963, its arming and assisting of Hussein's regime in the 1980s, its bombardment of Iraq in 1991, its imposition of sanctions in the 1990s and early 2000s, and its occupation of Iraq in 2003 have forced Iraqis to live on the edge of death for decades. However, the deaths of Iraqis have been dismissed as instances of collateral damage, or the casualties of violence perpetuated by a tyrant. While Iraqis lived with heavy bombardments, torture, and death, they also encountered everyday violence that has often been indiscernible. The daily violence, moreover, created the conditions of "slow death" for Iraqis, an in-between zone of "ongoingness, getting by, and living on, where the structural inequalities are dispersed and the pacing of their experience is uneven and often mediated by way of phenomena not prone to capture by a consciousness organized by archives of memorable impact."[5] The fear for one's life, the ongoing struggle with the loss of friends and homeland, the realities of environmental degradation and economic hardship, and the destruction of the social fabric meant that for decades Iraqis inhabited a national and imperial space predicated upon the ongoing erasure of life.

My interlocutors in London were acutely aware that the lives of Iraqis were valueless, and that their deaths in the thousands warranted little outrage or sympathy. Some of them compared Iraqis to flies; Iraqi lives were statistics, on a par with the lives of insects. The metaphor of flies and insects not only refers to the fact that Iraqi lives were expendable and insignificant, but also that their killing amounted to an extermination. Iraqis I met in London often wondered why imperial powers were unable to see them as human beings who feel pain at the untimely loss of friends and relatives. They knew that U.S. and British officials who supported Hussein, waged wars, allowed looting, and imposed sanctions were not going to be held accountable for the crimes they committed in Iraq, precisely because Iraqi lives were worthless. In addition, to my interlocutors, media explanations of Hussein's tyranny and the sectarian violence as products of internal disfunction and manifestations of primordial hatred were just another erasure of the role of the United States in perpetuating violence in Iraq for decades, and hence the dehumanization of the Iraqi people. The imperial powers by these analyses absolved themselves of any responsibility and blamed the violence on Iraqis themselves.

Not only did imperial violence produce conditions of precarity and death, it also resulted in the displacement of millions of Iraqis and prolonged their exile from home. The formation of diasporic Iraqi communities abroad since the late 1970s is deeply intertwined with the history of U.S. interventions in Iraq. Iraqis in London who had fled their country at different points were constantly battling the process of "dismemberment," which entails "the separation of persons from history, the literal injury or destruction of bodies . . . and the denial of membership . . . by forcing people to flee their country of citizenship."[6] Exile for Iraqis in London entailed the destruction of lives they had built in Iraq. While upper-middle-class Iraqis who had studied in the United Kingdom were better positioned than lower classes to start again, both groups left behind the homes, careers, and friendships and relations they had established over the decades. They also had to forgo the futures they had imagined in their homeland and the political projects they had fought for. The separation from homeland and history has been a source of anxiety and anguish for Iraqis in London, even though they realize that return is no longer possible. My interlocutors were long-distance nationalists who felt pain at the ongoing destruction of Iraq, the dispossession and hardships that characterized daily lives for Iraqis in Iraq, and the loss of cultural heritage.

Iraqis separated from their homeland also constantly struggled with the precarity of their legal status in the United Kingdom. As more and more Iraqis began to flee Iraq during the sanctions and the U.S. occupation, they found themselves unable to secure a visa, permanent residence, or citizenship in the United Kingdom. While Britain played a major role in vetoing any UN resolution to ease or lift the sanctions and was part of the occupying forces in 2003, it implemented measures against the admission of Iraqi refugees. Not only did denying Iraqis entry into Western countries shift the centers of exile for the Iraqi diaspora, with Syria and Jordan emerging as hubs for the displaced, it also constituted Iraqis as unwelcome guests who could not make legal claims in countries that were responsible for perpetuating the violence and economic hardships that had caused their exile. The denial of entry speaks to the processes of violence entailed in the definition of Iraqis as outsiders unworthy of protection and asylum.[7] Moreover, these conditions of dismemberment obscure the conditions through which Iraqis are produced as disposable human beings, as well as the imperial violence that led to their displacement.[8] The difficulty of securing a visa to the United Kingdom or other Western countries is part and parcel of the politics of erasure that Iraqis have grappled with for decades.

---

The ongoing violence in Iraq raised questions among my Iraqi interlocutors in London about what it means to be an Iraqi amid the destruction and fragmentation of their country. As they watched daily news about rampant corruption, sectarian killings, and violence brought about by the U.S. occupation, they saw the visions they had of their homeland and the lives they lived there erased. In order to challenge this status quo, they asserted their existence through narratives. The life stories that Iraqis have fashioned in exile show how they responded to the legacies of imperial interventions in Iraq through new notions of selfhood. Their narratives of selfhood were associated with shifting discourses informed by political events, religious differences, and gendered and classed sensibilities. These discourses included nostalgic reminiscences of a revolutionary time and the emancipation of women, which produced a discourse about a progressive Iraqi past; continuous political activism that aimed to reshape the contemporary Iraqi political sphere to break with the idealistic past and the sectarian present; intergenerational haunting that was informed both by Iraq's religious sphere and imaginations of the secular past; ongoing journeys between Iraq and London to define a notion of home; and performances of authenticity through tales of hardship, traditional food, and humor.

Catherine Lutz argues that "empire is in the details" and suggests that scholars look at "the many fissures, contradictions, historical particularities, and shifts in imperial processes"[9] to "make the human and material face and frailties of imperialism more visible, and in so doing ... make challenges to it more likely."[10] Though Iraqis are entangled in imperial formations, they remain invisible within this imperial legacy. Through narrating their lives and the futures they imagined, they aimed to write themselves back into the history of empire. Rather than focusing on spectacular violence or narratives of victimhood, Iraqis in this book have offered accounts that reflect their efforts to reckon with the past, envision futures, and carve out a sense of belonging amid destruction and loss. The ongoing violence in Iraq—brought about by imperial and national entanglement and spanning more than four decades—raises questions about what it means to be an Iraqi. The politics of erasure—whether the erasure of life, history, imperial violence, or homeland—poses a challenge to how Iraqis imagine themselves and interpret the past. My Iraqi interlocutors in London responded to the conditions of empire by narrating stories about how imperial interventions impacted their lives and political projects and led to their displacement. In looking at survivors of violence, Veena Das shows that "life was recovered not through some grand gestures in the realm of the transcendent but through descent into the ordinary."[11] Rather than describing moments of horror, Das invites us to describe "what happens to the subject and world when the memory of such events is folded into ongoing relationships."[12]

When I first arrived in London in 2006, I found two major discourses among Iraqis in London—namely, the communist discourse about the revolutionary past and a competing religious discourse that perceived Iraq as a land of holy cities. A third discourse, which encompassed the notion of endurance, was beginning to emerge at the time and has gained more popularity over the years. The discourse that Iraqi communists in London developed was situated in anticolonial struggle against British rule in Iraq and anti-feudal protests against the monarchy. Through their narratives, communists imagined Iraq as a place characterized by social and political vibrancy and cultural renaissance. The dominant political trends at the time focused on political projects that championed social and economic equality, political independence, and women's liberation. Iraqi communists perceived their revolutionary agenda as constituting a rupture with the traditional past and the colonial present. They cultivated a notion of Iraqi subjectivity that revolved around modernity and a promising future. Revolutionary men and women who marched together against the British presence in Iraq, who took part in the cultural scene of modern literature and art exhibitions, and who struggled for social justice through their fight for the downtrodden, emerged as the quintessential Iraqis. More importantly, this discourse developed as a response to the status quo in Iraq. Iraqi communists, while reflecting nostalgically about the "good old days," constantly compared the hopeful past of Iraq and its alternative futures to the impasse of the present, defined by sectarian violence, foreign occupation, and ethnic fragmentation.

In addition, this discourse was gendered and classed to a great extent in that the figure of the middle-class, unveiled, educated woman, who took part in demonstrations and worked toward the education of peasant women, emerged as the symbol of Iraqi modernity and the future. While modern women stood in contrast to traditional women who wore the veil and traditional garments, they also delineated a political project that pivoted around an increased role for women in the public sphere and around advocacy for gender reforms, especially with regard to the personal status code. The recollections of Iraqi communist women linked Iraq's independence from the British to the liberation of women in that the elimination of colonial rule and feudal realities through class struggle and anticolonial political reform would entail the end of women's subordination. Moreover, these gender aspirations were informed by the politics of class and the secularist/religious divides of the present. The disenchantment with ruling elites and politicians after 2003 for their failure to provide services and to quell sectarian divisions and rampant corruption was translated into Orientalist tropes that interpreted their incompetency as manifestations of backward religious beliefs and of affiliations with the uneducated lower-classes. Instead of seeing the status quo in Iraq within the parameters of the emerging alternative political discourse of those Iraqis who found themselves in exile in the 1990s, the older Iraqis in London who still yearned for the revolutionary past assumed essentialist interpretations of the present that eschewed political and historical explanations.

Imperial interventions in Iraq—represented by the British presence until the fall of the monarchy in 1958—fueled anticolonial struggles and inspired Iraqis to perceive themselves as revolutionaries who worked for political independence and social justice, but the communists' perception of an alternative future for Iraq after the British left were undermined when the United States began to play an increasing role in Iraqi affairs by the late 1950s. My Iraqi interlocutors and their compatriots were threatened with torture and death during the CIA-backed coup of 1963. For those who did not perish or serve sentences in prisons, the coup heralded the first phase of their exile. The return of the Ba'th Party to power in 1968 and the increasing persecution of the opponents of the regime in the 1970s marked the second phase of displacement for Iraqi communists. The United States' support of Saddam Hussein in the 1980s turned what Iraqis had thought was a temporary sojourn in Britain into a permanent exile. Not only did the U.S. empire leave the lives of Iraqis in ruins, but it also produced conditions in which Iraqis in exile could no longer visit or maintain unfettered connections with their country.

Though Iraqi communists shaped popular memory through their reminiscences about the 1950s as the golden age of a dynamic social and political landscape, this discourse failed to appeal to the younger generation in diaspora, who found a sense of belonging in Shi'i religious practices. My London interlocutors of the younger generation, who grew up in exile and learned about their country through their parents, were religious in their outlooks. To them, Iraq is a holy land they yearned to visit for religious reasons. Their sense of Iraqiness was deeply intertwined with religious events that took place in Iraq throughout the centuries. As such, this religious discourse that perceived Iraq through the prism of religion marked a shift from the secular imagination of Iraq. On the other hand, young Iraqis in Britain also saw Iraq through their parents' stories of daily life and common Iraqi experiences that they missed out on—such as enjoying the local food or strolls along the Tigris. Rather than grand ideals about the future, younger Iraqis were more concerned about carving out a subjectivity rooted in religious beliefs and British multiculturalism and retaining a sense of Iraqiness for their children. Instead of visions of bringing about radical transformation in their homeland, the younger generation in London was suspicious of political activism and looked for religious practice and normal daily life to create a sense of identity.

However, the religious discourse endorsed by young Iraqis not only marked a departure from the communists' secular project, but also aimed to break away from what they perceived to be the traditional Islam of their parents. While young Iraqis felt the need to constantly affirm a religious identity through regular religious practices and travels to Iraq, they fashioned a religious self that was nevertheless embedded in a modernist reading of Islam. Basing their religious practices and beliefs on reading and understanding the religious texts, rather than blindly following religious scholars, young Iraqis delineated a concept of traditional Islam versus modern Islam. The debate among them about traditional and modern Islam was embedded in the turn of events in Iraq after 2003. As it became apparent that the religious politicians who assumed power after the fall of Hussein's regime and who resorted to a sectarian discourse to mobilize people had failed to build a functioning state and to provide basic services to the citizens, young religious Iraqis in London began to be disenchanted with the religious establishment. In 2006, a few of them began to voice scathing critiques of politicians' use of religion for political ends and of the role of the religious establishment in public affairs; moreover, they advocated for the separation of religion from state and felt that religion had become a tool to exacerbate sectarian tensions, rather than a means to shape a pious self dedicated to the cultivation of networks of care and tolerance. By 2019, these rare voices became more dominant as young people thought religion should strictly revolve around the relationship between the individual and God without interfering in politics. While this critique broke with the vision that Islam held fundamental precepts for state governance, it did not renounce religion itself. Young Iraqis faulted the religious establishment and politicians for mischaracterizing Islam and believed that Islam itself offered lessons in acceptance of others, leading a life of integrity, and constructing spaces of solidarity.

This discourse, with its vision of a modernist understanding of religion and a celebration of the everyday life in Iraq, was classed as well. When young Iraqis talked about their early memories of Iraq and their parents' reminiscences about times of stability and plenty, they spoke of the experiences of middle-class Baghdadis. The Iraq they yearned for was a country where people from their background enjoyed status and prosperity. More importantly, they associated the corrupt and sectarian behavior of Iraqi politicians and their followers with lower classes from the south who did not have the capability to think independently or act with integrity. Though Iraqi communists and the religious youth seemed to inhabit different spaces, they shared the same classist view of Iraqi society. The world of the lower classes was either silenced or blamed for the ills in the Iraqi society and diaspora. Implicit in this attitude was the idea that middle- and upper-middle-class Baghdadis represented the true Iraq. Likewise, the religious discourse was also gendered. However, rather than looking to communist women as a source of inspiration and activism, young religious women turned to Muslim women as role models. While secular women related to Arab thinkers at the turn of the twentieth century who called for the education and unveiling of women, young religious women aspired to cultivate qualities of strength and independence associated with Prophet Muhammad's daughter and granddaughter. The figures of Fatima and Zainab in particular represented women who stood up to injustices, spoke their mind, and acquired formidable religious knowledge.

Younger Iraqis' efforts to fashion a religious Iraqi self implicated in classed and gendered sensibilities took place against the backdrop of U.S. imperialism. Young Iraqis who either left Iraq when they were very young or were born in the United Kingdom yearned to visit the country in order to formulate their own memories. However, U.S. interests in keeping Saddam Hussein in power in the 1980s and the 1990s prolonged their exile. Their daily lives, dictated by their parents' longing for Iraq, were punctuated by hopes of regime change so that they might go experience their homeland. U.S. interventions foreclosed that possibility in the 1980s and 1990s, but the invasion in 2003 provided the opportunity to visit Iraq for the first time in decades. Some of the young Iraqis chose not to visit in order to maintain the nostalgic picture they had formed. Others, however, decided to visit despite the chaos and violence. Though they felt emotional at seeing Baghdad and going to holy places, they also were disenchanted by the lack of public infrastructure and the destruction of their parents' homes and the country in general.

While the communist discourse delineated a past that became irrelevant in the present, and the religious discourse as a project of governance lost its appeal, a third narrative gained more popularity among Iraqis in London. The emerging discourse among Iraqis who did not belong to the upper-middle and middle classes revolved around the notion of endurance (*tahamul*)—of persistence and perseverance in conditions of chronic uncertainty, precarity, and destitution, which mostly affected the lower-middle and lower classes in Iraq. Iraqis in London who could not relate to the communist discourse of the older generation came to see Iraqis who had left Iraq after 2003 as representing the "real Iraq" because of their experiences of hardship and resilience. After spending decades in exile, Iraqis in London perceived their experience of Iraqiness as defined by an absence. Since the majority of them had arrived in London in either the late 1970s or early 1990s, they had not suffered like those who had stayed in Iraq until recently and had endured decades of persecution, the Iran-Iraq War, the Gulf War, the sanctions, the U.S. invasion, and the instability of the post-Saddam era.

Endurance emerged as the iconic condition of Iraqi subjectivity. In this framework, the more a person had endured through different regimes and conflagrations, the more the person was an Iraqi. The hierarchy of suffering conferred different shades of belonging and nationhood. A true Iraqi was no longer a revolutionary who had experienced the glorious 1950s, but one who had lived with dispossession and hardship and persevered against imperial erasure and death. Moreover, this discourse of suffering and endurance, like the previous discourses, was classed and gendered. Though the majority of people in Iraq had lived through wars, sanctions, and dictatorship, they had not experienced these conditions equally. Women from the lower-middle and lower classes were hit the hardest by economic precarity and political uncertainty. The figure of the Iraqi woman from the lower-middle class emerged as a powerful symbol of Iraqi endurance for her efforts to find legitimate ways to make ends meet and to hold the family together in times of hardship. These Iraqi women appeared as more authentic because they had sacrificed the most throughout the decades.

The discourse of endurance refers to the chronicity of conditions of dispossession brought about by imperial interventions. The imprisonment of family members following the first Ba'th coup, the loss of relatives in the Iran-Iraq War, the experience of heavy bombardments during wars that spanned four decades, the conditions of economic deprivation during the sanctions, the death of more friends during the invasion, and the legal precarity after displacement meant that Iraqis who stayed in Iraq until 2003 had lived constantly with the costs of empire. Not only did they have to contend with the realities of the imperialist destruction of their lives and livelihoods inside Iraq, but they also continued to experience imperial erasure in exile. During the sanctions and after the U.S. invasion in 2003, Iraqis became unwelcome guests who could not secure entry to Western countries, even though some of these countries—in particular the United States and Britain—were responsible for their exile. While Iraqis who arrived in London in the late 1970s and early 1990s managed to get the indefinite leave to remain and British citizenship relatively easily, Iraqis who arrived after 2003 experienced a precarious existence of living in legal limbo. As such, their hardships were perpetuated in exile by imperial practices that rendered these exiles as the other, persons whose humanity did not warrant a legitimate status or protection.

Living in the shadow of U.S. imperialism means that Iraqis in exile and in Iraq constantly inhabit a space defined by the denial of life and humanity. However, this imperial erasure is not always visible. While the British Mandate in Iraq and Britain's control of Iraqi affairs after the country's nominal independence in 1932 meant that the conditions of empire were acknowledged and visible, the U.S. empire with its perpetuation of wars and support of an authoritarian regime in Iraq is undeclared and unclear. Scholars and pundits who read the U.S. occupation of Iraq as marking a shift in the role that the United States envisioned for itself globally focus on a scenario of spectacular violence used directly to bring about regime changes. However, seeing the United States through the lens of its imperial practices since its inception and attending to the invisible ways that imperial violence has haunted Iraqis' lives for decades open a space to examine the continuation of the U.S. imperial legacy in different forms. To focus solely on the internal developments of Iraq to explain events such as the Iran-Iraq War, the invasion of Kuwait, the use of chemical weapons against the Kurds and Iranian soldiers, the persecution of Iraqis during Hussein's reign, and spiraling sectarian violence is to comfortably absolve the United States and other Western powers of any role they played in arming a brutal regime, prolonging wars, imposing sanctions, displacing people, and perpetuating exile. But it is in this context and through these details that empire materialized on the ground for Iraqis.

During my visits to London in 2018 and 2019, I found that, tragically, Iraqis there had begun to feel nostalgia for the days of Saddam Hussein's regime. Even Iraqis who had family members who disappeared and were killed under Hussein's reign thought that his rule was better than the status quo in Iraq. They believed that before the U.S. occupation there was at least a state in Iraq that managed to provide basic services like electricity and water, though inadequately in the 1990s and early 2000s. A common comment that I began to hear was, "We used to have one Saddam. Now, we have many Saddams." Iraqis were aghast at the level of violence perpetuated by opposing militias and the U.S. military. Saddam Hussein's regime was once the known, predictable source of danger in the country, but after 2003, no one knew where the danger would come from. And the corruption and partisan impasse in Iraq made things all the worse. The nostalgia for Hussein's reign did not spring from the desire to have a dictator, but simply to have a functioning state that could provide services to the people.

The irony of the situation was not lost on my interlocutors. They often told me that the United States had managed to make the unthinkable a reality yet again: Iraqis had reached a stage where they yearned for the tyrant who had destroyed their lives and their country.

# NOTES

## Introduction

1. http://georgewbush-whitehouse.archives.gov/news/releases/2003/03/20030319-17.html.

2. Nadine Naber (2012: 27) advances the concept of "diasporas of empire" to examine the impact of contemporary U.S. neocolonialism and imperialism on communities that were displaced as a result of imperial interventions.

3. Williams (2006).

4. Coutin (2016: 6–7).

5. Lieba Faier and Lisa Rofel (2014: 363) use the concept of "ethnographies of encounter" to explore "how culture making occurs through unequal relationships involving two or more groups of people and things that appear to exist in culturally distinct worlds."

6. Grewal (2005: 2–3) and Thomas (2011: 5).

7. Gutmann and Lutz (2018: 292).

8. Ibid., 292–93.

9. Maira (2018: 393).

10. Ibid.

11. Ibid.

12. Viet Thanh Nguyen furthers the discussion by linking the Vietnam War to the history of racism in the United States. He reminds readers of Martin Luther King Jr.'s argument that "the problem of racism, the problem of economic exploitation, and the problem of war are all tied together" (2016: 2). The interrelation between U.S. empire and the history of racism in the United States "has been written as a national tragedy or as part of an international history of slavery, but not necessarily as part of the history of U.S. empire. It is somebody else's empire." See Stoler (2018: 484).

13. McGranahan and Collins (2018: 10).
14. Stoler (2018: 478).
15. Ibid., 478–79.
16. McGranahan and Collins (2018: 1).
17. Jones (2017: 417).
18. Ibid., 418. See also Appel, Mason, and Watts (2015) and Mitchell (2011).
19. Wolfe-Hunnicutt (2018: 3).
20. U.S. officials were particularly concerned with the alliance between Qasim and the communists. After Qasim withdrew Iraq from the Baghdad Pact—an alliance between Turkey, Britain, Iran, and Pakistan, which Iraq joined in 1955—in 1959 and accepted military and economic aid from the Soviet Union, "the [U.S.] National Security Council formed a special working group on Iraq to monitor the situation and consider the options for bringing about a change in the government" (Wolfe-Hunnicutt (2018: 10). The turning point in U.S. foreign policy toward Qasim was Iraq's nationalization of 99.5 percent of its oil resources in December 1961. The nationalization decree did not impact the Iraq Petroleum Company's operation in existing fields. It only transferred ownership of oil fields that were not yet in production. While the U.S. State Department recognized Iraq's right to nationalize its oil, it feared the action would set a precedent in the region.
21. Wolfe-Hunnicutt (2018: 3).
22. Khalidi (2004: 41). See also Khalidi (2009: 151).
23. Batatu (1987: 988).
24. The number of communists killed is unsettled. Batatu quotes different sources that put the number between 340 and 5,000. Wolfe-Hunnicutt puts the number of executed communists at 5,000 (2018: 11).
25. For a detailed account of this history, see Wolfe-Hunnicutt (2017 and 2018).
26. Quoted in Jentleson (1994: 34).
27. Ibid., 35. See also, Wolfe-Hunnicutt (2017).
28. Jentleson (1994: 15).
29. Ibid. 42–49.
30. Ibid., 48.
31. Tripp (2007: 230).
32. Wolfe-Hunnicutt (2018: 15).
33. Tripp (2007: 236). Ali Allawi puts the number of Kurds who died during al-Anfal at two hundred thousand. See Allawi (2007: 38).
34. Quoted in Jentleson (1994: 69).
35. Ibid., 81–82.
36. Ibid., 84.
37. Ibid., 84.
38. Wolfe-Hunnicutt (2018: 16).

39. Gordon (2010: 89).
40. Ibid., 34.
41. Tripp (2007: 248).
42. Quoted in Haddad (2011: 74). The Hussein regime's response was swift and brutal. It sent the Republican Guard to put down the uprising in the south, where they "carried out indiscriminate mass executions of the population. Many tanks were painted with the slogan 'No Shi'is [will survive] after today' and there was widespread destruction of Shi'i shrines and other mosques in the Holy Cities [of Najaf and Karbala]. As many as 300,000 may have been killed in these operations" (Farouk-Sluglett and Sluglett 2001: 289). Around fifty thousand refugees fled to Saudi Arabia, and thousands sought refuge in Iran (Tripp 2007: 247).
43. Ibid.
44. Ibid.
45. Quoted in Haddad (2011: 76)
46. Gordon (2010: 37).
47. Ibid.
48. https://www.youtube.com/watch?v=RM0uvgHKZe8.
49. Gordon (2010: 87).
50. For a detailed account of the neoconservatives' objectives, see Harvey (2013: 190–208).
51. For a detailed account of torture at Abu Ghraib, see Hersh (2004).
52. Watson Institute, "Costs of War," https://watson.brown.edu/costsofwar/costs/human/civilians/iraqi.
53. "Iraq: The Human Cost," http://web.mit.edu/humancostiraq/.
54. For a history of the rise of the Islamic States, see Saleh (2015).
55. Jones (2012: 209).
56. Ibid., 209.
57. Ibid., 210, 217.
58. Ibid., 213.
59. Ibid., 213.
60. Ibid., 213.
61. Ibid., 215.
62. Ibid., 216.
63. Ibid., 216.
64. Ibid., 217.
65. Wolfe-Hunnicutt (2018: 11).
66. United States Army (2007: v, x).
67. Ibid., vi.
68. Ajami (2006: 51).
69. Gelb (2003).

70. Burns (2003).

71. Good (2003).

72. Thomas (2011: 6).

73. The subject, in this framework, is "at once a product and agent of history; the site of experience, memory, storytelling and aesthetic judgment; an agent of knowing as much as of action; and the conflicted site for moral acts and gestures amid impossibly immoral societies and institutions." See Biehl, Good, and Kleinman (2007: 14).

74. Franz Fanon called attention to the connection of colonialism and subjectivity back in 1963. He asserts, "Because it is a systematic negation of the other person and a furious determination to deny the other person all attributes of humanity, colonialism forces the people it dominates to ask themselves the question constantly: 'In reality, who am I?'" (Fanon 1963: 250). Fanon postulated that the solution to the problem of colonialism and the problem of subjectivity was armed resistance.

75. Sara Pursley (2019: 33) argues that while Michel Foucault's notions of biopolitics and discipline have influenced studies of British policy in Egypt and India, the case of Iraq reflects the British resort to another form of power in Iraq—namely, necropolitics.

76. For a study of nation building in Iraq as a disciplinary project, see Sara Pursley (2019). Pursley shows that the debate among Iraqi educators in the first half of the twentieth century, in particular about reforming the family through shaping the youth in the school and the military, was a Foucauldian project aiming to mold subjects worthy of sovereignty.

77. Ali (2018: 58–60).

78. Biehl, Good, and Kleinman (2007: 15).

79. Ibid., 5.

80. Parts of this section appeared in Saleh (2018: 515–17).

81. Al-Rasheed (1992).

82. Al-Rasheed (2005).

83. Al-Rasheed (1994).

84. There are no accurate statistics on the number of Iraqis who arrived in London in the early 1950s to the 1960s. Al-Rasheed (1994) puts the number of Iraqi Assyrians in London in 1994 at three to four thousand. During my fieldwork (2006–2008), Iraqi Jews estimated that their community consisted of five thousand members.

85. Al-Rasheed (2005: 318). Jordan has a large Iraqi community as well. Joseph Sassoon estimates that before 2003, there were 250,000 to 350,000 Iraqis living in Jordan (2009).

86. For works on the transnational connections between diasporic communities and their homelands, see, for instance, Schiller and Fouron (2001), Shipley (2013), and Brah (1996).

87. Clifford (2013).

88. Al-Ali (2007) and Al-Rasheed (1994, 2005).

89. Nina Glick Schiller and Georges Eugene Fouron employ the concept of "long-distance nationalism" to refer to the experiences of Haitians in New York who "live their lives across borders" and who remain committed to Haiti even though they are settled abroad. What defines the experiences of Haitians in New York are not only personal ties to Haiti but also "a deep love for the country." See Schiller and Fouron (2001: 3–4).

90. Freud (1989: 586).

91. Quoted in Garcia (2010: 75).

92. Freud (1989: 589).

93. Scott (2013).

94. Quoted in Pickering and Keightley (2006: 920).

95. hooks (1999: 42–43).

96. Ibid., 43.

97. Amoah (1997: 85).

98. Collins (1990: 7).

99. Amoah (1997: 84).

100. Ibid., 85.

101. Ibid., 95.

102. Ibid., 97. Emphasis in the original. In a similar vein, Latina feminists found the practice of *testimonios* "a crucial means of bearing witness and inscribing into history those lived realities that would otherwise succumb to the alchemy of erasure" (The Latina Feminist Group 2001: 2). To them, providing testimonies was a liberatory act that aimed to offer politicized accounts of history and selfhood. Like Black feminists, Latina feminists strove to disrupt essentialist and homogenizing misconceptions about their communities and histories. In this framework, the narration of life stories became a venue to gain nuanced understandings of differences and political events. Through narratives and *testimonios*, the disenfranchised can "assert themselves as political subjects through others, often outsiders, and in the process . . . emphasize particular aspects of their collective identity" (13). Indeed, the Latina Feminist Group invites us to approach testimonies "as disclosures not of personal lives but rather of the political violence inflicted on whole communities" (13). Testimonies provide *testimoniadoras* (producers of testimonies) with an opportunity to theorize oppression and subjectivity, draw global connections between events, and build networks of resistance to imperialism, racism, and sexism (19).

## Chapter 1

1. The British first invaded Iraq in 1914. Though Iraq became nominally independent in 1932, it remained under British control until the fall of the monarchy in 1958.

2. Bashkin (2009: 104).

3. Ibid., 89.

4. Arab nationalists in Iraq saw Islam as the catalyst that led to a glorious Arab empire in the past. However, this reading of Islam and past glory was based on a secular understanding of Islam.

5. For the role of schools as disciplinary spaces, see Adely (2012) and Pursley (2019).

6. Under the Ottomans, the tribal leaders and landlords could not secure land tenure. The Ottoman land reforms weakened the position of the tribal sheikhs, a process that was reversed under the British. See Farouk-Sluglett and Sluglett (2001: 30).

7. Ibid., 33.

8. According to Batatu, the population of Baghdad more than doubled between 1922 and 1947. See Batatu (1978: 473).

9. Ibid., 134.

10. Ibid., 134.

11. Ibid., 135.

12. The Portsmouth Treaty "enabled the British government to remain influential in military advising and to maintain its position as the sole supplier of arms to the Iraqi army." See Bashkin (2009: 114).

13. Batatu (1978: 550). For a detailed historical account of the treaty and the Wathba, see Batatu (1978: 545–57).

14. Muhammad Mahdi al-Jawahiri was a prominent Iraqi poet. His poem "My Brother, Ja'far" became a classical Iraqi poem.

15. For a detailed account of al-Dulaimi's book, see Ali (2018) and Efrati (2012).

16. Ali (2018: 58).

17. See Efrati (2012: 154).

18. Ali (2018: 58).

19. Egger (1986: ix).

20. El-Ariss (2018: 31–49).

21. The chief of political police in 1949 estimated that 50 percent of the youth of all classes advocated communist doctrines. See Batatu (1978: 465).

22. The population of Baghdad was half a million at the time.

23. Batatu (1978: 806).

24. Angry mobs dragged the bodies of the regent and the prime minister at the time in the streets of Baghdad.

25. See Farouk-Sluglett and Sluglett (2001: 76–78).

26. Personal status questions during the monarchy period were settled under the Tribal and Criminal and Civil Disputes Regulation, which did not grant women any rights in terms of marriage, divorce, child custody, and inheritance. For a detailed account of the Tribal and Criminal and Civil Disputes Regulation, see Efrati (2012), chapters 1 and 2.

27. Sara Pursley offers a different reading of the Personal Status Code and argues that it did not in fact improve the situation of women. See Pursley (2019), chapter 7.

28. See Efrati (2012: 161–62).

29. The law remained in effect despite amendments under different regimes after 1963. It was only after the fall of Saddam Hussein that there were serious efforts to annul it. Despite these efforts, the law remained in effect. However, it was amended so that the testimony of two women equals the testimony of one man and that a man inherits twice the share of a woman. For more details on the law, see Ali (2018), Al-Ali (2007), and Efrati (2012).

30. Tripp (2007: 155).

31. Writing on revolution in Serbia, Jessica Greenberg argues that when "people mobilized the idea of revolution, they also invoked the ideas of a desirable form of total political transformation and the utopian reorganization of society." See Greenberg (2014: 9).

32. Farouk-Sluglett and Sluglett (2001: 53), and Tripp (2007: 147–48).

33. Wolfe-Hunnicutt (2011: 99).

34. Ibid., 99–101.

35. Quoted in Batatu (1978: 982).

36. Ibid.

37. Hamid Naficy, writing about the Iranian diaspora in the United States, argues that the fixation in television dramas on Iran prior to the Iran-Iraq War and on pre-Islamic symbols serves to deal with three losses for Iranian exiles, namely, the loss "to the Islamic Republic, to the war, and to exile." The idealization of the good old days shields the self from these losses and the effects of exile. See Hamid Naficy (1993: 131).

38. The ICP was liquidated in Iraq, and it mainly operated in exile, primarily in Eastern Europe and Britain.

39. At the time, the Iraqi Forum was overwhelmed with work because the British government granted asylum to Iraqis in the 1990s in large numbers. It provided refugees with interpreters, found them suitable lodging, filed asylum paperwork (since most of those Iraqis did not speak English), and familiarized them with the British system, including schooling, the health system, and social and housing benefits.

40. For a discussion on the politics of disenchantment among Arab Marxists, see Bardawil (2020)

41. For a detailed account of the Iraqi opposition, See Ali A. Allawi (2007), chapter 2.

42. For a discussion of the emergence of a distinct Shi'i identity in Iraq under the monarchy as a response to a history of marginalization and exclusion, see Haddad (2014).

43. Speaking of classical Western tales of homecoming, Svetlana Boym (2011) argues that homecoming is usually accompanied by contradictions and misrecognitions. The nostalgic imagines a mythical return and a reunion with an enchanted world, but is disappointed to find a world she cannot read or recognize.

44. An abaya is a loose black gown worn by women.

## Chapter 2

1. Svetlana Boym differentiates between restorative and reflective nostalgia. She argues that restorative nostalgia "does not think of itself as nostalgia, but rather as truth and tradition. Reflective nostalgia dwells on the ambivalences of human longing and belonging and does not shy away from the contradictions of modernity. Restorative nostalgia protects the absolute truth, while reflective nostalgia calls it into doubt" (2001: xviii).

2. Tripp (2007: 150).

3. Both Qasim and the communists knew that the Arab nationalists outnumbered them in Mosul, so, to thwart the coup, Qasim allowed the communists to travel from Baghdad to Mosul to hold a rally organized by the ICP-inspired Peace Partisans. Thousands of communists went to Mosul to participate in the rally. They shouted, "Our sole leader is Abd Karim Qasim" and "There is no Za'im [leader] other than Karim," writes Batatu (1978: 866–89). The leaders of the coup were forced into action by this show of power on the part of the communists. In their first manifesto, which was broadcast over Mosul Radio, they declared that Qasim had "betrayed" the 1958 Revolution and "warred against Arab nationalism," among other grievances (881). In response, the head of the communist-led unions and organizations—including the General Union of Students, the Federation of Peasants' Associations, the Peace Partisans, and the League for the Defense of Women's Rights—appealed to the people to put down "treason" and to Qasim to mobilize the masses (883). Fearful that the army officers in Baghdad would stand with the leaders of the coup, Qasim gave "the People's Resistance Forces a free hand." At the same time, he "afforded the Communists and their tens of thousands of supporters the run of the streets in Baghdad and other towns. This completed the paralysis of the nationalists and conservatives."

4. Ibid., 866.
5. Ibid., 866. See also Tripp (2007: 151).
6. Batatu (1978: 887).
7. Tripp (2007: 201).
8. Jabar (2003: 225).
9. Allawi (2007: 31).
10. Tripp (2007: 237).
11. Ibid., 237.
12. Ibid., 204–5.
13. Ibid., 205.
14. Ibid., 206.
15. Ibid., 248.
16. Chalabi's family left Iraq after the fall of the monarchy and established business networks in Jordan, Lebanon, and Switzerland. From exile, Chalabi was involved in the Iraqi political scene since the 1960s. After the collapse of Petra Bank, of which

he was in charge, Chalabi fled Jordan to London, where he emerged as a leading figure in the opposition, given his contacts with different groups in the opposition. See Allawi (2007: 41–42).

17. Iyad Allawi, who established the INA in 1990, hailed from a prominent Shi'i family. He was aggravated by the power of the Iraqi Communist Party and joined the Ba'th at an early age in the late 1950s. After a falling out with the Ba'th regime in the 1970s, he fled to London. Throughout the 1980s, he kept his distance from the opposition, given their Islamist-leaning and close relations with Iran. See Allawi (2007: 51).

18. Allawi (2007: 53).
19. Ibid., 67.
20. Ibid., 67.
21. Quoted in Allawi (2007: 62).
22. Ibid., 67.
23. Tripp (2007: 270).
24. Ibid., 271.
25. Ibid., 271.
26. Ibid., 271.
27. On the role of the CPA in institutionalizing a sectarian quota system, see Haddad (2011), chapter 7.
28. See Haddad (2011: 251n19).

## Chapter 3

1. I employ "South Asia" on purpose to protect the identity of Ali and his father.
2. With regard to the relevance of history, not only in terms of how it appears in the present, but also how it circulates affectively in the present, see Thomas (2019: 19).
3. Dodge (2003: 67).
4. The curriculum—which focused on Islamic philosophy, jurisprudence, al-Hadith, logic, language, interpretation of the Quran, and history among other subjects—aimed to provide religious students with the tools to meet the spiritual needs of their congregation.
5. Corboz (2015: 192–93).
6. Saleh (2013: 59).
7. Jabar (2003: 75).
8. Ibid., 76.
9. Tripp (2007: 155).
10. Jabar (2003: 27).
11. Ibid., 202–6.
12. Baumann (1999: 76–80).
13. Haddad (2011: 65).
14. Ibid., 73.

15. Ibid., 75.
16. Ibid., 82.
17. Ibid., 83.
18. Ibid., 85; and Cockburn (2008: 70).
19. Deeb (2006: 130).
20. Abu Bakr and Omar are the first and second caliphs in Islam, respectively. Aisha and Hafsa were wives of Prophet Mohammed that Shi'is associate with Sunnism because they stood against Ali, the fourth caliph and first Shi'i imam.
21. By using the term "brothers in religion," Ali employs a gendered understanding of a religious community as consisting of men, reproducing a religious narrative that perceives Muslims as brothers in religion. As such, Ali's narrative, informed by language use in traditional Islam, is exclusionary in its connotation, though he champions an inclusive, modern reading of Islam.
22. For debates among pious Muslim women on the construction of a pious self through religious practices and modernist understanding of religion, see Mahmood (2005) and Deeb (2006), respectively.
23. Svetlana Boym defines nostalgia as a "sentiment of loss and displacement" and as a "romance with one's own fantasy." See Boym (2001: xiii).

## Chapter 4

1. The three provinces that became Iraq in 1921—Mosul, Baghdad, and Basra—were under Ottoman rule from the sixteenth century until the fall of the Ottoman Empire in 1918.
2. Quoted in Babakhan (2002).
3. Saleh (2013: 49).
4. Rogers Brubaker addresses the nation as a category of practice in that nationhood is institutionalized in the practices of a state. Critical of the imagined community framework, he advances the idea that the imagination of a nation is better understood through practices and policies adopted by the ruling elites (Brubaker 1996: 88). He further argues that nationality laws are instruments of social closure to differentiate between citizens and aliens (Brubaker 1996: 21–23). The Iraqi Nationality Law, however, did not merely define the citizen and the noncitizen. As I argue (2013: 49), it was an instrument of internal differentiation, through which ruling elites facilitated political closures and constructed internal others within the very category of the Iraqi citizen.
5. Nakash (1994).
6. Tripp (2007: 195).
7. There are only various estimates of the number of Iraqis deported. It is estimated that between forty thousand and four hundred thousand Iraqis were deported in the early 1980s. See Ali Babakhan (2002: 198–99). According to Kanan Makiya, there were

two million Iraqis who were considered *taba'iyya*, or about 15 percent of the population. See Makiya (1998: 136).

8. Shaban (2002).

9. Kashani-Sabet (2002: 165–66).

10. Qaimar is a dairy dish Iraqis eat in the morning; pacha is a dish made of Iraqi bread and meat.

11. For further details on the trope of "the good Arab girl" and "the good Iraqi girl," see Naber (2012) and Campbell (2016), respectively.

12. During our interviews, Hadjar always perceived herself as a Muslim feminist who championed women's rights. She asserted that being who she was, she would not have embraced her Muslim heritage if Islam were truly antifeminist. Hadjar advocates the adoption of a modern reading of Islam. Such a critical rereading would show that Islam has always emphasized women's rights. She believed that there was an antifeminist tradition in the Islamic community, but not the Islamic faith. To her, the Quran emphasized equality between genders and appreciated women's needs and strengths. Islam abounds with stories about strong women, such as the Virgin Mary, Queen of Sheba, Hagar (the wife of Abraham), and Khadija, the first wife of the Prophet, a widow who was older than him. Khadija's support of him throughout the prophecy proved indispensable to the success of Muhammad and the spread of Islam. To Hadjar, Khadija was a powerful woman who played an important role in the history of Islam, but her role is dismissed by patriarchal cultural practices. Hadjar also read the tragedy of Karbala through a feminist lens. To her, an important element of the story, which is often ignored, is the fact that Imam Hussein always went to his sister, Zainab, for comfort and military advice. After his death, Zainab played an important role in carrying the message of her brother.

13. For a discussion of the importance of sacred localities in the construction of religious subjectivity, local history, and identity, see Schielke and Stauth (2008: 7–24), Grewal (2013), and Ali (2019).

14. During the sanction years (1990–2003), direct flights to and from Iraq were suspended. When Hadjar went to Iraq for the first time, she had to fly to Amman and take a taxi to Baghdad.

15. Tahrir Square, where the Monument of Freedom by the prominent Iraqi sculptor Jawad Salim stands, is an iconic location of Baghdad. The monument commemorates the achievements of the 1958 Revolution.

16. The prayer reads "Hail upon you, O father of Abdullah." Imam Hussein was also known as the father of Abdullah.

17. 'Umrah is little Hajj.

18. Sunni Muslims believe that Omar and Abu-Bakr were the rightful caliphs to succeed Prophet Muhammad after this death, while Shi'i Muslims believe that Imam

Ali and his offspring from his wife Fatima, the Prophet's daughter, were the rightful successors.

19. Interestingly, when I last saw Hadjar, she talked about how she only felt free when she went on pilgrimage to Mecca. She said that being in Europe, she was always aware that she was not completely free. Though she was a woman who could freely express her opinion, travel around, and do things, she was not as free as she would like to be. For instance, she talked about how she was not free to pray whenever it was time for prayer, how she had to hide in a corner to pray, and how people were curious about what she was doing. She also mentioned the way wearing the hijab singled her out as different and made people have outlandish ideas about her (such as that she was hiding a bomb or that she did not have hair). She wished people in the United Kingdom would see beyond her religious difference and realize that she was a normal human being who loved to have fun. In Mecca, by contrast, she felt free in her "Muslimness." While she always tried to be flexible and to integrate in Europe, she was just a Muslim like everyone else around her in Mecca. When it was time to pray, everyone prayed together. To her, the sense of freedom she yearned for in Britain was the feeling that she did not have to worry about anything. She also talked about Iraq as a place where she did not have freedom because, though she was from there, the way she dressed and spoke marked her as someone coming from abroad. She constantly tried to prove to people that she was an Iraqi and to hide the fact that she was living abroad.

20. Wadi al-Salam is considered the largest cemetery in the world. Shi'i Muslims deem it a blessed land and aspire to be buried there.

21. For questions about burial rituals among Turkish migrant communities in Germany, see Osman Balkan (2015).

22. Like Ali, Hadjar became disappointed with the Iraqi religious leaders and politicians who employed Shi'ism as a means to gain power and wealth and to impose strict religious practices. She believed that these politicians misunderstood the true message of Islam, which emphasized that rulers worked for the well-being of the community and that "there is no compulsion in religion." To her, the bankruptcy of the religious political project necessitated the separation of religion from politics. Her experience in the United Kingdom led her to believe that a secular state was the solution to the impasse in Iraq, as it would allow freedom of religion and enable an atmosphere of coexistence of diverse groups of people.

## Chapter 5

1. Elizabeth Povinelli (2011) has focused on how people experience dispossession and precarity, which are endemic to our times, and how they endure through these experiences. She advances the notion of "economies of abandonment" to understand how late liberalism came to be defined by state practices and policies that unequally distributed life and death among populations. The concept of zones of abandonment focuses

on how liberal states deal with populations within the confines of the nation-state and at its borders. However, liberal states—in this case, the United States—are also empires that have relegated people in the rest of the world to zones of abandonment, of bringing death in the name of spreading freedom and democracy.

2. Tripp (2007: 206).

3. Marr (2004: 161–68).

4. Gordon (2010: 89–91).

5. Ibid., 89–91.

6. Ibid., 34.

7. The Green Zone is a fortified area in the center of Baghdad that served as the headquarters of the Coalition Provisional Authority during the U.S. occupation of Iraq and is still the center of international and Iraqi governmental institutions and organizations.

8. For a discussion on humor, subject formation, and precarity among migrants crossing the U.S.-Mexico border, see De León (2015: 92). For a study on humor and national politics, see Shipley (2017).

9. When Mosul fell to the Islamic State in 2014, Rasha called me and was heartbroken that more suffering had befallen Iraqis and that the country would further disintegrate. Likewise, when the great majority of Kurds voted for secession from Iraq in 2017, Rasha was concerned about the diminished prospect for a unified Iraq, though intellectually she supported the idea of Kurdish independence. When the Iraqi forces finally liberated Mosul in 2017, Rasha was ecstatic, especially when she heard stories about people from south Iraq sending aid to Mosul. Likewise, she was happy when the referendum in Kurdistan failed, since it meant that Iraq would remain a united country, although Kurdistan was de facto separated from Iraq. Despite her feeling that the Iraq she loved was gone, Rasha still held to the hope that a unified Iraq inhabited by Iraqis in solidarity with each other was still imaginable.

## Conclusion

1. Thinking about the notion of sovereignty, J. A. Mbembe argues that "war, after all, is as much a means of achieving sovereignty as a way of exercising the right to kill." He asks, "under what practical conditions is the right to kill, to allow to live, or to expose to death exercised?" Speaking of racialized politics of colonial violence, Mbembe advances the argument that "sovereignty means the capacity to define who matters and who does not, who is *disposable* and who is not." See Mbembe (2003: 12, 27).

2. Shakhsari (2013: 340). Emphasis in the original.

3. Ibid.

4. Butler (2010: xviii–xix).

5. Berlant (2011: 99–100).

6. Coutin (2016: 4).

7. Holmes and Castañeda (2016).
8. Ibid.
9. Lutz (2006: 593).
10. Ibid., 594.
11. Das (2007: 7).
12. Ibid., 8.

# REFERENCES

Abraham, Nabeel, Sally Howell, and Andrew Shryock. 2011. *Arab Detroit 9/11: Life in the Terror Decade*. Detroit: Wayne State University Press.
Abraham, Nicolas. 1994. *The Shell and the Kernel: Renewals of Psychoanalysis*. Chicago: University of Chicago Press.
Abrahamian, Ervand. 2013. *The Coup: 1953, the CIA, and the Roots of Modern U.S.-Iranian Relations*. New York: New Press.
Abu-Lughod, Lila. 1999. *Veiled Sentiments: Honor and Poetry in a Bedouin Society*. Berkeley: University of California Press.
———. 2005. *Dramas of Nationhood the Politics of Television in Egypt*. Chicago: University of Chicago Press.
Adelkhah, Fariba. 2000. *Being Modern in Iran*. New York: Columbia University Press in association with the Centre d'Etudes et de Recherches Internationales.
Adely. Fida. 2012. *Gendered Paradoxes: Educating Jordanian Women in Nation, Faith, and Progress*. Chicago: University of Chicago Press.
Agee, James. 1941. *Let Us Now Praise Famous Men*. Boston: Houghton Mifflin.
Ahmad, Attiya. 2017. *Everyday Conversions: Islam, Domestic Work, and South Asian Migrant Women in Kuwait*. Next Wave: New Directions in Women's Studies. Durham, NC: Duke University Press.
Ahuja, Neel. 2016. *Bioinsecurities: Disease Interventions, Empire, and the Government of Species*. ANIMA. Durham, NC: Duke University Press.
Ajami, Fouad. 2006. *The Foreigner's Gift: The Americans, the Arabs, and the Iraqis in Iraq*. New York: Free Press.
Al-Ali, Nadje Sadig. 2007. *Iraqi Women: Untold Stories from 1948 to the Present*. London: Zed Books.

———. 2009. *What Kind of Liberation? Women and the Occupation of Iraq*. Berkeley: University of California Press.

Al-Ali, Nadje Sadig, and Deborah Al-Najjar. 2013. *We Are Iraqis Aesthetics and Politics in a Time of War*. Syracuse, NY: Syracuse University Press.

Al-Ali, Zaid. 2014. *The Struggle for Iraq's Future: How Corruption, Incompetence and Sectarianism Have Undermined Democracy*. New Haven, CT: Yale University Press.

Al-Dewachi, Omar. 2017. *Ungovernable Life: Mandatory Medicine and Statecraft in Iraq*. Stanford, CA: Stanford University Press.

Alexander, M. Jacqui. 2005. *Pedagogies of Crossing: Meditations on Feminism, Sexual Politics, Memory, and the Sacred*. Perverse Modernities. Durham, NC: Duke University Press.

Ali, Zahra. 2018. *Women and Gender in Iraq: Between Nation-Building and Fragmentation*. Cambridge: Cambridge University Press.

———. 2019. "Being a Young British Iraqi Shii in London: Exploring Diasporic Cultural and Religious Identities between Britain and Iraq." *Contemporary Islam*: 1–19. https://doi.org/10.1007/s11562-018-0433-y.

Allan, Diana. 2014. *Refugees of the Revolution: Experiences of Palestinian Exile*. Stanford, CA: Stanford University Press.

Allawi, Ali A. 2007. *The Occupation of Iraq: Winning the War, Losing the Peace*. New Haven, CT: Yale University Press.

Al-Mohammad, Hayder. 2007. "Ordure and Disorder: The Case of Basra and the Anthropology of Excrement." *Anthropology of the Middle East* 2 (2): 1–23.

———. 2010. "Towards an Ethics of Being-With: Intertwinements of Life in Post-Invasion Basra." *Ethnos* 75 (4): 425–46.

———. 2012. "A Kidnapping in Basra: The Struggles and Precariousness of Life in Postinvasion Iraq." *Cultural Anthropology* 27 (4): 597–614.

Alonso Bejarano, Carolina. 2019. *Decolonizing Ethnography: Undocumented Immigrants and New Directions in Social Science*. Durham, NC: Duke University Press.

Al-Rasheed, Madawi. 1992. "Political Migration and Downward Socio-Economic Mobility: The Iraqi Community in London." *New Community* 18 (4): 537–50.

———. 1994. "The Myth of Return: Iraqi Arabs and Assyrian Refugees in London." *Journal of Refugee Studies* 7 (2–3): 199–219.

———. 1998. *Iraqi Assyrian Christians in London: The Construction of Ethnicity*. New York: Edwin Mellen Press.

———. 2005a. "Diaspora: Iraqi." In *Encyclopedia of Global Migration*. Santa Barbara, CA: Clio/ABC.

———. 2005b. *Transnational Connections and the Arab Gulf*. London: Routledge.

Aly, Ramy M. K. 2015. *Becoming Arab in London: Performativity and the Undoing of Identity*. London: Pluto Press.

Amoah, Jewel. 1997. "Narrative: The Road to Black Feminist Theory." *Berkeley Journal of Gender Law & Justice*. https://doi.org/10.15779/z38fp3b.
Anderson, Benedict. 1991. *Imagined Communities: Reflections on the Origin and Spread of Nationalism*. London: Verso.
Andersson, Ruben. 2014. *Illegality, Inc.: Clandestine Migration and the Business of Bordering Europe*. Oakland: University of California Press.
Ansari, Humayun. 2004. *The Infidel Within: Muslims in Britain since 1800*. London: Hurst & Co.
Antoon, Sinan. 2018. "Difficult Variations: Saadi Youssef's Impossible Returns." *International Journal of Contemporary Iraqi Studies* 12 (2): 199–211. https://doi.org/10.1386/ijcis.12.2.199_1.
Anwar Lori, Noora. 2019. *Offshore Citizens: Permanent Temporary Status in the Gulf*. Cambridge: Cambridge University Press.
Anzaldúa, Gloria. 2012. *Borderlands / La Frontera: The New Mestiza*. Fourth edition. San Francisco: Aunt Lute Books.
Appadurai, Arjun. 1996. *Modernity at Large Cultural Dimensions of Globalization*. Minneapolis: University of Minnesota Press.
Appel, Hannah, Arthur Mason, and Michael Watts. 2015. *Subterranean Estates: Life Worlds of Oil and Gas*. Ithaca, NY: Cornell University Press.
Arato, Andrew. 2009. *Constitution Making under Occupation the Politics of Imposed Revolution in Iraq*. New York: Columbia University Press.
Asad, Talal. 1973. *Anthropology and the Colonial Encounter*. New York: Humanities Press.
———. 1993. *Genealogies of Religion: Discipline and Reasons of Power in Christianity and Islam*. Baltimore: Johns Hopkins University Press.
———. 2003. *Formations of the Secular: Christianity, Islam, Modernity*. Stanford, CA: Stanford University Press.
Asher, Kiran. 2013. "Latin American Decolonial Thought, or Making the Subaltern Speak." *Geography Compass* 7 (12): 832–42. https://doi.org/10.1111/gec3.12102.
Atiyya, Ghassan. 1973. *Iraq, 1908–1921: A Socio-political Study*. Beirut: Arab Institute for Research and Publication.
Axel, Brian Keith. 2001. *The Nation's Tortured Body: Violence, Representation, and the Formation of a Sikh "Diaspora."* Durham, NC: Duke University Press.
Babakhan, Ali. 2002. "The Deportation of Shi'is During the Iran-Iraq War: Causes and Consequences." In *Ayatollahs, Sufis and Ideologues: State, Religion and Social Movements in Iraq*. London: Saqi.
Bald, Vivek. 2013. *Bengali Harlem and the Lost Histories of South Asian America*. Cambridge, MA: Harvard University Press.
Balkan, Osman. 2015. "Burial and Belonging." *Studies in Ethnicity and Nationalism* 15 (1): 120–34.

Ballantyne, Tony. 2006. *Between Colonialism and Diaspora: Sikh Cultural Formations in an Imperial World*. Durham, NC: Duke University Press.

Bardawil, Fadi A. 2020. *Revolution and Disenchantment: Arab Marxism and the Binds of Emancipation*. Durham, NC: Duke University Press.

Bashkin, Orit. 2009. *The Other Iraq: Pluralism and Culture in Hashemite Iraq*. Stanford, CA: Stanford University Press.

Batatu, Hanna. 1978. *The Old Social Classes and the Revolutionary Movements of Iraq: A Study of Iraq's Old Landed and Commercial Classes and of Its Communists, Ba'thists, and Free Officers*. Princeton, NJ: Princeton University Press.

———. 1981. "Iraq's Underground Shi'a Movements: Characteristics, Causes and Prospects." *The Middle East Journal* 35 (4): 578–94.

———. 1991. "The Old Social Classes Revisited." In *The Iraqi Revolution of 1958: The Old Social Classes Revisited*. London: I.B. Tauris.

Baumann, Gerd. 1999. *The Multicultural Riddle Rethinking National, Ethnic, and Religious Identities*. Zones of Religion. New York: Routledge.

Beck, Sam. 2013. *Toward Engaged Anthropology*. New York: Berghahn Books.

Beck, Sam, and Carl A. Maida. 2015. *Public Anthropology in a Borderless World*. New York: Berghahn Books.

Behar, Ruth. 1993. *Translated Woman: Crossing the Border with Esperanza's Story*. Boston: Beacon Press.

———. 1996. *The Vulnerable Observer: Anthropology That Breaks Your Heart*. Boston: Beacon Press.

———. 2013. *Traveling Heavy: A Memoir in between Journeys*. Durham, NC: Duke University Press.

Behar, Ruth, Deborah A. Gordon, and Catherine Lutz. 1995. *Women Writing Culture*. Berkeley: University of California Press.

Benjamin, Walter. 1969. *Illuminations*. New York: Schocken Books.

Berlant, Lauren Gail. 2011. *Cruel Optimism*. Durham, NC: Duke University Press.

Bernal, Victoria. 2017. "Diaspora and the Afterlife of Violence: Eritrean National Narratives and What Goes without Saying." *American Anthropologist* 119 (1): 23–34.

Biehl, João Guilherme. 2005. *Vita: Life in a Zone of Social Abandonment*. Berkeley: University of California Press.

Biehl, João Guilherme, Byron Good, and Arthur Kleinman. 2007. *Subjectivity: Ethnographic Investigations*. Berkeley: University of California Press.

Biehl, João, and Peter Locke. 2017. *Unfinished: The Anthropology of Becoming*. Durham, NC: Duke University Press.

Bishara, Amahl. "Watching U.S. Television from the Palestinian Street: The Media, the State, and Representational Interventions." *Cultural Anthropology* 23 (3): 488–530.

Bocco, Riccardo, Hamit Bozarslan, Peter Sluglett, and Jordi Tejel. 2012. *Writing the Modern History of Iraq Historiographical and Political Challenges*. Hackensack, NJ: World Scientific.
Bonilla, Yarimar. 2015. *Non-Sovereign Futures: French Caribbean Politics in the Wake of Disenchantment*. Chicago: Chicago University Press.
Boym, Svetlana. 2001. *The Future of Nostalgia*. New York: Basic Books.
Brah, Avtar. 1996. *Cartographies of Diaspora: Contesting Identities*. London: Routledge.
Brubaker, Rogers. 1996. *Nationalism Reframed: Nationhood and the National Question in the New Europe*. Cambridge: Cambridge University Press.
Buch Segal, Lotte. 2016. *No Place for Grief: Martyrs, Prisoners, and Mourning in Contemporary Palestine*. Philadelphia: University of Pennsylvania Press.
Burns, John F. 2003. "How Many People Has Hussein Killed?" *New York Times*, January 26.
Butler, Judith. 2004. *Precarious Life: The Powers of Mourning and Violence*. London: Verso.
——. 2005. *Giving an Account of Oneself*. New York: Fordham University Press.
——. 2010. *Frames of War: When Is Life Grievable?* London: Verso.
Calhoun, Craig J., Frederick Cooper, Kevin W. Moore, and Social Science Research Council. 2006. *Lessons of Empire: Imperial Histories and American Power*. New York: New Press.
Campbell, Madeline Otis. 2016. *Interpreters of Occupation: Gender and the Politics of Belonging in an Iraqi Refugee Network*. Syracuse, NY: Syracuse University Press.
Cannell, Fenella. 2010. "The Anthropology of Secularism." *Annual Review of Anthropology* 39 (1): 85–100.
Carter, Jon Horne. 2019. "Carceral Kinship: Future Families of the Late Leviathan." *Journal of Historical Sociology* 32 (1): 26–37. https://doi.org/10.1111/johs.12222.
Carter, Rebecca Louise. 2019. *Prayers for the People: Homicide and Humanity in the Crescent City*. Chicago: The University of Chicago Press.
Cavarero, Adriana. 2000. *Relating Narratives: Storytelling and Selfhood*. London: Routledge.
Chan, Shelly. 2018. *Diaspora's Homeland: Modern China in the Age of Global Migration*. Durham, NC: Duke University Press.
Chatterjee, Partha. 1993. *The Nation and Its Fragments: Colonial and Postcolonial Histories*. Princeton, NJ: Princeton University Press.
Chatterjee, Piya. 2001. *A Time for Tea: Women, Labor, and Post/Colonial Politics on an Indian Plantation*. Durham, NC: Duke University Press.
Chatty, Dawn. 2010. *Displacement and Dispossession in the Modern Middle East*. Cambridge: Cambridge University Press.

Choy, Timothy K. 2005. "Articulated Knowledges: Environmental Forms after Universality's Demise." *American Anthropologist* 107 (1): 5–18. https://doi.org/10.1525/aa.2005.107.1.005.

Clarke, Kamari Maxine. 2012. *Globalization and Race Transformations in the Cultural Production of Blackness*. Durham, NC: Duke University Press.

Clifford, James. 1994. "Diasporas." *Cultural Anthropology* 9 (3): 302–38.

———. 1997. *Routes: Travel and Translation in the Late Twentieth Century*. Cambridge, MA: Harvard University Press.

———. 2013. *Returns: Becoming Indigenous in the Twenty-First Century*. Cambridge, MA: Harvard University Press.

Cockburn, Patrick. 2006. *The Occupation*. London: Verso.

———. 2008. *Muqtada: Muqtada al-Sadr, the Shia Revival, and the Struggle for Iraq*. New York: Scribner.

Cohn, Bernard S. 1987. *An Anthropologist among the Historians: And Other Essays*. Delhi: Oxford University Press.

Collins, Patricia Hill. 1990. *Black Feminist Thought: Knowledge, Consciousness, and the Politics of Empowerment*. Boston: Unwin Hyman.

Comaroff, John L. 1992. *Ethnography and the Historical Imagination*. Boulder: Westview Press.

Corboz, Elvire. 2015. *Guardians of Shi'ism: Sacred Authority and Transnational Family Networks*. Edinburgh: Edinburgh University Press.

Coronil, Fernando. 1997. *The Magical State: Nature, Money, and Modernity in Venezuela*. Chicago: University of Chicago Press.

Coronil, Fernando, and Julie Skurski. 2006. *States of Violence*. Ann Arbor: University of Michigan Press.

Coutin, Susan Bibler. 2000. *Legalizing Moves: Salvadoran Immigrants' Struggle for U.S. Residency*. Ann Arbor: University of Michigan Press.

———. 2016. *Exiled Home: Salvadoran Transnational Youth in the Aftermath of Violence*. Durham, NC: Duke University Press.

Cox, Aimee Meredith. 2015. *Shapeshifters: Black Girls and the Choreography of Citizenship*. Durham, NC: Duke University Press.

Crapanzano, Vincent. 1980. *Tuhami, Portrait of a Moroccan*. Chicago: University of Chicago Press.

———. 2011. *The Harkis: The Wound That Never Heals*. Chicago: University of Chicago Press.

Das, Veena. 2000. *Violence and Subjectivity*. Berkeley: University of California Press.

———. 2007. *Life and Words Violence and the Descent into the Ordinary*. Berkeley: University of California Press.

Davis, Eric. 2005. *Memories of State: Politics, History, and Collective Identity in Modern Iraq*. Berkeley: University of California Press.

Dawn, C. Ernest. 1973. *From Ottomanism to Arabism; Essays on the Origins of Arab Nationalism.* Urbana: University of Illinois Press.

De León, Jason. 2015. *The Land of Open Graves: Living and Dying on the Migrant Trail.* Oakland: University of California Press.

De Regt, Marina. 2017. "From Yemen to Eritrea and Back: A Twentieth Century Family History." *Northeast African Studies* 17 (1): 25–50. https://doi.org/10.14321/nortafristud.17.1.0025.

Deeb, Lara. 2006. *An Enchanted Modern Gender and Public Piety in Shi'i Lebanon.* Princeton, NJ: Princeton University Press.

Dodge, Toby. 2003. *Inventing Iraq: The Failure of Nation-Building and a History Denied.* New York: Columbia University Press.

———. 2005. *Iraq's Future: The Aftermath of Regime Change.* London: Routledge.

———. 2012. *Iraq: From War to a New Authoritarianism.* London: Routledge.

Efrati, Noga. 2008. "Competing Narratives: Histories of the Women's Movement in Iraq, 1910–1958." *International Journal of Middle East Studies* 40 (3): 445–66. https://doi.org/10.1017/S0020743808081373.

———. 2012. *Women in Iraq: Past Meets Present.* New York: Columbia University Press.

Egger, Vernon. 1986. *Fabian in Egypt: Salama Musa and the Rise of the Professional Classes in Egypt, 1909–39.* Lanham, MD: University Press of America.

El-Ariss, Tarek. 2018. *The Arab Renaissance: A Bilingual Anthology of the Nahda.* New York: The Modern Language Association of America.

El-Shaarawi, Nadia. 2015. "Living an Uncertain Future: Temporality, Uncertainty, and Well-Being among Iraqi Refugees in Egypt." *Social Analysis* 59 (1): 38–56. https://doi.org/10.3167/sa.2015.590103.

Faier, Lieba, and Lisa Rofel. 2014. "Ethnographies of Encounter." *Annual Review of Anthropology* 43 (1): 363–77. https://doi.org/10.1146/annurev-anthro-102313-030210.

Fanon, Frantz. 2004. *The Wretched of the Earth.* New York: Grove Press.

Farouk-Sluglett, Marion, and Peter Sluglett. 1991. "The Historiography of Modern Iraq." *American Historical Review* 96 (5): 1408–21. https://doi.org/10.2307/2165278.

———. 2001. *Iraq since 1958: From Revolution to Dictatorship.* London: I.B. Tauris.

Fassin, Didier. 2011. "Policing Borders, Producing Boundaries. The Governmentality of Immigration in Dark Times." *Annual Review of Anthropology* 40 (1): 213–26. https://doi.org/10.1146/annurev-anthro-081309-145847.

———. 2013. "Why Ethnography Matters: On Anthropology and Its Publics." *Cultural Anthropology* 28 (4): 621–46. https://doi.org/10.1111/cuan.12030.

———. 2017. *If Truth Be Told: The Politics of Public Ethnography.* Durham, NC: Duke University Press.

Feldman, Ilana. 2015. "Looking for Humanitarian Purpose: Endurance and the Value of Lives in a Palestinian Refugee Camp." *Public Culture* 27 (3 [77]): 427–47. https://doi.org/10.1215/08992363-2896171.

———. 2018. *Life Lived in Relief: Humanitarian Predicaments and Palestinian Refugee Politics*. Oakland: University of California Press.

Fernea, Elizabeth Warnock. 1989. *Guests of the Sheik: An Ethnography of an Iraqi Village*. New York: Doubleday.

Fernea, Robert A. 1970. *Shaykh and Effendi; Changing Patterns of Authority among the El Shabana of Southern Iraq*. Cambridge, MA: Harvard University Press.

Fernea, Robert A., and William Roger Louis. 1991. *The Iraqi Revolution of 1958: The Old Social Classes Revisited*. London: I.B. Tauris.

Fiddian-Qasmiyeh, Elena. 2014. *The Ideal Refugees: Gender, Islam, and the Sahrawi Politics of Survival*. Gender, Culture, and Politics in the Middle East. Syracuse, NY: Syracuse University Press.

Fisher, Andrew B., and Matthew D. O'Hara. 2009. *Imperial Subjects: Race and Identity in Colonial Latin America*. Durham, NC: Duke University Press.

Foucault, Michel. 1978. *The History of Sexuality*. New York: Pantheon Books.

———. 1979. *Discipline and Punish: The Birth of the Prison*. New York: Vintage Books.

———. 1980. *Power/Knowledge: Selected Interviews and Other Writings, 1972–1977*. New York: Pantheon Books.

Franzén, Johan. 2011. *Red Star over Iraq: Iraqi Communism before Saddam*. New York: Columbia University Press.

Freud, Sigmund. 1995. *The Freud Reader*. New York: W.W. Norton.

Friedman, Andrew. 2013. *Covert Capital: Landscapes of Denial and the Making of U.S. Empire in the Suburbs of Northern Virginia*. Berkeley: University of California Press.

Gamboni, Dario. 2007. *The Destruction of Art: Iconoclasm and Vandalism since the French Revolution*. London: Reaktion.

Garcia, Angela. 2010. *The Pastoral Clinic: Addiction and Dispossession along the Rio Grande*. Berkeley: University of California Press.

———. 2017. "The Rainy Season: Toward a Cinematic Ethnography of Crisis and Endurance in Mexico City." *Social Text* 35 (1 [130]): 101–21. https://doi.org/10.1215/01642472-3728020.

Gelb, Leslie. 2003. "The Three-State Solution." *New York Times*, November 25.

Ghannam, Farha. 2002. *Remaking the Modern: Space, Relocation, and the Politics of Identity in a Global Cairo*. Berkeley: University of California Press.

———. 2013. *Live and Die like a Man: Gender Dynamics in Urban Egypt*. Stanford: Stanford University Press.

Gilroy, Paul. 1993. *The Black Atlantic: Modernity and Double Consciousness.* Cambridge, MA: Harvard University Press.

Go, Julian. 2008. *American Empire and the Politics of Meaning: Elite Political Cultures in the Philippines and Puerto Rico during U.S. Colonialism.* Durham, NC: Duke University Press.

Goldstein, Alyosha. 2014. *Formations of United States Colonialism.* Durham, NC: Duke University Press.

Goldstein, Daniel M. 2000. "Names, Places, and Power: Collective Identity in the Miss Oruro Pageant, Cochabamba, Bolivia." *PoLAR: Political and Legal Anthropology Review* 23 (1): 1–24. https://doi.org/10.1525/pol.2000.23.1.1.

Good, Erica. 2003. "Stalin to Saddam: So Much for the Madman Theory." *New York Times*, May 4.

Gopinath, Gayatri. 2005. *Impossible Desires: Queer Diasporas and South Asian Public Cultures.* Durham, NC: Duke University Press.

Gordon, Avery. 2008. *Ghostly Matters: Haunting and the Sociological Imagination.* Minneapolis: University of Minnesota Press.

Gordon, Joy. 2010. *Invisible War: The United States and the Iraq Sanctions.* Cambridge, MA: Harvard University Press.

Graham-Brown, Sarah. 1999. *Sanctioning Saddam: The Politics of Intervention in Iraq.* London: I.B. Tauris in association with MERIP.

Grandin, Greg. 2006. *Empire's Workshop: Latin America, the United States, and the Rise of the New Imperialism.* New York: Metropolitan Books.

Greenberg, Jessica. 2014. *After the Revolution: Youth, Democracy, and the Politics of Disappointment in Serbia.* Stanford, CA: Stanford University Press.

Grewal, Inderpal. 2005. *Transnational America Feminisms, Diasporas, Neoliberalisms.* Durham, NC: Duke University Press.

Grewal, Zareena. 2013. *Islam Is a Foreign Country: American Muslims and the Global Crisis of Authority.* New York: New York University Press.

Gupta, Akhil, and James Ferguson. 1997. *Culture, Power, Place: Explorations in Critical Anthropology.* Durham, NC: Duke University Press.

Gutmann, Matthew, and Catherine Lutz. 2018. "The Empire of Choice and the Emergence of Military Dissent." In *Ethnographies of U.S. Empire*, edited by Carole McGranahan and John F. Collins, 291–312. Durham, NC: Duke University Press.

Haddad, Fanar. 2011. *Sectarianism in Iraq: Antagonistic Visions of Unity.* New York: Columbia University Press.

———. 2014. "A Sectarian Awakening: Reinventing Sunni Identity in Iraq after 2003." *Hudson Institute* (blog). August 4. https://www.hudson.org/research/10544-a-sectarian-awakening-reinventing-sunni-identity-in-iraq-after-2003.

Hafez, Sherine. 2019. *Women of the Midan: The Untold Stories of Egypt's Revolutionaries*. Public Cultures of the Middle East and North Africa. Bloomington: Indiana University Press.
Hall, Stuart. 1990. "Cultural Identity and Diaspora." In *Identity: Community, Culture, Difference*. London: Lawrence & Wishart.
Hall, Stuart, and Paul Du Gay. 1996. *Questions of Cultural Identity*. London: Sage.
Hall, Stuart, David Held, and Anthony G. McGrew. 1992. *Modernity and Its Futures*. Cambridge: Polity Press in association with the Open University.
Harlow, Barbara, and Mia Carter. 2003. *Archives of Empire*. Durham, NC: Duke University Press.
Harrison, Faye Venetia. 2010. *Decolonizing Anthropology: Moving Further toward an Anthropology of Liberation*. Arlington, VA: Association of Black Anthropologists, American Anthropological Association.
Harvey, David. 2005. *A Brief History of Neoliberalism*. Oxford: Oxford University Press.
———. 2013. *The New Imperialism*. Oxford: Oxford University Press.
Hashemi, Nader, and Danny Postel. 2017. *Sectarianization: Mapping the New Politics of the Middle East*. New York: Oxford University Press.
Hersh, Seymour. 2004. "Torture at Abu Ghraib." *New Yorker*, May 10. https://www.newyorker.com/magazine/2004/05/10/torture-at-abu-ghraib.
Hirschkind, Charles. 2006. *The Ethical Soundscape: Cassette Sermons and Islamic Counterpublics*. New York: Columbia University Press.
Ho, Engseng. 2006. *The Graves of Tarim: Genealogy and Mobility across the Indian Ocean*. Berkeley: University of California Press.
Holmes, Seth, and Heide Castañeda. 2016. "Representing the 'European Refugee Crisis' in Germany and Beyond: Deservingness and Difference, Life and Death." *American Ethnologist* 43 (1): 12–24.
Holston, James. 1999. *Cities and Citizenship*. Durham, NC: Duke University Press.
hooks, bell. 1989. *Talking Back: Thinking Feminist, Thinking Black*. Boston, MA: South End Press.
Immerwahr, Daniel. 2019. *How to Hide an Empire: A History of the Greater United States*. New York: Farrar, Straus and Giroux.
Inhorn, Marcia C. 2018. *America's Arab Refugees: Vulnerability and Health on the Margins*. Stanford, CA: Stanford University Press.
Ismael, Tareq Y. 2008. *The Rise and Fall of the Communist Party of Iraq*. Cambridge: Cambridge University Press.
Izzo, Justin. 2019. *Experiments with Empire: Anthropology and Fiction in the French Atlantic*. Theory in Forms. Durham, NC: Duke University Press.
Jabar, Faleh, A. 2002. *Ayatollahs, Sufis and Ideologues: State, Religion and Social Movements in Iraq*. London: Saqi.

———. 2003. *The Shi'ite Movement in Iraq*. London: Saqi.
Jacob, Wilson Chacko. 2011. *Working out Egypt: Effendi Masculinity and Subject Formation in Colonial Modernity, 1870–1940*. Durham, NC: Duke University Press.
Jansen, Jan C., and Jürgen Osterhammel. 2019. *Decolonization: A Short History*. Translated by Jeremiah Riemer. Princeton, NJ: Princeton University Press.
Jentleson, Bruce W. 1994. *With Friends Like These: Reagan, Bush, and Saddam, 1982–1990*. New York: W.W. Norton.
Jones, Toby Craig. 2012. "America, Oil, and War in the Middle East." *Journal of American History* 99 (1): 208–18. https://doi.org/10.1093/jahist/jas045.
———. 2017. "After the Pipelines: Energy and the Flow of War in the Persian Gulf." *South Atlantic Quarterly* 116 (2): 417–25. https://doi.org/10.1215/00382876-3829500.
Kang, Hyun Yi. 2002. *Compositional Subjects: Enfiguring Asian/American Women*. Durham, NC: Duke University Press.
Kaplan, Amy, and Donald E. Pease. 1993. *Cultures of United States Imperialism*. Durham, NC: Duke University Press.
Kashani-Sabet, Firoozeh. 2002. "Cultures of Iranianness: The Evolving Polemic of Iranian Nationalism." In *Iran and the Surrounding World: Interpretations in Culture and Cultural Politics*, edited by Nikki R. Keddie and Rudi Mathee, 162–81. Seattle: University of Washington Press.
Keddie, Nikki R., and Rudolph P. Matthee. 2002. *Iran and the Surrounding World: Interactions in Culture and Cultural Politics*. Seattle: University of Washington Press.
Khadduri, Majid. 1960. *Independent Iraq, 1932–1958: A Study in Iraqi Politics*. New York: Oxford University Press.
———. 1969. *Republican Iraq: A Study in Iraqi Politics since the Revolution of 1958*. London: Oxford University Press.
Khalidi, Rashid. 1991. *The Origins of Arab Nationalism*. New York: Columbia University Press.
———. 2004. *Resurrecting Empire: Western Footprints and America's Perilous Path in the Middle East*. Boston: Beacon Press.
———. 2009. *Sowing Crisis: The Cold War and American Dominance in the Middle East*. Boston: Beacon Press.
Khalili, Laleh. 2007. *Heroes and Martyrs of Palestine: The Politics of National Commemoration*. Cambridge: Cambridge University Press.
———. 2012. *Time in the Shadows: Confinement in Counterinsurgencies*. Stanford, CA: Stanford University Press.
Khanna, Ranjana. 2003. *Dark Continents: Psychoanalysis and Colonialism*. Durham, NC: Duke University Press.
Khoury, Dina Rizk. 2013. *Iraq in Wartime: Soldiering, Martyrdom, and Remembrance*. New York: Cambridge University Press.

Kim, Jodi. 2010. *Ends of Empire: Asian American Critique and the Cold War*. Minneapolis: University of Minnesota Press.

Klein, Naomi. 2007. *The Shock Doctrine: The Rise of Disaster Capitalism*. New York: Metropolitan Books/Henry Holt.

Kunreuther, Laura. 2014. *Voicing Subjects: Public Intimacy and Mediation in Kathmandu*. Berkeley: University of California Press.

Lalami, Laila. 2005. *Hope and Other Dangerous Pursuits*. Chapel Hill, NC: Algonquin Books of Chapel Hill.

Langwick, Stacey A. 2008. "Articulate(d) Bodies: Traditional Medicine in a Tanzanian Hospital." *American Ethnologist* 35 (3): 428–39. https://doi.org/10.1111/j.1548-1425.2008.00044.x.

The Latina Feminist Group. 2001. *Telling to Live: Latina Feminist Testimonios*. Latin America Otherwise. Durham, NC: Duke University Press.

L'Estoile, Benoit de, Federico G. Neiburg, and Lygia Sigaud. 2005. *Empires, Nations, and Natives: Anthropology and State-Making*. Durham, NC: Duke University Press.

Limbert, Mandana E. 2010. *In the Time of Oil Piety, Memory, and Social Life in an Omani Town*. Stanford, CA: Stanford University Press.

Lomas, Laura. 2008. *Translating Empire: José Martí, Migrant Latino Subjects, and American Modernities*. Durham, NC: Duke University Press.

López, Tiffany Ana, and Karen Mary Davalos. 2009. "Editors' Commentary: Knowing, Feeling, Doing: The Epistemology of Chicana/Latina Studies." *Chicana/Latina Studies* 8 (1–2): 8–22.

Louis, William Roger, and Roger Owen. 2002. *A Revolutionary Year: The Middle East in 1958*. London: I.B. Tauris.

Lowe, Lisa. 2015. *The Intimacies of Four Continents*. Durham, NC: Duke University Press.

Löwy, Michael. 2005. *Fire Alarm: Reading Walter Benjamin's On the Concept of History*. London: Verso.

Lutz, Catherine. 2006. "Empire Is in the Details." *American Ethnologist* 33 (4): 593–611. https://doi.org/10.1525/ae.2006.33.4.593.

Lutz, Catherine, and Andrea Mazzarino. 2019. *War and Health: The Medical Consequences of the Wars in Iraq and Afghanistan*. New York: New York University Press.

Mahmood, Saba. 2005. *Politics of Piety: The Islamic Revival and the Feminist Subject*. Princeton, NJ: Princeton University Press.

———. 2016. *Religious Difference in a Secular Age: A Minority Report*. Princeton, NJ: Princeton University Press.

Maira, Sunaina. 2009. *Missing: Youth, Citizenship, and Empire after 9/11*. Durham, NC: Duke University Press.

———. 2018. "Radicalizing Empire: Youth and Dissent in the War on Terror." In *Ethnographies of U.S. Empire*, edited by Carole McGranahan and John F. Collins, 391–410. Durham, NC: Duke University Press.

Makdisi, Ussama Samir. 2000. *The Culture of Sectarianism: Community, History, and Violence in Nineteenth-Century Ottoman Lebanon*. Berkeley: University of California Press.

Makdisi, Ussama Samir, and Paul A. Silverstein. 2006. *Memory and Violence in the Middle East and North Africa*. Bloomington: Indiana University Press.

Makiya, Kanan. 1998. *Republic of Fear: The Politics of Modern Iraq*. Berkeley: University of California Press.

Malkki, Liisa H. 1995. *Purity and Exile: Violence, Memory, and National Cosmology among Hutu Refugees in Tanzania*. Chicago: University of Chicago Press.

Marr, Phebe. 2004. *The Modern History of Iraq*. Boulder, CO: Westview Press.

Mbembe, Achille. 2001. *On the Postcolony*. Studies on the History of Society and Culture 41. Berkeley: University of California Press.

———. 2003. "Necropolitics." *Public Culture* 15 (1): 11–40.

McClintock, Anne. 1995. *Imperial Leather: Race, Gender, and Sexuality in the Colonial Contest*. New York: Routledge.

McCoy, Alfred W., and Francisco A. Scarano. 2009. *Colonial Crucible: Empire in the Making of the Modern American State*. Madison: University of Wisconsin Press.

McDowall, David. 1996. *A Modern History of the Kurds*. London: I.B. Tauris.

McGranahan, Carole, and John F. Collins. 2018. *Ethnographies of U.S. Empire*. Durham, NC: Duke University Press.

Mirzoeff, Nicholas. 2005. *Watching Babylon: The War in Iraq and Global Visual Culture*. London: Routledge.

———. 2011. *The Right to Look: A Counterhistory of Visuality*. Durham, NC: Duke University Press.

Mitchell, Timothy. 2011. *Carbon Democracy: Political Power in the Age of Oil*. London: Verso.

Moraga, Cherríe, and Gloria Anzaldúa. 2015. *This Bridge Called My Back: Writings by Radical Women of Color*. Albany: State University of New York Press.

Muttitt, Greg. 2012. *Fuel on the Fire: Oil and Politics in Occupied Iraq*. New York: New Press.

Naber, Nadine Christine. 2012. *Arab America: Gender, Cultural Politics, and Activism*. New York: New York University Press.

Naficy, Hamid. 1993. *The Making of Exile Cultures: Iranian Television in Los Angeles*. Minneapolis: University of Minnesota Press.

Nakash, Yitzhak. 1994. *The Shi'is of Iraq*. Princeton, NJ: Princeton University Press.

Napolitano, Valentina. 2002. *Migration, Mujercitas, and Medicine Men Living in Urban Mexico*. Berkeley: University of California Press.

Nguyen, Mimi Thi. 2012. *The Gift of Freedom: War, Debt, and Other Refugee Passages*. Durham, NC: Duke University Press.

Nguyen, Viet Thanh. 2016. *Nothing Ever Dies: Vietnam and the Memory of War*. Cambridge, MA: Harvard University Press.

Nixon, Rob. 2011. *Slow Violence and the Environmentalism of the Poor*. Cambridge, MA: Harvard University Press.

Noble, Denise. 2008. "Postcolonial Criticism, Transnational Identifications and the Hegemonies of Dancehall's Academic and Popular Performativities." *Feminist Review* 90: 106–27.

Olszewska, Zuzanna. 2015. *The Pearl of Dari: Poetry and Personhood among Young Afghans in Iran*. Bloomington: Indiana University Press.

Ong, Aihwa. 1999. *Flexible Citizenship: The Cultural Logics of Transnationality*. Durham, NC: Duke University Press.

Pandolfo, Stephania. 2018. *Knot of the Soul: Madness, Psychoanalysis, Islam*. Chicago: Chicago University Press.

Parla, Ayşe. 2019. *Precarious Hope: Migration and the Limits of Belonging in Turkey*. Stanford, CA: Stanford University Press.

Pearlman, Wendy. 2003. *Occupied Voices: Stories of Everyday Life from the Second Intifada*. New York: Thunder's Mouth Press/Nation Books.

———. 2017. *We Crossed a Bridge and It Trembled: Voices from Syria*. New York: Custom House.

Perdigon, Sylvain. 2015. "'For Us It Is Otherwise': Three Sketches on Making Poverty Sensible in the Palestinian Refugee Camps of Lebanon." *Current Anthropology* 56 (S11): S88–96. https://doi.org/10.1086/682354.

Perry, Imani. 2018. *Vexy Thing: On Gender and Liberation*. Durham, NC: Duke University Press.

Peteet, Julie Marie. 2005. *Landscape of Hope and Despair: Palestinian Refugee Camps*. Philadelphia: University of Pennsylvania Press.

Pickering, Michael, and Emily Keightley. 2006. "The Modalities of Nostalgia." *Current Sociology* 54 (6): 919–41.

Povinelli, Elizabeth A. 2002. *The Cunning of Recognition: Indigenous Alterities and the Making of Australian Multiculturalism*. Politics, History, and Culture. Durham, NC: Duke University Press.

———. 2011. *Economies of Abandonment Social Belonging and Endurance in Late Liberalism*. Durham, NC: Duke University Press.

———. 2017. "Bleak House: An Afterword." *Social Text* 35 (1 [130]): 131–36. https://doi.org/10.1215/01642472-3728201.

Puar, Jasbir, ed. 2012. "Precarity Talk: A Virtual Roundtable with Lauren Berlant, Judith Butler, Bojana Cvejić, Isabell Lorey, Jasbir Puar, and Ana Vujanović." *TDR/ The Drama Review* 56 (4): 163–77. https://doi.org/10.1162/DRAM_a_00221.

Puar, Jasbir K., and Amit S. Rai. 2002. "Monster, Terrorist, Fag: The War on Terrorism and the Production of Docile Patriots." *Social Text* 20 (3): 117–48. https://doi.org/10.1215/01642472-20-3_72-117.

Pursley, Sara. 2019. *Familiar Futures: Time, Selfhood, and Sovereignty in Iraq.* Stanford, CA: Stanford University Press.

Radovic-Fanta, Jelena. 2017. "Living on Standby: Endurance and Anticipation in Chile's Aconcagua Valley: Living on Standby." *Journal of Latin American and Caribbean Anthropology* 22 (2): 357–75. https://doi.org/10.1111/jlca.12255.

Raschig, Megan. 2017. "Triggering Change: Police Homicides, Community Healing, and the Emergent Eventfulness of the New Civil Rights." *Cultural Anthropology* 32 (3): 399–423. https://doi.org/10.14506/ca32.3.07.

Roberts, Brian Russell, and Michelle Ann Stephens. 2017. *Archipelagic American Studies.* Durham, NC: Duke University Press.

Rofel, Lisa. 1999. *Other Modernities: Gendered Yearnings in China after Socialism.* Berkeley: University of California Press.

Roitman, Janet. 2013. *Anti-Crisis.* Durham, NC: Duke University Press.

Rossington, Michael, Anne Whitehead, and Linda R. Anderson. 2007. *Theories of Memory: A Reader.* Baltimore: Johns Hopkins University Press.

Ruhaimi, Abdul-Halim al-. 2002. "The Da'wa Islamic Party: Origins, Actors, and Ideology." In *Ayatollahs, Sufis and Ideologues: State, Religion and Social Movements in Iraq.* London: Saqi.

Russel y Rodríguez, Mónica. 2007. "Messy Spaces: Chicana Testimonio and the Undisciplining of Ethnography." *Chicana/Latina Studies* 7 (1): 86–121.

Said, Edward W. 1993. *Culture and Imperialism.* New York: Knopf.

———. 1994. *Orientalism.* 25th anniversary ed. New York: Vintage Books.

———. 2000. *Reflections on Exile and Other Essays.* Cambridge, MA: Harvard University Press.

Saleh, Zainab. 2013. "On Iraqi Nationality: Law, Citizenship, and Exclusion." *Arab Studies Journal* 21 (1): 48–78.

———. 2015. "The Islamic State in Iraq and Greater Syria (ISIS)." In *Oxford Islamic Studies Online.* Oxford: Oxford University Press.

———. 2018. "'Toppling' Saddam Hussein in London: Media, Meaning, and the Construction of an Iraqi Diasporic Community" *American Anthropologist* 120 (3): 512–22. https://doi.org/10.1111/aman.13007.

Sassoon, Joseph. 2011. *The Iraqi Refugees: The New Crisis in the Middle East.* London: I.B. Tauris.

———. 2012. *Saddam Hussein's Ba'th Party: Inside an Authoritarian Regime.* New York: Cambridge University Press.

Sawyer, Lena. "Engendering 'Race' in Calls for Diasporic Community in Sweden." *Feminist Review* 90: 87–105.

Sawyer, Suzana. 2004. *Crude Chronicles: Indigenous Politics, Multinational Oil, and Neoliberalism in Ecuador*. Durham, NC: Duke University Press.

Sayigh, Rosemary. 2015. *Too Many Enemies: The Palestinian Experience in Lebanon*. London: Zed Books.

Schielke, Joska Samuli. 2015. *Egypt in the Future Tense: Hope, Frustration, and Ambivalence before and after 2011*. Bloomington: Indiana University Press.

Schielke, Samuli, and Georg Stauth. 2009. *Dimensions of Locality: Muslim Saints, Their Place and Space*. Bielefeld: Transcript Verlag.

Schiller, Nina Glick. 2001. *Georges Woke up Laughing: Long-Distance Nationalism and the Search for Home*. Durham, NC: Duke University Press.

Scott, David. 1999. *Refashioning Futures: Criticism after Postcoloniality*. Princeton, NJ: Princeton University Press.

———. 2014. *Omens of Adversity: Tragedy, Time, Memory, Justice*. Durham, NC: Duke University Press.

Shaban, Abud-Hussein. 2002. *Men Hwa Al-Iraqi? Ishaliat al-Jinsiya Wa La-Jinsiya Fi al-Qanun al-Iraqi Wa al-Duwali*. London: Center for Oriental Studies.

Shakhsari, Sima. 2013. "Transnational Governmentality and the Politics of Life and Death." *International Journal of Middle East Studies* 45 (2): 340–42. https://doi.org/10.1017/S0020743813000081.

———. 2014. "The Queer Time of Death: Temporality, Geopolitics, and Refugee Rights." Edited by Rachel A Lewis and Nancy A Naples. *Sexualities* 17 (8): 998–1015. https://doi.org/10.1177/1363460714552261.

Shankar, Shalini. 2008. *Desi Land: Teen Culture, Class, and Success in Silicon Valley*. Durham, NC: Duke University Press.

Shipley, Jesse Weaver. 2013. *Living the Hiplife: Celebrity and Entrepreneurship in Ghanaian Popular Music*. Durham, NC: Duke University Press.

———. 2017. "Parody after Identity: Digital Music and the Politics of Uncertainty in West Africa." *American Ethnologist* 44 (2): 249–62.

Shohat, Ella. 2006. *Taboo Memories, Diasporic Voices*. Durham, NC: Duke University Press.

Silverstein, Paul A. 2004. *Algeria in France: Transpolitics, Race, and Nation*. Bloomington: Indiana University Press.

———. 2018. *Postcolonial France: Race, Islam, and the Future of the Republic*. London: Pluto Press.

Simpson, Audra. 2014. *Mohawk Interruptus: Political Life across the Borders of Settler States*. Durham, NC: Duke University Press.

Slate, Nico. 2012. *Colored Cosmopolitanism: The Shared Struggle for Freedom in the United States and India*. Cambridge, MA: Harvard University Press.

Smith, Neil. 2003. *American Empire: Roosevelt's Geographer and the Prelude to Globalization*. Berkeley: University of California Press.

Sontag, Susan. 2003. *Regarding the Pain of Others*. New York: Farrar, Straus and Giroux.
Spivak, Gayatry. 1988. "Can the Subaltern Speak?" In *Marxism and the Interpretation of Culture*, 271–313. Chicago: University of Illinois Press.
Stein, Rebecca L. 2008. *Itineraries in Conflict: Israelis, Palestinians, and the Political Lives of Tourism*. Durham, NC: Duke University Press.
Stewart, Kathleen. 1988. "Nostalgia: A Polemic." *Cultural Anthropology* 3: 227–41.
———. 2007. *Ordinary Affects*. Durham, NC: Duke University Press.
Stiglitz, Joseph E. 2008. *The Three Trillion Dollar War: The True Cost of the Iraq Conflict*. New York: W.W. Norton.
Stoler, Ann Laura. 2006. "Refractions Off Empire: Untimely Comparisons in Harsh Times." *Radical History Review* 2006 (95): 93–107. https://doi.org/10.1215/01636545-2006-95-93.
———. 2010. *Carnal Knowledge and Imperial Power: Race and the Intimate in Colonial Rule*. Berkeley: University of California Press.
———. 2013. *Imperial Debris: On Ruins and Ruination*. Durham, NC: Duke University Press.
———. 2016. *Duress: Imperial Durabilities in Our Times*. Durham, NC: Duke University Press.
Stoler, Ann Laura, with Carole McGranahan. 2018. "Disassemblage: Rethinking U.S. Imperial Formations." In *Ethnographies of U.S. Empire* edited by Carole McGranahan and John F. Collins. Durham, NC: Duke University Press.
Taussig, Michael T. 1986. *Shamanism, Colonialism, and the Wild Man: A Study in Terror and Healing*. Chicago: University of Chicago Press.
———. 1997. *The Magic of the State*. New York: Routledge.
———. 1999. *Defacement: Public Secrecy and the Labor of the Negative*. Stanford: Stanford University Press.
———. 2004. *My Cocaine Museum*. Chicago: University of Chicago Press.
———. 2006. *Walter Benjamin's Grave*. Chicago: University of Chicago Press.
Terry, Jennifer. 2017. *Attachments to War: Biomedical Logics and Violence in Twenty-First-Century America*. Durham, NC: Duke University Press.
Thiranagama, Sharika. 2011. *In My Mother's House: Civil War in Sri Lanka*. Philadelphia: University of Pennsylvania Press.
Thomas, Deborah A. 2011. *Exceptional Violence Embodied Citizenship in Transnational Jamaica*. Durham, NC: Duke University Press.
———. 2016. "Time and the Otherwise: Plantations, Garrisons and Being Human in the Caribbean." *Anthropological Theory* 16 (2–3): 177–200. https://doi.org/10.1177/1463499616636269.
———. 2019. *Political Life in the Wake of the Plantation: Sovereignty, Witnessing, Repair*. Durham, NC: Duke University Press.

Thomas, Deborah A., and Tina Campt. 2008. "Gendering Diaspora: Transnational Feminism, Diaspora and Its Hegemonies." *Feminist Review* 90: 1–8.

Thompson, Elizabeth. 2013. *Justice Interrupted: The Struggle for Constitutional Government in the Middle East*. Cambridge, MA: Harvard University Press.

———. 2018. "The 1948 Wathba Revisited: Comrade Fahd and the Mass Appeal of Iraqi Communism." *International Journal of Contemporary Iraqi Studies* 12 (2): 127–45. https://doi.org/10.1386/ijcis.12.2.127_1.

Thorpe, Helen. 2017. *The Newcomers: Finding Refuge, Friendship, and Hope in an American Classroom*. New York, NY: Scribner.

Tinker Salas, Miguel. 2009. *The Enduring Legacy: Oil, Culture, and Society in Venezuela*. Durham, NC: Duke University Press.

Tripp, Charles. 2007. *A History of Iraq*. Cambridge: Cambridge University Press.

Trouillot, Michel-Rolph. 2015. *Silencing the Past: Power and the Production of History*. Boston: Beacon Press.

Tsing, Anna Lowenhaupt. 2011. *Friction: An Ethnography of Global Connection*. Princeton, NJ: Princeton University Press.

Tuck, Eve, and K. Wayne Yang. 2012. "Decolonization Is Not a Metaphor." *Decolonization: Indigeneity, Education & Society* 1 (1). https://jps.library.utoronto.ca/index.php/des/article/view/18630.

Turner, Victor W. 1970. *The Forest of Symbols: Aspects of Ndembu Ritual*. Ithaca, NY: Cornell University Press.

United States Army. 2007. *Instructions for American Servicemen in Iraq during World War II*. Chicago: University of Chicago Press.

Van Doorn, Niels. 2015. "Forces of Faith: Endurance, Flourishing, and the Queer Religious Subject." *GLQ: A Journal of Lesbian and Gay Studies* 21 (4): 635–66. https://doi.org/10.1215/10642684-3123725.

Vogler, Gary. 2017. *Iraq and the Politics of Oil: An Insider's Perspective*. Lawrence: University Press of Kansas.

Vora, Neha. 2013. *Impossible Citizens: Dubai's Indian Diaspora*. Durham, NC: Duke University Press.

———. 2018. "Diaspora." In *The International Encyclopedia of Anthropology*. Hoboken, NJ: John Wiley & Sons.

Wedeen, Lisa. 1999. *Ambiguities of Domination: Politics, Rhetoric, and Symbols in Contemporary Syria*. Chicago: University of Chicago Press.

Williams, William Appleman. 2006. *Empire as a Way of Life: An Essay on the Causes and Character of America's Present Predicament, along with a Few Thoughts about an Alternative*. Brooklyn: IG Publishing.

Wolfe-Hunnicutt, Brandon. 2017. "Oil Sovereignty, American Foreign Policy, and the 1968 Coups in Iraq." *Diplomacy & Statecraft* 28 (2): 235–53. https://doi.org/10.1080/09592296.2017.1309882.

———. 2018. *U.S.-Iraq Relations, 1920–2003*. Vol. 1. Oxford Research Encyclopedia of American History. https://doi.org/10.1093/acrefore/9780199329175.013.463.

Wool, Zoë H. 2017. "In-Durable Sociality: Precarious Life in Common and the Temporal Boundaries of the Social." *Social Text* 35 (1 [130]): 79–99. https://doi.org/10.1215/01642472-3728008.

Wool, Zoë H., and Julie Livingston. 2017. "Collateral Afterworlds: An Introduction." *Social Text* 35 (1 [130]): 1–15. https://doi.org/10.1215/01642472-3727960.

Wright, Michelle M. 2003. *Becoming Black Creating Identity in the African Diaspora*. Durham, NC: Duke University Press.

Yergin, Daniel. 2008. *The Prize: The Epic Quest for Oil, Money, & Power*. New York: Free Press.

Youssef, Saʿdī. 2012. *Nostalgia, My Enemy: Poems*. Minneapolis: Graywolf Press.

Zengin, Aslı. 2019. "The Afterlife of Gender: Sovereignty, Intimacy and Muslim Funerals of Transgender People in Turkey." *Cultural Anthropology* 34 (1): 78–102. https://doi.org/10.14506/ca34.1.09.

Zubaida, Sami. 1991. "Community, Class, and Minorities in Iraqi Politics." In *The Iraqi Revolution of 1958: The Old Social Classes Revisited*, 197–210. London: I.B. Tauris.

———. 2002. "The Fragments Imagine the Nation: The Case of Iraq." *International Journal of Middle East Studies* 32 (2): 205–15.

# INDEX

Abd al-Salam Aref, 52
Abu Bakr, 126, 131, 166, 228n20, 229–30n18
Abu Ghraib prison, 14, 75, 168
Afghanistan, 7–8
agency, 135
Ahl al-Bait Center, 92
Al-Bakr, Ahmed Hasan, 183
Ajami, Fouad, 17
Albright, Madeleine, 13
Algiers Agreement, 93
Al-Husri, Sati, 101
Ali, Imam, 115, 145–46, 163, 166
Allawi, Ali, 220n33
Allawi, Iyad, 96–98, 227n17
al-Qaeda, 1–2, 13, 99
Al-Rasheed, Madawi, 9, 222n84
al-Thawara City, 53
al-Wathba (The Leap), 37–38, 47–49, 51, 58, 77, 85
Amara (Iraq), 95
Amin, Qasim, 46
Amman (Jordan), 26, 162, 186–87; Iraqi communities in, 25, 27
Amoah, Jewel, 32

Amoco, 11
Anfal-al campaign, 141, 220n33
Anglo-Iraqi Treaty, 47, 120
anticolonial movements, 33
Arab nationalists, 39, 51, 56, 87–88, 92–96, 101, 224n4, 226n3
Arab Muslims, 88
Arabs, 56, 87–88, 144, 151, 154–55, 167
Arab uprisings, 107
Aramean Christians, 88
Ashura, 125, 159, 166
Asia, 8
Assyrians, 88
AT&T, 11
Ataturk, Mustafa Kemal, 105
Australia: Iraqi enclaves in, 24
authentic citizenship: notion of, 35–36, 180
authenticity, 195, 211; "authentic" Iraqis, 179–80; economic deprivation, 23; economic and legal precarity, notion of, 195–96, 208; political subjectivity, 23; suffering and endurance, link with, 35–36
Aziz, Tariq, 150

Baghdad (Iraq), 12, 15, 21, 23, 27, 32, 39, 46–47, 52, 55, 61, 65–67, 69, 73, 75, 88–90, 92–93, 95, 99–100, 107, 115, 133, 144–45, 147, 151, 162–65, 172, 178–80, 182–83, 189–90, 195, 198, 200, 215–16, 224n24, 226n3, 228n1; corruption and bribes in, 174; Green Zone, 177, 191, 231n7; population of, 224n8, 224n22; post-war state of insecurity in, 173–74; Scud missiles, 141; Shi'i merchants, 149; siege of, 108; street demonstrations, 87; Tahrir Square, as iconic location, 229n15; uprisings in, 85–86
Baghdad Pact, 220n20
Bakr-al, Ahmad Hasan, 58, 90
Barzani, Mulla Mustafa, 93
Basra (Iraq), 95, 202, 228n1; Scud missiles, 141
Ba'th coups, 29, 34, 40, 57, 83–84, 178, 208, 217; CIA-backed, 182, 213
Ba'th Party, 9, 15, 20, 56, 73–74, 76, 81, 85, 90–94, 96, 101, 111, 120, 138–40, 180, 183, 190, 227n17; ascent of, 57–58; Arab unity and Islam, emphasis on, 86; Iraqis of Iranian origin, deportation of, 151
Batatu, Hanna, 220n24, 224n8
belonging, 6, 36, 68, 117, 133, 158, 160, 165; political, 181; suffering, hierarchy of, 216
biopolitics, 222n75
Black feminists, 31, 223n102
Black women, 32
Boym, Svetlana, 225n43, 226n1, 228n23
Britain, 3, 6, 9–13, 19–21, 26–27, 33, 37, 47, 80–81, 83, 86, 91, 93, 96, 102, 107, 128–29, 131, 157, 164–65, 171, 177, 179–80, 185, 189, 193, 198, 200, 209, 215, 217, 220n20, 225n38, 230n19, 230n22; as civil state, 104; as de facto home, 28; idealistic view of, 168; inclusion, as place of, 167; indefinite leave to remain (ILR), 178; Iraqi communists, exodus of, 95; Iraqi enclaves in, 24–25, 28; Iraqi legal status in, precarity of, 210; Iraqi refugees, measures against, 210; MI6 (intelligence agency), 97; multiculturalism of, 122–23, 146, 168, 214; necropolitics, 222n75; other in, 144; as secular state, 105; as safe haven, 25. *See also* England, Scotland, Wales
Brubaker, Rogers, 228n4
Brzezinski, Zbigniew, 10
Burns, John, 18
Bush, George H. W., 12, 17, 95–96
Bush, George W., 1–2, 13, 99–100, 162

Cambodia, 8
Carter, Jimmy, 10
Central Intelligence Agency (CIA), 9, 40, 56, 89, 180, 182, 213
Chalabi, Ahmed, 96–99, 226–27n16
Cheysson, Claude, 12–13
Chicana feminists, 31
civil state: components of, 103–4
class, 4–5, 21–22, 24, 30, 36, 45, 50, 64, 117, 198; class divisions, 85, 88; class struggle, 51, 212–13; and gender, 19, 23, 70–71, 211–12, 215–16; politics of, 213; progressive self, 44; and religion, 132; and selfhood, 83; and subjectivity, 70–71; and women, 49
Clinton, Bill, 13, 99
Coalition of Democracy in Iraq, 79, 81–82, 94, 96, 98, 100–102, 105, 107
Coalition Provisional Authority (CPA), 14, 16, 100, 191, 231n7
Cold War, 4
Collins, Patricia Hill, 32
colonialism, 49, 50, 86, 98, 146; subjectivity, 222n74
communism, 4, 9, 29–30, 33, 38, 41, 43, 51, 52, 59–60, 63–65, 69, 73, 82,

84, 86, 89–90, 92–94, 96, 101, 109, 117–19, 132, 134, 178, 214–15, 220n24; Arab nationalists, rivalry between, 39, 56, 87–88; campaign against, 40; and exodus, 95; "good old days," 212–13; idealized past, 133; onslaught against, 81, 91; oppression of, 183; persecution of, 40, 79; repression of, 58. *See also* Iraqi Communist Party (ICP)

Constitutional Monarchy Movement, 99

Damascus (Syria), 62, 91, 145, 159–60, 163, 198; Iraqi communities in, 25; refugees in, 177
Das, Veena, 211–12
Da'wa Party, 29, 92, 94, 96, 109–11, 120, 124
deportation, 29, 137–38, 144, 149, 163, 169, 228–29n7
deportees: legal exclusion of in Iran, 154–55; social prejudice against, 155–56; as stateless, 154–55
Detroit (Michigan): Iraqi communities in, 25
diaspora, 5, 18–19, 20–21, 24–28, 34, 43–44, 62–63, 82–83, 91, 199, 201, 207–9
diasporas of empire, 219n2
disappeared, 137, 218 [re Iraqis
disassemblage, 8
dismemberment, 209–10
displacement, 22, 25, 33, 35, 96, 102, 134, 143, 169, 180, 198, 209–11, 218; legal precarity after, 217
dispossession, 5, 22–23, 180–81, 208, 210, 230–31n1; endurance, 217
double exile, 128
Dulaimi-al, Naziha, 49–50

East Asia, 122
economies of abandonment, 230–31n1
Egypt, 10, 19, 38–39, 50, 56, 86, 222n75

Eisenhower Doctrine, 52
empowerment: and storytelling, 31
endurance (*tahamul*): Arabic concept of, 194; notion of, 212, 216; and dispossession, 217; enduring subject, 36, 181; as classed and gendered, 23; Iraqi women, as quintessential figure of, 23, 217; subjectivity, as iconic condition of, 216
England, 201. *See also* Britain
erasure, 5, 16–18, 32, 200, 202, 209–11; exile, 217; of women, 31, 70. *See also* politics of erasure
ethnographies of encounter, 219n5
Europe, 26, 103, 189, 192, 196, 201, 207, 225n38; Iraqi enclaves in, 24, 115
exile, 5–6, 20–22, 25, 34, 60, 62, 89, 91, 95, 98, 169, 209, 213, 215–18, 225n37; contradictions of, 147; exclusion in, 146; first phase, 83–84; marginalization in, 146; as the other, 217; phases of, 83; second phase, 84; as term, 27; U.S. invasion of Iraq, 161
exilic politics, 91, 96
exodus, 24, 92, 95–96, 122, 207–8
Exxon, 11

Fadhallah, Mohammed Hussein, 158–59
Faier, Lieba, 219n5
Faith Campaign, 186
Fanon, Frantz, 222n74
Federation of Peasants' Associations, 226n3
Fifth Brigade, 88
Finland, 200
Foucault, Michel, 222n75, 222n76
Fouron, Georges Eugene, 223n89
France, 10–11, 86
Freedom Monument, 69
Free Officers, 52
Freud, Sigmund, 29–30

Gelb, Leslie, 17
gender, 4–5, 21–22, 24, 30, 36, 46, 132, 147, 166; and class, 19, 23, 211–12, 215–16; discourse on, 54, 159–60; disparity, 181–82; gender equality, 45, 82–83, 86, 96, 103, 229n12; gender reforms, 44, 212; gender rights, 106; gender segregated, 124; "good Iraqi girl," 158; politics of class, 213; religious discourse, as gendered, 215, 228n21; and subjectivity, 70–71
General Motors, 11
General Security, 76
General Union of Students, 226n3
Good, Erica, 18
Gordon, Roy, 13
Grand Library of Baghdad: ransacking of, 108
Greenberg, Jessica, 225n31
Guatemala, 8
Gulf War, 1, 6, 25, 35, 59, 84, 95, 117, 122, 134, 173, 180, 185, 194–95, 216

Haiti, 223n89
Hakim-al Muhammad Baqir, 92
Halabia massacre, 141
home, 6, 107, 133, 144, 163, 169, 211; as elastic notion, 165; generational shifts, 146; and journeying, reenacted through, 146; as shifting and contested concept, 145, 164
homecoming, 145–46, 225n43
Honduras, 8
hooks, bell, 31–32
*hawza* (seminaries), 118
hybrid identities, 164
hybridity, 145
Hussein, Abbas, 126
Hussein, Imam, 115, 125–26, 128, 145–46, 159–63, 229n12
Hussein, Saddam, 2–3, 6, 10, 12–13, 16–17, 23, 28, 32, 35, 37, 39, 58, 60, 62, 67, 69, 73, 75–77, 92, 95–96, 98–99, 101, 109, 114, 116, 120–21, 130–33, 148, 153, 157, 165, 169, 171, 174, 178, 180, 187–88, 195–96, 198, 203, 205, 216, 221n42; authoritarianism of, 147; chemical weapons, use of, 11, 15; deportation campaign of, 137, 149, 152; deserters, execution of, 139–40; expulsion campaign of, 144, 151–52; displacement under, 143; fall of, 27, 29–30, 42–44, 59, 65–66, 102–3, 105, 145–46, 161, 163, 185, 190, 199, 214, 225n29; glorification of, 111; idealization of, 30–31; khaki, association with, 139; nostalgia for, 38, 218; opposition to, 93–94, 122–23; Persian nationality, denaturalization campaign against, 146; as predictable source of danger, 218; religion, suspicion of, 110; removal of, 42; rise of, 18, 24–25, 33–34, 83, 84, 91, 143, 183, 184; Shi'i establishment, persecution of, 115, 124–26; Shi'i-led opposition against, 149–50; songs glorifying of, 139–40; statue, toppling of, 61, 100, 129, 189; student indoctrination, 139; ultimatum to, 100; US support of, 1, 7, 24, 84, 117, 122, 134, 207–9, 213, 215

identity, 31, 62, 65, 123, 125, 143, 165, 169, 197, 214; belonging, 145; identity cards, 149; national, 2, 16; as hybrid, 164; as multiple, 164; as shifting, 167
identity crisis, 144
*imama* (religious establishment), 130
imagined community, 228n4
imperial encounter, 7
imperialism, 7–8, 22–23, 146, 215, 217–18, 223n102
India, 19, 222n75
inequality, 19–20, 22, 47, 85, 181

intifada uprisings, 49, 85
Iran, 11–13, 15, 29, 77, 93, 122, 125, 141, 144, 146, 156–57, 160, 168, 220n20, 227n17; deportation camps, 153; exodus to, 92; Iraqis in, 20–21; green card, 154–55; Iraqi deportees in, 154; Iraqis in, as unwelcome guests, 20, 154; Islamic Republic, loss to, 225n37; Islamic Revolution in, 10, 92, 149–52
Iran-Iraq War, 1, 6, 10, 15, 20, 35, 59–60, 77, 93, 134, 137–38, 139, 153–54, 157, 171, 180, 184–85, 194–95, 207, 216–18, 225n37; Scud missiles, 141
Iraq, 1, 8, 11–12, 25, 37, 59, 64, 68, 77–80, 91, 101, 107, 113, 121, 125, 130, 145, 153–54, 157, 160, 162, 164, 166–67, 178, 181, 193, 199, 200, 204, 211, 225n38, 226–27n16, 229n14, 230n19; Amiriyya Shelter, bombing of, 185–86; anticolonial sentiment, 44; as Arab nation, 51; Arab nationalism, 85, 224n4; bombardment of, 173; British colonial rule, 19–20, 33, 150; British invasion of, 9, 114, 223n1; under British mandate, 45–46, 217; British occupation of, 168, 177; British presence in, 70, 212–13; civil state, 103–4; collateral damage, 208; colonialism, 49–50; disillusionment with, 60, 62; displacement, 96, 102; division, fear of, 202; dual-use technologies, 15; enduring subject, notion of, 23; food rationing, 173; foreign occupation of, 108; fragmentation of, 22, 210, 212; gender equality, issue of, 96; "good old days" in, 21, 26, 30, 33, 43, 70–71, 116, 183, 212, 225n37; as holy land, 213–14; idealized past of, 43–44, 56, 60, 62, 65, 69–70, 82, 84, 106, 116–18, 133, 146, 184; infrastructure, damage to, 185; instability in, 195, 216; Iraqis of Iranian origin, deportation campaign against, 137–38; "Iranians" in, anxiety over, 150; Iraqis as term, erasure of, 17; Kurds, secession from, 203, 231n9; looting in, 61–62, 171–72; mass exodus from, 96; mass graves, 29–30; melancholia, 45; monarchy, fall of, 2, 9, 24, 39, 52–53, 55–56, 61, 70, 87, 92, 120, 182, 213, 223n1; mourning, 29–30; nation building, 222n76; necropolitics, 222n75; nostalgia, 30, 34, 44–45; oil fields, nationalization of, 10, 56, 220n20; as "open wound," 29, 67; Ottoman Iraq, 20, 228n1; Persian nationality, denaturalization campaign against, 146; of Persian nationality, as second-class citizens, 151, 169; postcolonial chaos, 39; "real" Iraq, 194, 216; real Iraqis in, 128–29; regime change, 6–7, 13, 34, 60, 96–100, 123, 161, 169, 185, 207; religious scholars, role of, 118–20; as rentier state, 103–4; revolution in, 52–53; rumors, as source of information in, 140; sanctions against, 13, 26, 95, 99, 172–73, 180, 184–85, 188, 208, 210, 216, 218; secret police, 38; sectarianism in, 43–44, 97, 108, 126, 134; sectarian violence in, 3, 4, 14, 16, 17, 18, 27–32, 35, 71, 102, 105, 116, 133–34, 177, 196–98, 201, 209, 212, 218; secularism in, 62–63, 230n22; as sheep, 117, 131–32; "shock and awe" campaign against, 13; shortages in, as common, 174; social fabric, destruction of, 209; state institutions, looting and destruction of, 13–14; suicide bombings, 114; "true" Iraq, 179–80, 215; uprisings in, 185, 221n42; U.S. bombardment of, 208; U.S. imperialism, 215, 217–18; U.S. interventions

Iraq (*continued*)
in, 22, 24, 39, 56, 83, 108, 134, 207–8, 216; U.S. invasion of, 7, 17–18, 27, 61, 100, 161, 188, 196, 207, 216; U.S. occupation of, 5–6, 14, 18, 23, 30, 34–35, 42, 44, 60, 66, 100, 169, 180, 208, 210–11, 217–18; weapons of mass destruction (WMD), 99–100; women in, 46, 48–52, 55, 212–13

Iraqi Assyrians, 24

Iraqi Communist Party (ICP), 15, 19, 33, 37–41, 45, 49–51, 57–60, 63–65, 69–70, 81–82, 84–86, 88–89, 91, 94, 97–98, 101, 114, 226n3, 227n17; Ba'th Party, alignment with, 90; in exile, 225n38; liquidation of, 77, 92–93, 110, 225n38

Iraqi Forum, 59–60, 93, 123, 225n39

Iraqi Governing Council (IGC), 100, 190

Iraqi National Accord (INA), 96–97, 99, 227n17

Iraqi Nationality Certificate, 151

Iraqi Nationality Law, 20, 146, 150–51, 169, 228n4

Iraqiness, 116, 122, 156, 164–65; absence, defined by, 195, 216; alternative imaginations about, 181; double exile, 128; notion of, 128, 214; religious events, intertwined with, 214; and selfhood, 167

Iraq Liberation Act (ILA), 99

Iraq National Congress (INC), 96–97, 99–100

Iraqi Personal Status Code, 42–43

Iraqis: as authentic, 23; enforced absence, 25–26; in exile, 25; indefinite leave (ILR), 28; Iraqi self, as classed and gendered, 36; long-distance nationalism, 27–28, 223n89; new Iraqi man and modern Iraqi woman, notion of, 83, 85; pious self, 21

Iraqis in London, 5–6, 18–19, 23, 26, 29–34, 41, 59–60, 62, 64, 70, 80–84, 102, 115, 116, 118, 123, 125, 126–28, 131–33, 157–58, 164, 168, 178–79, 181, 196, 198, 201, 207, 211; and authenticity, 180; authentic citizenship, 36; authenticity, 35–36; class discourse, 212–13, 215; communist discourse, 212, 216; cultural heritage, loss of, 210; as different from parents, 22; dismemberment, process of, 209; endurance, notion of, 212, 216; and exile, 25; fragmentation of, 197; gender discourse, 212–13; "I'm an Iraqi" campaign, 197; Iraqi subjectivity, 35; modernity of, 21–22; Muslim women, as role models, 215; as permanent home, 27–28; regime change, support of, 161; religious discourse, 212, 214–16; religious establishments disenchantment with, 214–15; strong Iraqi woman, trope of in, 194–95

Iraqi Women's League (IWL), 41–42, 49, 54, 69–70. *See also* League for the Defense of Women's Rights

Iraq Petroleum Company, 9, 54, 220n20

Islam, 86, 116–17, 126–27, 128, 131–32, 214–15, 224n4, 228n21, 229n12

Islamism, 101

Islamic Movement of Kurdistan, 99

Islamic Republic, 225n37

Islamic Revolution, 10, 92, 149–52

Islamic State, 14, 68, 231n9

Israel, 24, 86, 172

Italy, 10

Jawahir-al, Muhammad Mahdi, 48, 224n14

Jones, Toby, 9, 14

Jordan, 10, 14, 26, 179, 192–93, 210, 226–27n16; Iraqis in, 222n85

journeying, 146

Kadhim, Imam, 190
Karbala (Iraq), 12, 95, 114, 125–26, 145, 151, 160, 163, 165, 221n42
Kennedy, John F., 9
Khalisi-al Mahdi, 120
Khan, Genghis, 108
Khan, Hulagu, 108
Kho'i Foundation, 92
Khomeini, Ayatollah, 125
*khums* (religious taxes), 119
King, Martin Luther Jr., 219n12
Kirkuk (Iraq), 12
Kufa (Iraq), 126
Kurdish Democratic Party (KDP), 93, 96, 99
Kurdistan, 11–12, 96, 166, 231n9
Kurds, 10–12, 15, 17, 24, 51, 58, 64–65, 76–77, 87–88, 91–92, 94–98, 100, 144, 150, 158, 166–67, 201–2, 220n33; chemical weapons against, 141, 218; displacement of, 93; secession, 203, 231n9; Kurdish revolt, 93
Kuwait, 1, 10, 13, 32–33, 58, 185; Iraqi invasion of, 11–12, 15, 59, 91, 171–72, 218

Latina Feminist Group, 223n102
Latina feminists, 223n102
Latin America, 8
Law 80, 54
League for the Defense of Women's Rights, 49, 50–51, 54, 226n3. *See also* Iraqi Women's League
League of Nationalist Youth, 85
Lebanon, 1, 114, 122, 204, 226–27n16
Lockheed Martin, 11
Locke, John, 104
London (England), 62, 79, 93–94, 101, 114, 140, 143, 145–47, 157, 165, 168, 171, 175, 177–79, 192–93, 200–201, 211, 218; as center of Hussein opposition, 91; Iraqi Assyrians in, 222n84; Iraqi Jews in, 24, 222n84; Iraqi opposition groups in, 92, 95, 100, 122; Shi'i Iraqi community in, 130; *turba* fights, 123. *See also* Iraqis in London
long-distance nationalism, 27–28, 223n89
Lutz, Catherine, 211

Manifesto of March, 93
marginalization, 146, 179–81
marginalized groups, 31–32
Mashhad (Iran), 154
Mbembe, J. A., 231n1
Mecca, 126, 145, 159–60, 163, 165–66, 230n19
Medina (Saudi Arabia), 160, 166
melancholia, 29–30, 45
Middle East, 8–9, 17, 24, 26, 42, 56, 144, 207; oil, 7; U.S. militarism in, 14
militant Islamism, 96
Mobil, 11
mobility, 20, 146, 180, 183
modernity, 5, 21, 44–45, 50, 70–71; nation building, tied to, 63; women, as symbol of, 212
Monument of Freedom, 229n15
Mosul (Iraq), 9, 68, 184, 226n3, 228n1; as conservative city, 85; Islamic State, 231n9
Mosul massacre, 88
Mosul Radio, 226n3
mourning, 29; nostalgia, 30
Muhammad, Prophet, 114, 125, 147, 215, 229n12, 229–30n18
Mukhabarat (Iraqi intelligence agency), 74, 188
multiculturalism, 122–23, 146, 168, 214
Musa, Salama, 49–50
Muslim Brotherhood, 120

Naber, Nadine, 219n2
Naficy, Hamid, 225n37
Nagl, John A., 16

Najaf (Iraq), 12, 95, 119, 125, 145, 151, 160, 163, 165, 168–69, 172, 221n42
narratives, 4–5, 17–19, 21, 24, 33, 91, 183, 212, 223n102; communist, 34; empowerment, as technique of, 31; as gendered and classed, 83; as idealized, 43–44; importance of, 211; sectarian, 34; of selfhood, 6, 211; as tool of liberation, 32; of victimhood, 83, 124
Nasiriyya (Iraq), 12, 95
Nasser, Gamal Abd, 86–87
Nasserists, 87
National Action Charter, 90
nationalism, 146; Arab, 39, 51, 56, 87–88, 92–96, 101, 224n4, 226n3; Kurdish, 96; Persian, 144
National Patriotic Front, 81, 90–91
National Security Council, 220n20
nation-state, 7, 44, 130–31, 164–65, 167
Native Americans, 8
neoconservatives, 13; rise of, 99
necropolitics, 222n75
New York, 122; Haitians in, 223n89
Nguyen, Viet Thanh, 219n12
Nicaragua, 8
1958 Revolution, 9, 42, 69–70, 87, 226n3, 229n15
1920 Revolt, 114, 119
Non-Aligned Movement, 75
nostalgia, 34, 37, 44–45, 84, 117–18, 133, 135, 173, 183, 187, 200, 211–12, 218; as defined, 228n23; mourning, 30; restorative v. reflective, 226n1

obscurantism, 98, 118–19
Omar, 126, 131, 166, 228n20, 229–30n18
Operation Desert Storm, 12, 185
Operation Iraqi Freedom, 100
Orientalism, 119
Ottoman Empire, 228n1
Ottomans, 144, 146, 150–51, 224n6

Pahlavi, Mohammad Reza: overthrowing of, 10
Pakistan, 220n20
Paris (France), 122
Patriot Union of Kurdistan (PUK), 93, 96, 99
Peace Partisans, 226n3
Pershmerga, 93, 96
Personal Status Code, 54, 224n27
Petra Bank, 226–27n16
Philippines, 8
"Pictures from the Battlefield," 140
pilgrimage, 145–46, 151, 160
Poland, 184
politics of erasure, 32, 210–11. *See also* erasure
polygamy, 55
Popular Army, 184–85
Portsmouth Treaty, 37, 47–48, 224n12
Povinelli, Elizabeth, 230–31n1
Powell, Colin, 12
precarity, 20, 37, 194, 201, 209, 230–31n1; authenticity, 195–96, 208; displacement, 217; economic, 187, 195–96; legal, 180, 195–96, 210, 217; of women, 216–17
public sphere: women in, 212–13
Pursley, Sara, 222n75, 222n76, 224n27

Qasim, Abdul Karim, 9, 53, 56, 58, 87–88, 92–93, 120, 182–83, 220n20, 226n3; removal of, 89
quietism, 114–15, 120–21
Qum (Iran), 151

racism, 8, 223n102; and Vietnam War, 219n12
Ramadan, Taha Yasin, 94
Reagan, Ronald, 10–11
refugees, 14, 59–60, 93, 95, 131, 177, 179, 192–94, 196, 198, 200, 210, 221n42
regime change, 6–7, 13, 34, 60, 96–100, 123, 140, 161, 169, 171, 207, 215–16; sanctions, link to, 185

Republican Guard, 122, 221n42
Revolutionary Command Council, 58
Revolution of 1958. *See* 1958 Revolution
Rofel, Lisa, 219n5
Rumsfeld, Donald, 2, 10
Rusafi-al, Maʻruf, 46

Sadr-al, Muhammad Sayyid Baqir, 92, 101, 109
Salahuddin Conference, 97
Salim, Jawad, 229n15
Samoa, 8
*sarifas* (shantytowns), 53, 47, 49, 85–86
Sassoon, Joseph, 222n85
Saudi Arabia, 10, 15, 165–66
Schiller, Nina Glick, 223n89
Scotland, 201. *See also* Britain
Scott, David, 30
sectarianism, 64–65; and secularism, 104
secularism, 5, 62, 105, 230n22; enlightenment, link to, 63; sectarianism, as antidote to, 104
selfhood, 5–6, 19, 21, 44, 46, 106, 117, 144, 164, 167, 180, 201, 211; as classed, 83; as gendered, 83; intergenerational haunting, 118; journeying, reenacted through, 146
self-making, 24
September 11 attacks, 8, 13–14, 99
Serbia, 225n31
settler colonialism, 8
sexism, 223n102
Shawaf-al, Abd Awahhab, 88
Shiʻi doctrine, 166
Shiʻi Islam, 158
Shiʻis, 12–13, 15–17, 20–22, 51, 58, 64–65, 91–98, 100, 103, 113–14, 116–24, 126–31, 145–47, 151–52, 164, 190, 197–98, 201–2, 228n20; Hussein, opposition-led campaign against, 149–50; younger generation, turn to, 213
Shiʻism, 114, 147, 160, 230n22

Shiʻi Muslims, 143–44, 155, 229–30n18, 230n20
Shiites, 15
Shirazi-al, Sayyid Sadiq Husseini, 124
Shultz, George, 11
Sistani-al, Sayyid Ali, 130
South Asia, 115, 117, 121–22, 124, 127
South East Asia, 122
sovereignty, 231n1
Soviet Union, 40, 105; fall of, 95. *See also* USSR
spatial imagination, 28
State Sponsors of Terrorism, 10
Stewart, Kathleen, 30
Stoler, Ann, 8
storytelling: empowerment, as technique of, 31; homeland, connecting with, 31; people of color, 32
subjectivity, 36, 118, 145, 147, 163–66, 169, 180, 194, 212, 223n102; colonialism, 222n74; endurance, 216; and gender, 70–71; generational shifts, 146
Suez Canal, 86
Suez Crisis, 86
Sunni Arabs, 150
Sunni Muslims, 229–30n18
Sunnis, 14, 16–17, 45, 64, 97, 100, 120, 125–29, 197, 198, 201–2, 228n20
Supreme Council for the Islamic Revolution in Iraq (SCIRI), 92, 94, 96, 99
survivor's guilt, 78
Sweden, 131
Switzerland, 226–27n16
Syria, 14, 56, 177, 179, 193, 198, 200, 210

*tabaʻiyya* (Iraqi of Iranian origin), 144, 146, 161; as deportation of the merchants, 149–50; expulsion campaign against, 149
*tahamul*. *See* endurance
Talabani, Jalal, 93
Tanker War, 10
technocrat: as term, 190

Tehran (Iran), 62, 91
*testimonios*, 223n102
Third World, 7, 19, 46, 52, 83
Train of Death, 56
transnationalism, 146–47
Tribal and Criminal and Civil Disputes Regulation, 224n26
Tribal Dispute Act, 120
Turkey, 12, 105, 220n20

Ulloum-al, Sayyid Bahr, 94
Umayyad dynasty, 114, 126
United Nations (UN), 11–13, 26, 99–100, 157, 172, 184, 199, 210; High Commissioner for Refugees, 177, 194; Security Council, 185
United States, 4, 9–13, 25–26, 39, 56, 59, 62, 67, 83, 93, 96–97, 104, 108, 117, 122, 134, 141, 172, 185–86, 188–90, 209, 213, 230–31n1; expansion and global domination, 8; genocidal violence, as central to, 8; imperialism of, 7–8, 22–23, 215, 217–18; Iranian diaspora in, 225n37; Iraq, invasion and occupation of, 5–7, 14, 17–18, 23, 27, 30, 34–35, 42, 44, 60–61, 66, 100, 161, 169, 180, 188, 196, 207–8, 210–11, 216–18; Iraqi enclaves in, 24; militarism of, 7, 14; military-industrial complex, 7, 15; racism, and Vietnam War, 219n12; as secular state, 105
U.S. Iraq Business Forum, 11
USSR, 81. *See also* Soviet Union

*velayat-e-faqih*, 92
Vietnam, 8
Vietnam War, 15; American racism, link to, 219n12

Wadi al-Salam cemetery, 125, 230n20
Wales, 81. *See also* Britain
Warda, Abu, 79, 113–14
War on Terror, 8, 99
weapons of mass destruction (WMD), 99–100
We Are Iraqis, 177
West Germany, 10
Wolfe-Hunnicut, Brandon, 220n24
women, 32, 47–48, 51, 55, 57, 59, 62–63, 80, 90, 106, 110, 113, 128–29, 159, 179–80, 187, 215, 224n26, 224n27, 225n29; and class, 49; deported, 152; economic precarity and political uncertainty, hardest hit by, 216–17; emancipation of, 211; as erased, 31, 70; gender equality, 96, 212–13; as heads of household, 194–95; Iraqi endurance, as symbol of, 217; Kurdish women, as independent, 166–67; *mahram* (male legal guardian), 204; as misrepresented, 31; modernity, as marker of, 21, 33, 34, 71, 147, 160, 212; as quintessential figure, 23; women's liberation, 4, 20, 30, 44, 50, 195, 212; women's rights, 6, 21, 42–46, 49, 54, 69–70, 83, 86, 229n12
World War I, 9, 114
World War II, 45, 63, 69

Yusuf, Yusuf Salman (aka Fahd), 101

Zahawi-al, Jamil Sidqi, 46
Zainab, Sayyida, 159–60
Zionism, 98
*ziyyara* (pilgrimage), 133
zones of abandonment, 230–31n1

The authorized representative in the EU for product safety and compliance is:
Mare Nostrum Group
B.V Doelen 72
4831 GR Breda
The Netherlands

www.ingramcontent.com/pod-product-compliance
Lightning Source LLC
Chambersburg PA
CBHW031803220426
43662CB00007B/510